DISCOVERING BLACK AMERICA

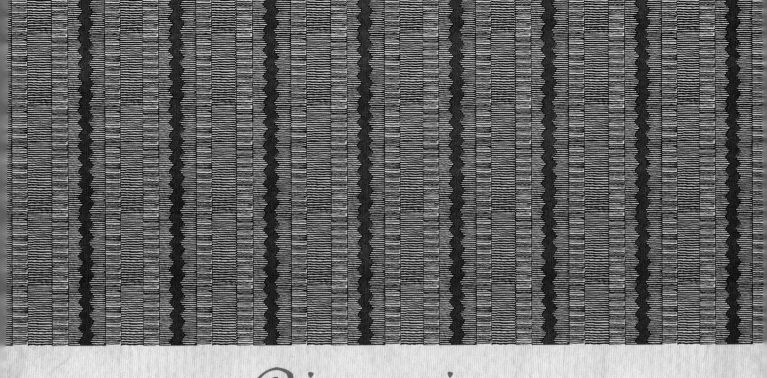

Discovering
BLACK AMERICA

From the AGE OF EXPLORATION to the TWENTY-FIRST CENTURY

Linda Tarrant-Reid

ABRAMS BOOKS FOR YOUNG READERS

NEW YORK

Library of Congress Cataloging-in-Publication Data

Tarrant-Reid, Linda.
Discovering Black America : from the age of exploration to the
twenty-first century / Linda Tarrant-Reid.
p. cm.
Includes bibliographical references and index.
ISBN 978-0-8109-7098-4
1. African Americans—History—Juvenile literature. 2. African
Americans—Biography—Juvenile literature. I. Title.
E185.T198 2012
973'.0496073—dc23
2011052201

Text copyright © 2012 Linda Tarrant-Reid
For illustration credits, see page 232.

Book design by Alissa Faden
Art directed by Maria T. Middleton

Printed and bound in China
10 9 8 7 6 5 4 3 2 1

Abrams Books for Young Readers are available at special discounts when purchased in quantity for
premiums and promotions as well as fundraising or educational use. Special editions can also be
created to specification. For details, contact specialsales@abramsbooks.com or the address below.

THE ART OF BOOKS SINCE 1949
115 West 18th Street
New York, NY 10011
www.abramsbooks.com

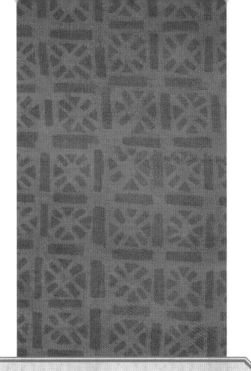

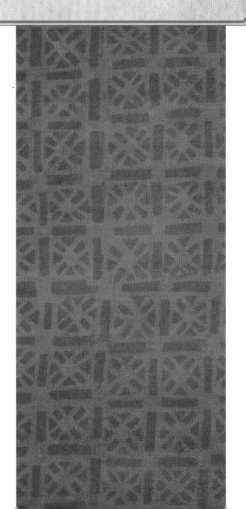

To Gale Claudette Colden
1948 TO 2009

CONTENTS

Untitled pen and ink and tempera drawing on rice paper by
Tom Feelings, from his book *The Middle Passage: White
Ships/Black Cargo*, published in 1995

INTRODUCTION

Writing and researching *Discovering Black America* has been an extraordinary journey. As a journalist and naturally curious person, I had my work cut out for me. But I was determined to uncover the narrative of the men, women, and children of African descent who were brought over to America as enslaved workers or were born into slavery on American soil, as well as those who were free people of color who chose to come of their own will. This book follows their experiences and those of their descendants up to the twenty-first century.

IN RESEARCHING AND writing *Discovering Black America*, I had to decide where to start (the first black man to set foot on American soil seemed a good place), where to end (the first black person elected to serve as president of the United States), and then to fill in what lay between, bringing forth some very important people, places, and events. Many of the people I cover are well known, a number are less so, and some are obscure—but all have contributed to the African American experience. This book, however, is not intended as an exhaustive review of African American history, but rather a journey in which the reader visits both familiar and unfamiliar territory and learns some new information and maybe even gains a new perspective. My goal has been to tell significant portions of the story with an expanded view of what really happened as African Americans traveled from the age of exploration to slavery to freedom and beyond.

Of course, we all are taught American history in school, but not always a complete history and, in some instances, not an accurate history. And we certainly have not been taught the full story, because history is constantly being updated and corrected as new evidence comes to light and new discoveries are made. My friend and colleague Tonya Bolden refers to how history is often taught these days as "flashcard history," in which you learn only the answer to a question and not the full story behind the question. For example, when asked, "Who was the first person to die in the American Revolution?" you may respond "Crispus Attucks." Which is the correct answer. But did you know that he was a black man living in Boston at the time? Do you know what it was like to be a free black person living in the North? And do you understand the circumstances under which this black man died in colonial Boston in the late 1700s? What was happening there?

And why? History is not a series of people, places, and events recounted in isolation. There is a context in which each event takes place that helps us to better understand the whole story.

Discovering Black America is a journey that I invite you to take with me. We'll meet new people, revisit big moments in history, learn about the struggles endured by an enslaved people, and witness their journey to freedom against the most challenging circumstances. On the way, we will learn lessons from the lives of these African Americans, such as perseverance, ingenuity, and the importance of working together to achieve common goals. We can use these lessons to make our own lives better, no matter our own histories.

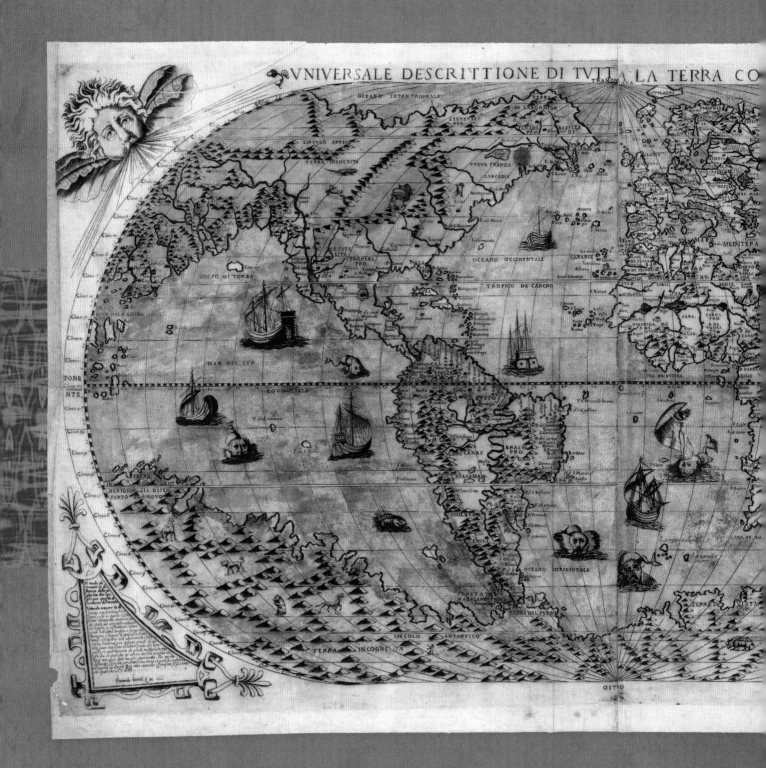

PART 1

Exploration of the New World and Settlements in Colonial America

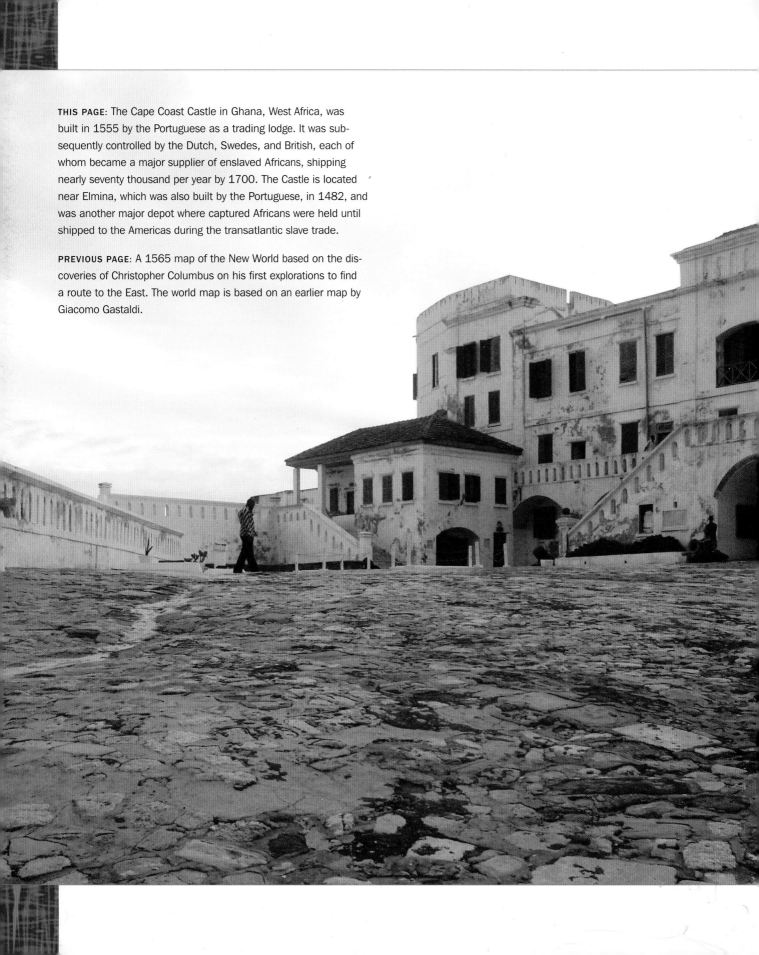

THIS PAGE: The Cape Coast Castle in Ghana, West Africa, was built in 1555 by the Portuguese as a trading lodge. It was subsequently controlled by the Dutch, Swedes, and British, each of whom became a major supplier of enslaved Africans, shipping nearly seventy thousand per year by 1700. The Castle is located near Elmina, which was also built by the Portuguese, in 1482, and was another major depot where captured Africans were held until shipped to the Americas during the transatlantic slave trade.

PREVIOUS PAGE: A 1565 map of the New World based on the discoveries of Christopher Columbus on his first explorations to find a route to the East. The world map is based on an earlier map by Giacomo Gastaldi.

IN THE FIFTEENTH century, European seamen embarked on a period of discovery called the Age of Exploration. Portuguese, Spanish, Dutch, French, and British ships sailed on expeditions to the African continent and to the Americas, or the New World, as it was called. The explorers were in search of a water route to the lucrative markets in the Far East—Asia, as we now know it—India, China, Japan, and Indonesia. European countries also wanted to expand their empires and exploit the rich resources of newly discovered territories.

Africa, with its gold mines, natural resources, and massive geography, held a particular attraction for the Europeans. In the opening decades of the 1400s, Prince Henry of Portugal, a missionary and politician, sponsored expeditions to the West African coast to search for gold and North Africa to learn more about the Muslim presence in the hopes of converting the population to Christianity and establishing Portuguese colonies.

Trade agreements between the Portuguese and the African rulers were negotiated, and one of the results was the birth of the slave trade. From 1440 to 1640, Portugal was the primary supplier of slave labor to the New World. Slave castles, sometimes referred to as forts, were constructed on the West African coast. The first such European structure was São Jorge da Mina, St. George of the Mine, built on the Gold Coast of modern-day Ghana in 1482 by the Portuguese. Known as Elmina, the trade center first operated as a depot where gold, ivory, spices, and other African goods were bartered. Later, humans were traded, too, between Africans and Europeans.

Pizarro Going to Peru by Constantino Brumidi, created between 1878 and 1880, illustrates the journey of Francisco Pizarro, the Spaniard who conquered lands in the New World for Spain.

Slavery had been in existence in Africa since ancient times and was exploited by warring factions as part of the spoils of war. The conquerors would take their enemies captive and enslave them. On other occasions, slaves were acquired through kidnapping neighboring tribe members, or from families who sold their kin for money. In these ancient times, the slaves—men, women, and children—were used as a labor force to farm the land and as domestic servants in the home. However, the slaves still held a degree of social status: "Some served in royal courts, . . . as officials, soldiers, servants, and artisans . . . Under a system known as 'clientage,' slaves owed a share of their crop or their labor to an owner or a lineage [relative of an owner]. Yet they owned the bulk of their crop and were allowed to participate in the society's political activities. These slaves were often treated no differently than other peasant or tenant farmers."

This system was not adopted when the British colonized North America in the seventeenth century, and slavery became institutionalized as "chattel slavery": Blacks were treated as property without the rights or privileges afforded a human being, based solely on their skin color.

The Black Explorers

THE EARLIEST BLACKS to arrive in North America were not the shackled Africans who were forced to migrate from Africa to the New World during the journey called the Middle Passage in the seventeenth and eighteenth centuries. Some of the first Africans or people of African descent to step foot on the American continent were navigators, translators, and other seamen who worked aboard European ships during the Age of Exploration in the fifteenth century. Some who sailed were free, while others were enslaved.

Historians have documented that on Christopher Columbus's first voyage to the New World in 1492, Pedro Alonzo (Alonso) Niño, a black man of Spanish descent, was the pilot or the navigator of the *Niña*, one of the three ships Columbus outfitted for his voyage to the New World. Juan Las Canarias or Las Canerias, a black sailor, who most likely came aboard in the

Juan Garrido, a free black explorer, was a member of Ponce de León's expeditions to Puerto Rico and the Caribbean. Garrido also joined Hernán Cortés in the fight to conquer Mexico, and in this sixteenth-century engraving, Garrido (far left) and Cortés meet with Mexican officials.

Canary Islands, reportedly accompanied Columbus on the *Santa María*, although some historical accounts place Pedro Alonzo Niño on the *Santa María*.

Esteban Gómez sailed under a Spanish flag into the "narrows claimed by Giovanni da Verrazano in 1525," becoming the first known person of African descent to explore the lower Hudson River around what is now New York City. Juan Garrido, a free black explorer also of African descent, traveled with Juan Ponce de León's expedition to Puerto Rico, Florida, and the Caribbean between 1508 and 1519, and with the Hernán Cortés expedition to Mexico in 1521. And Estevanico, an enslaved black Moor, accompanied Andrés Dorantes de Carranza and Álvar Núñez Cabeza de Vaca on explorations of Florida, Texas, and the Gulf of Mexico and across the Southwest to the site of Mexico City in 1528 with the Pánfilo de Narváez expedition (more than 275 years before Lewis and Clark's expedition crossed the United States).

Estevanico, Black Stephen, and Esteban the Moor are just some of the names the infamous black conquistador is known by in historical accounts. Born in Azemmour, Morocco, around 1503, Estevanico was enslaved after the Portuguese attacked his village in 1513. He was purchased by Andrés Dorantes de Carranza, the Spanish aristocrat and explorer, who was part of the Pánfilo de Narváez expedition. Estevanico traveled with his master on the ill-fated journey, during which their boat ran aground off the coast of present-day Galveston Island, Texas, in 1528. All four survivors—Carranza, Estevanico, Núñez Cabeza de Vaca, and Alonso Castillo Maldonado—were captured by the Native Americans who inhabited the island.

Estevanico, or Esteban of Azemmour, as the Moor was known, traveled to the New World in the 1500s with the Pánfilo de Narváez expedition. Though no actual depictions of him exist, this bust fits the surviving written descriptions.

During their captivity, the explorers, at the insistence of their hosts, became medicine men and were compelled to cure the sick in the village. After moderate success, the men gained a reputation among the Native Americans as healers. After escaping their captors in 1534, the group traveled to various Indian villages and healed the sick.

As their reputation as healers grew, Estevanico was appointed the intermediary because he had learned to speak the dialects of the many tribes and was well respected in the Indian communities. "Estevanico's abilities, and the position of the men as wanderers in a new world where their very survival was in question, made his status that of companion rather than slave."

As they traveled across the American Southwest, the medicine men were given many gifts in gratitude for their miraculous acts. Two sacred gourds and an engraved copper rattle from the medicine men of the Arbadaos tribe were particularly noteworthy. These gifts lent credibility to the explorers' healing abilities among some Native American tribes. Estevanico and his shipmates were also told of extravagant riches in the country to the north.

After more than eight years, which included their captivity and journey across the vast territories of Texas and Mexico, the explorers met up with a group of Spaniards who escorted them to San Miguel de Culiacán and then on to Mexico City. Estevanico became quite a celebrity and was hired as a translator and a guide on an expedition headed by the Franciscan fray (friar) Marcos de Niza to search for the fabled riches in the Seven Cities of Gold.

Hernando de Alarcón, a contemporary of Estevanico's who would later investigate his death, described the Moroccan's departure from Mexico City on March 7, 1539, with his entourage:

> [Estevanico] was wearing certain things which did ring, . . . bels and feathers on his armes and legs, and he was flanked by a pair of what were probably Spanish greyhounds. The animals must have been a comforting presence to [Estevanico], since this breed of gazehound is descended from the North African saluki, a dog believed by Moroccans to possess baraka, or a blessing.

It was also reported that Estevanico carried with him four green dinner plates, which he treasured and took his meals on. His charisma, his mastery of dialects, and his decadence made him a legendary figure in his own time.

Estevanico traveled ahead of the main expedition, sending Native American messengers back to Fray Niza, informing him that the journey was going well. When Estevanico arrived at a Zuni pueblo (a settlement of Native Americans) in present-day New Mexico in the town of Hawikuh (Hawikkuh), the first of the Seven Cities of Gold, he was met with distrust and barred from entering the settlement by the Zuni chiefs. Estevanico had sent messengers ahead of the entourage to present the chiefs with his copper rattle and sacred gourds, which were adorned with feathers. The chiefs were offended by the offering and believed it signified evil or death and refused entry to Estevanico and his group. Estevanico was held captive by the Zunis and was killed while trying to escape.

Over the next hundred years, black seamen continued to travel to the New World on board European vessels. During the eighteenth century, many of them settled in the ports of New York, Boston, and Philadelphia, helping to create communities of free blacks.

Dividing Up the New World

THE SPANISH CONQUISTADORS explored the North American continent from Florida to California, including the Yucatán and Baja peninsulas, in the sixteenth century. A group of British investors, under a charter granted by King James I in 1606, formed the Virginia Company of London and the Virginia Company of Plymouth to explore the East Coast of North America and establish colonies. The Virginia Company of London annexed an area that stretched from Cape Fear, North Carolina, on the southeastern coast to the Long Island Sound in the Northeast. The company named the colony Virginia.

The Virginia Company of Plymouth's first colony overlapped with that of the Virginia Company of London, and it included land from the Chesapeake Bay to Maine, where the company initially established the Popham

Colony at the Kennebec River in 1607. That settlement failed, and the Plymouth Company reorganized and founded the Plymouth Colony in 1620 in Massachusetts.

The Dutch claimed a territory in 1614 that they called New Netherland, which spanned the area from the Delaware Bay—including the modern-day states of Delaware, Pennsylvania, New Jersey, New York, western Connecticut, and Massachusetts—to Cape Cod. The capital of New Netherland was New Amsterdam, present-day Manhattan in New York City.

JAMESTOWN, THE FIRST SURVIVING BRITISH COLONY

Jamestown, Virginia, the first permanent British settlement in the New World, was founded in 1607. The earliest documented Africans to arrive at Jamestown came in late August of 1619. They had been captured in a war between the Portuguese and the Kingdom of Ndongo and the Kingdom of Kongo, part of what is known today as Angola and the coastal regions of the Congo, located in West Central Africa. The lucrative Portuguese and Spanish slave business continued and shipped hundreds of thousands of captive Africans from slaving stations in Luanda and from other locations along the western coast of Africa, including Elmina in Ghana, to the Spanish colonies in the New World.

These dispossessed passengers who in 1619 sailed into Old Point Comfort (today, Fort Monroe, Virginia) had been taken from the Portuguese slaver the *San Juan Bautista*. The slave ship was on its way to Veracruz, Mexico, with its cargo of Africans and imported goods, when it was overrun by privateers from the Dutch *White Lion* and the British *Treasurer*. The pirates divided up the ship's cargo, each taking twenty or thirty of the African captives, and traveled together to the British colony of Jamestown. The *White Lion* was the first vessel to arrive at Point Comfort, Virginia, where "20. and odd Negroes" disembarked, according to a letter written in January 1620 by settler John Rolfe, describing the Africans' arrival to the Virginia Company treasurer Sir Edwin Sandys.

The Africans were sold to the local plantation owners, who desperately needed help planting, growing, and harvesting their cash crop of tobacco. The African arrivals were treated like indentured servants rather than slaves, since slavery did not yet exist in Virginia. At this time, an indentured

Queen Nzinga of the Kingdom of Kongo meets with the Portuguese governor of Luanda to broker a treaty after Portugal conquered the African country. The agreement was breached by the Portuguese and the slave trade expanded rapidly in the region, and the Kingdom of Kongo became a major supplier of the enslaved. The sketch is by Italian priest Giovanni Antonio Cavazzi, who witnessed the event in the 1600s.

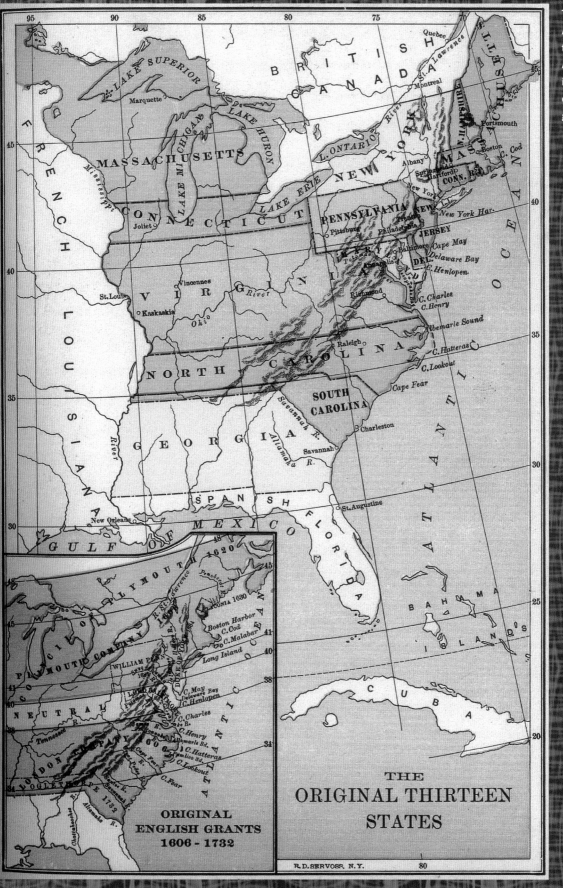

This colonial North America map shows the East Coast of America with the inset showing the original territories granted by England.

THE
ORIGINAL THIRTEEN
STATES

ORIGINAL
ENGLISH GRANTS
1606 – 1732

R. D. SERVOSS, N.Y.

About the latter end of August, a Dutch man of Warr, the White Lion, of the burden of a 160 tunnes [tons] arrived at Point-Comfort, the Commandors name Capt Jope, his pilott for the West Indies one Mr. Marmaduke an Englishman.

. . . He brought not any thin [thing] but 20. and odd Negroes, wch [which] the Governor (Sir George Yeardley) and Cape Merchant (Abraham Peirsey) bought for victualle [supplies, mainly food] (whereof he was in greate need as he pretended) at the best and easyest rate they could.

The first Africans landed at Jamestown, Virginia, in August of 1619, according to Captain John Smith, a resident of the settlement. This is an early-twentieth-century interpretation by artist Howard Pyle.

servant, whether black or white, man, woman, or child, was an individual who worked for no wages in exchange for free passage to the colonies. The indentured servant was obligated to work at least four to seven years and sometimes longer. At the end of the term, he or she would gain freedom, along with money or land, clothing, farm tools, and food. The Africans who arrived in 1619 worked a number of years and then received their freedom, along with a parcel of land.

The second man-of-war—the British ship the *Treasurer*—arrived in Point Comfort three or four days after the *White Lion* left port. Rolfe noted that the *Treasurer* left hastily because the crew was refused provisions that they needed, but not before leaving behind an African woman named Angelo, who disembarked from the ship. Historians believe other Africans stayed behind, too, because more than twenty-one Africans are documented in the 1620 census. It is estimated that a total of thirty-two disembarked from the two ships.

Researchers suggest that Angela was the Christian name given to her at her baptism in Africa before she was shipped to the Americas. A misspelling on the listing of the Africans on board the vessel that transported her to the New World made the name masculine—Angelo. Her name also appeared as Angelo in the 1625 muster (a record of persons living in a household) of Captain William Pierce, compounding a mistake that would never be undone, as was the case for so many of her African brethren who would be given new names in the New World.

Angelo and her companions had a rough trip. Kidnapped from their homeland in West Central Africa in the Ndongo or Kongo regions by marauding Imbangala rebels and sold into slavery to the Portuguese, the Africans began their forced migration, known as the Middle Passage, on the *San Juan Bautista*. It would have been a cruel and inhumane journey.

Packed tightly, like sardines in a can, the captives would have been crammed side by side, on their backs, with chained hands and feet, during the grueling trip that took from five to twelve weeks to cross the Atlantic Ocean. Men, women, and children were separated and the rebellious among them were beaten or killed. Some of the tortured souls committed suicide by jumping into the sea or died of disease, which was rampant in the close quarters of a slave ship.

Living in the Kingdom of Ndongo, between two rivers, the Lukal and the Lutele, Angelo's family may have been farmers who raised livestock and grew vegetables or weavers who made textiles and baskets. Surrounded by rows of steep cliffs, the district was made up of several towns where people gathered in marketplaces to buy and sell goods. Angelo's family and her neighbors would have been familiar with the Europeans, since by then the Portuguese had been in West Africa for many years trading with the tribal chiefs for gold and other goods.

When Angelo arrived in Jamestown and was purchased by Captain William Pierce, it was most likely to work in his household. She was not a slave and was probably considered a servant, although she was not paid for her work. Angelo's duties may have included cleaning the house; washing,

Enslaved workers—men, women, and children—at work on a tobacco plantation in Virginia.

sewing, or mending clothes; preparing and serving meals; and taking care of the children, if there were any in the household. If she worked outside the home in the fields, as some women did, she helped with the cultivation and harvesting of tobacco, which was the colony's primary and most lucrative crop.

The fact that the Africans of the *Treasurer* and the *White Lion* all came from the same regions in West Central Africa may explain why they were able to survive in the harsh New World environment. They shared a similar culture and ethnic identity as well as language and skills (they were craftspeople, farmers, or cattlemen). This shared background helped the Africans support each other as they adapted to their new surroundings and survive in an inhospitable land.

A FAMILY NAMED JOHNSON

Two years after the first group of Africans arrived in Jamestown, Antonio arrived from Angola in 1621 aboard the vessel *James* and was purchased by Richard Bennett to work on his tobacco plantation as an indentured servant. "Antonio, the Negar" appears in the 1625 census as part of the Bennett household.

Antonio, or Anthony as he was called, survived the brutal attack by the Powhatan Indians on the colonists of Jamestown on March 22, 1622. The same year, "Mary a Negro Woman" arrived on the ship Margaret and John and became a servant at Warresquioake (Wariscoyack), the Bennett plantation. After 1625, Anthony and Mary married and took Johnson as their last name. They also earned their freedom around this time. They had four children in a union that lasted more than forty years.

During their life together, the Johnsons and their two boys and two girls amassed a huge parcel of land (eight hundred acres), and on it they raised cattle and tobacco. Primary sources such as census records and court documents trace the lives of Mary and Anthony Johnson of Pungoteague Creek (today it is incorporated into Accomack County) in Northampton County, Virginia, and in Somerset County, Maryland, where the family moved in 1665.

FREE BLACK PLANTERS

Along with the Johnson family, there were other free black planters who lived in Northampton County, Virginia. By 1664, the county tax list (persons sixteen and older) indicated that sixty-two blacks lived in the county. By 1677, the number had risen to seventy-five, making up 16 percent of the Northampton community.

SOME OF THE FREE BLACK PLANTERS OF NORTHAMPTON COUNTY

Sebastian Cane	Francis Payne (Pane or Paine)	Lony Longo
Bashaw Ferdinando	Emanuel (Manuel Driggus [Rodriggus])	Anthony Johnson
John Francisco	Thomas Driggus	Mary Johnson
Susan (Susanna) Grace	Mary Rodriggus	John Johnson
William Harman	Tony King	Richard Johnson
Philip Mongum	Sara King	Jane Gossall

Court Records from Northampton County, 1651–1654, Involving the Anthony Johnson Family:

- In 1635, John Upton of Warresquioake County (by then, the plantation where Anthony and Mary worked was defunct, and the area where the plantation existed was now part of the county of the same name) petitioned for 1,650 acres, based on thirty-three headrights (the granting of 50 acres of land to persons who settled in Virginia or to persons who paid for the transportation and expenses of persons who settled in Virginia). Included on his list of thirty-three people were "Antho[ny], a Negroe and Mary, a Negroe." This record is not necessarily an indication of Anthony and Mary's status as free or indentured, because headright certificates circulated sometimes for as long as a decade before being processed, which involved the surveying and claiming of the property. (Upton may have accumulated or purchased the headrights from another person and saved them until he could "make a sizable claim.")

- The Johnsons moved to Northampton County on Pungoteague Creek, and records indicate that in 1651, Anthony Johnson claimed 250 acres of land due him for five headrights.

- In 1652, John Johnson, the oldest son, claimed 450 acres next to his father's land.

- In February 1653, a fire destroyed the Johnson plantation and Anthony and Mary petitioned the court for relief. The court excused Mary and her two daughters from paying "Taxes and Charges in Northampton County for public use" for "their natural lives."

- On October 8, 1653, Anthony Johnson was in court in a dispute with Lieutenant John Neale over a cow. The matter was resolved in Anthony Johnson's favor.

- In 1654, Richard Johnson, another son, claimed a 100-acre tract adjacent to his father's and brother's holdings, bringing the total Johnson family land holdings to 800 acres.

- Also in 1654, Anthony Johnson's slave, John Casor, told white planter Captain Samuel Gouldsmith, who had business with Johnson at his plantation, that he was being held against his will; he had come to Virginia as an indentured servant, not as a slave. It was not uncommon for black planters to own slaves; the enslavement of blacks by blacks occurred in the New World as well as in Africa. Two other white planters, Robert and George Parker, believed Casor's story and took him to their plantation to work. Johnson was disturbed by this, since Casor's story was untrue. After a family meeting, it was decided that the Johnsons would give Casor his freedom as an indentured servant and discharge "John Casor Negro from all service, claims and demands. . . ." But Johnson had a change of heart and decided to go to court for the return of his property.

- On March 8, 1655, Anthony Johnson made a complaint against Robert Parker in the Northampton County Court. Johnson claimed that Parker had detained his servant John Casor through false pretenses, under which he claimed that Casor was a free man. Through evidence from a deposition given by Captain Gouldsmith, John Casor was returned to Anthony Johnson, and Robert Parker had to pay for all the charges in the suit.

- In 1665, the entire Johnson family moved to Somerset County, Maryland, where Anthony leased a 300-acre plantation, which he named Tonies Vineyard. His sons became successful landowners after their father died, and their mother renewed the lease on the plantation for ninety-nine years.

- In 1677, John Jr., the grandson of Anthony Johnson, purchased 44 acres of land and named it Angola, after his grandfather's birthplace.

- John Jr. married Elizabeth Low in 1681 in Sussex County, Delaware. John Jr.'s sister, Susan, married John Puckham, an Indian, in 1682 in Somerset County, Maryland.

The free blacks of Virginia were living a life of comfort and prosperity as property owners and tobacco growers. There were no strict codes forbidding them from conducting business, buying property, or marrying whomever they wanted. There were interracial marriages between the African and white indentured servant populations and the African and Native American populations. Small at first, the free black community expanded as members married and had families.

DUTCH NEW AMSTERDAM

The Dutch West India Company founded a colony along the eastern coast of the United States, extending from Delaware to Massachusetts, and called it New Netherland. Situated in a harbor originally discovered by Henry Hudson in 1609, and later explored by Adriaen Block and Hendrick Christiaensen from 1611 to 1614, the colony's capital, New Amsterdam, was settled in 1624. Today we know it as Manhattan in New York City.

The first Africans were brought to New Amsterdam between 1625 and 1626 to clear the land and to build forts, roads, and housing for the new white settlers. They were referred to by the Dutch as "Company slaves" or "Company Negroes." Unlike the Africans brought to America by the British, these first eleven Africans were not indentured servants and were paid wages, but they were not free to return to their homes either. Based on some of their surnames—D'Angola, Congo, and Portuguese—these Africans probably came from Angola, the Congo, and Portugal.

"The Company's slaves acted as the colony's municipal workers, building and repairing fortifications, roads, warehouses, and other structures of the corporate state . . . In 1635, five black workers petitioned The Hague in the Netherlands, for an increase in their wages to make their pay comparable to the white workers." The court granted their request, and this ruling opened the door for blacks in New Netherland to settle their disputes with the Dutch West India Company in court.

The Company Negroes were also important from a military perspective; they helped the Dutch fight in conflicts with the Native Americans, the original residents of Manhattan Island. At first there existed a fragile peace between the Dutch and their Native American neighbors, but attacks increased as the colonists moved north from their original fort in Lower Manhattan into lands inhabited by the Indians.

Willem Kieft, one of the early directors of New Netherland, decided to create a buffer zone between the white colonists and the Indians and began to grant land to the blacks who had fought in these conflicts. The land grants, which were given from 1643 to 1664, totaled more than 130 acres, with the northernmost parcel of 18 acres owned by Manuel Trumpeter, situated near what is modern-day Manhattan's Fifth Avenue and Washington Square Park.

In 1644, eleven of the Company Negroes petitioned the Dutch West India Company for their emancipation and received a form of "half-freedom" for themselves and their wives, as well as grants of land. Their children remained enslaved. In return for the land, the Negroes had to pay the company an annual payment in farm goods and continue to work for the company when needed. Paulo D'Angola, Gracia D'Angola, Simon Congo, Big Manuel, Little Manuel, Manuel De Gerrit de Reus, Anthony Portuguese, Pieter San Tome, Jan Francisco, Little Anthony, and Jan Fort Orange were the eleven freed Negroes, and they had been among the first group of blacks brought to New Amsterdam by the Dutch.

THE BRITISH COLONIES

The colony of Plymouth in Massachusetts was founded in 1620 by the Virginia Company of Plymouth and settled by the Pilgrims, followers of the teachings of French theologian John Calvin. The Pilgrims wanted reform in the Church of England. When this did not happen and it became much more difficult for them to practice their religion—a pure form of Protestantism—they left England. After Jamestown, Plymouth was the second permanent British colony established in North America. English Puritans, also seeking religious freedom, settled in Salem, Massachusetts, in 1629, founding the Massachusetts Bay Colony. In 1691, the colonies of Plymouth and Maine became part of the Massachusetts Bay Colony. And, in 1664, the British took over the Dutch colony of New Netherland after positioning troops and negotiating with the colony's leaders. It was renamed New York. The colony of Carolina was established in 1663 by eight proprietors who were granted a charter by King Charles II of England. Four of the proprietors were affiliated with the Royal African Company. Carolina was divided into two colonies, North and South Carolina, in 1729. Georgia was made a British penal colony in 1732 and a royal colony in 1752. The British colonies now reached from Georgia to Massachusetts.

A slave auction scene set in the late seventeenth or early eighteenth century at a slave
market in Lower Manhattan, interpreted by artist Howard Pyle in the early twentieth
century

Chattel Slavery

IN 1641, MASSACHUSETTS became the first colony to recognize slavery as a legal institution. Connecticut approved a law legalizing slavery in 1650, and Virginia ruled in 1661 that a child born to a slave would also be a slave.

By the mid-1600s, slavery was evolving into a race-based institution: The enslaved were identified by the color of their skin. This was illustrated in the Hugh Gwyn case of Northampton County, Virginia. In 1640, three of Gwyn's servants ran away to Maryland. When they were captured, the court ordered that the two white laborers be given thirty lashes and four years extra service. The "negro named John Punch" received not only thirty lashes, but he was also ordered to "serve his said master or his assigns for the time of his natural Life here or elsewhere."

This verdict in the Gwyn case set the stage for the birth of "chattel slavery," in which enslaved Africans were designated as property—able to be "mortgaged, inherited, and/or sold separately from the land." Blacks in colonial America would no longer be viewed as indentured servants.

The system of indentured servitude had evolved because of Britain's stagnating economy in the early 1600s. A lack of jobs and a population increase resulted in a higher rate of unemployment. Crime and poverty escalated. One strategy was to contract large numbers of the unemployed, craftspeople, criminals, the homeless, and itinerant workers into indentured service and ship them to the new British colonies in America to ease Britain's economic burdens.

In Virginia and Maryland, the flow of indentured servants had begun to decline by the mid-1660s. "There were several reasons for this growing shortage of white workers. In England the birth rate had fallen in the 1640s and the population grew slowly for the rest of the century. There were fewer young people to compete for available jobs and wages." The economy began to grow, and there was more work in England.

This economic shift made England a more attractive alternative than the American colonies for those British citizens trying to earn a living. At the same time, opportunities to become landowners in Virginia and Maryland had decreased as good land became more scarce and less accessible.

No. 5.

THE LASH.

An enslaved man being whipped by a white overseer, circa 1863. Beatings, maimings, and other forms of physical abuse were used by slaveholders to instill fear and to control African workers.

"Indentured servants did continue to arrive in the Chesapeake [the area around Jamestown, Virginia], where planters were willing to purchase convicts and other less desirable immigrants and to pay premium prices for carpenters, tailors, bricklayers, blacksmiths, and other skilled craftsmen. But by the 1680s, the larger planters realized that for the main business of producing, slaves were considerably cheaper than white servants."

Thus began the harsh and inhumane campaign to bring slavery to the American colonies. Early America's buildings and roads would be constructed at the expense of the Africans' freedom. The enslaved would also tend the livestock, plant and harvest crops, and manage and perform household chores.

SLAVERY

THIS PAGE: *Cutting the Sugar Cane, Antigua*, by William Clark, 1823. Europeans introduced sugarcane to the New World in the 1490s. Plantations spread throughout the Caribbean and South America. By the 1750s, British and French plantations and their slave labor produced most of the world's sugar and other by-products, including molasses and rum.

PREVIOUS PAGE: *Slaves Waiting for Sale—Richmond, Virginia*, 1861, an oil painting by Eyre Crowe

THE TRANSATLANTIC SLAVE trade began in 1518 when King Charles I of Spain sanctioned the importation of Africans to Spanish colonies in the Americas and the Caribbean by granting licenses, or *asientos,* to companies to import slaves. The British began importing slave labor to their colonies in America in the seventeenth century. In all, an estimated ten million— and, in some estimates, twenty-five million—Africans were forced to migrate to the Americas (North, Central, and South America) and the Caribbean over the course of three centuries.

The enslaved Africans brought to North America came originally from West Central Africa: Angola and the Kongo regions, and later on from Senegambia (present-day Senegal and Gambia). The Africans were also shipped from Sierra Leone, the Ivory Coast, the Gold Coast (Ghana), Mali, the Bight of Biafra (eastern Nigeria, Cameroon, and the Gulf of Guinea), and the Bight of Benin (southern Ghana, Togo, Benin, and southwest Nigeria). More of the enslaved came from central and southwest Africa (the Congo, northern Angola, and Zaire).

From 1700 to the early 1800s, the importation of African slaves to the Americas was at its peak. An estimated six million Africans were brought to the New World during this period, of which three hundred thousand to five hundred thousand were imported by the British to their American colonies.

The British looked to the Caribbean and South America, where the Portuguese and Spanish used African slave labor to plant and harvest sugarcane, as a model for what they wanted to do in their colonies. "By the 1560s, the slave population was larger than the white population in the Spanish island colonies of Hispaniola [present-day Haiti and the Dominican Republic] and Cuba. In Brazil and the West Indies, the need for enslaved Africans also increased."

Sugarcane plantations required many workers to cultivate the crop, strong workers to wield large machetes to cut through the thick, tough sugarcane stalks during harvest, and workers to process the cane into sugar. "The need for slave labor was great because few Europeans were willing to migrate to the hot climate and do the grueling, backbreaking work that plantation agriculture required." The labor was often dangerous because of the sharp tools and machinery used to process the cane. Diseases brought over by the Europeans, such as smallpox and scarlet fever, spread quickly and decimated the island population.

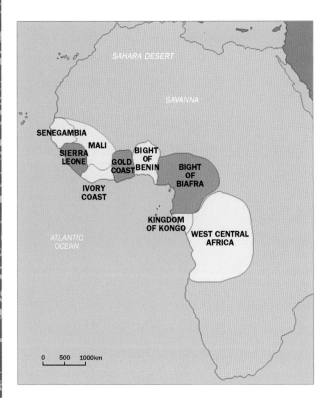

Map of the regions on the west coast of the African continent from which the enslaved were shipped. These areas were the major suppliers of enslaved Africans during the Atlantic slave trade in the seventeenth and eighteenth centuries.

The importation of the enslaved to the American colonies was facilitated by the Royal African Company of London, a private British slaving company, under an exclusive 1672 charter with the British government in which 5,000 enslaved Africans were transported between 1680 and 1686. In 1698, the British Parliament abolished the Royal African Company's monopoly and opened up slave trading to every British citizen.

The total number of Africans transported on British ships to the American colonies increased dramatically from "8,000 to 45,000 annually" after the Royal African Company's charter was abolished. "In the first nine years following the end of the company's monopoly, the port at Bristol shipped an average of 18,000 slaves a year." Bristol, Liverpool, and London were major British ports in the Atlantic slave trade. About 1.5 million Africans were transported from Liverpool, which was considered the European capital of the slave trade, between the 1780s and the end of the British slave trade in 1807.

From its Bristol, Liverpool, and London ports, Great Britain exported manufactured and luxury products to America. British goods were traded for slaves in West Africa. Enslaved Africans were then transported to the West Indies and the British colonies in the Americas. This export/import system of trade between England, Africa, and the colonies was called "triangular trade."

British ships filled with gold, ivory, spices, and hardwoods from West Africa returned to England, while other British ships, packed with enslaved Africans from West Africa, sailed to the West Indies. Still other British ships ladened with teas, spices, furniture, cloth, and tools sailed directly to Boston.

From the West Indies, ships sailed to ports in Charleston, South Carolina; Philadelphia, Pennsylvania; New York, New York; and Boston, Massachusetts, transporting enslaved Africans, sugar, and molasses bound for the northern ports.

Fish, flour, livestock, and lumber were loaded onto ships in Philadelphia and New York, bound for the West Indies. Rum, iron, gunpowder, cloth, and tools were also shipped from these cities to the West African coast.

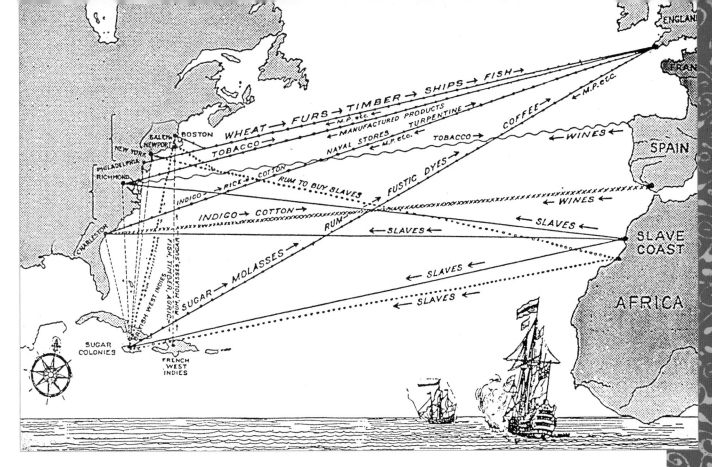

On the final leg of the trade route, British ships carried sugar, molasses, and wood from the West Indies; rice, silk, indigo (a blue dye), and tobacco from Charleston; and whale oil, lumber, and furs from Boston back to England.

Triangular trade routes between England, Spain, their American colonies, and Africa in the seventeenth and eighteenth centuries. Ships sailed from England to the Caribbean islands bringing manufactured products (M.P. on diagram), and returned to Great Britain with sugar, molasses, rum, and coffee. Other ships carried enslaved men, women, and children from the west coast of Africa to the Caribbean, South America, and the American colonies. The ships leaving the American colonies were ladened with cotton, tobacco, indigo, furs, timber, and fish to be sold to the European market.

SLAVE SOCIETY IN COLONIAL AMERICA

THE LIFE OF an enslaved person in the colonies by the mid-1700s was shaped by where he or she lived. In New England (Massachusetts, Connecticut, Rhode Island, and New Hampshire), many people lived on small farms, although the climate was cold and the soil was not very fertile. The colonists planted crops to feed their cattle and pigs, and potatoes and corn to sell in the markets. The farmers also bartered for goods and labor among themselves.

Sequences of Legal Maneuvers and Laws That Limited the Rights of Negroes and Slaves in Virginia

1640 All persons, except Africans, will be provided with arms and ammunition.

1660 The term "Negro Slave" first appears in law.

1661 The institution of slavery is acknowledged in law.

1662 Slavery is an inherited condition flowing from the mother.

1667 Baptism does not exempt blacks from bondage.

1669 A slave resisting his master, or anyone else by his master's order, can be killed and the master or his agent will not be charged with a felony.

1670 Free Africans and Indians cannot purchase white servants (Christians), but can purchase any from their own nation.

1680 An act for preventing Negro Insurrections. Slaves are forbidden to carry weapons, or come and go from their master's property without a certificate.

1682 An act for preventing rioting or rebellion by Negroes. No slave or Negro can stay on another's plantation, without permission from his owner, more than four hours or the master or overseer will pay a fine.

—William Waller Hening, *Hening's Statutes, Being a Collection of All the Laws of Virginia from the First Session of the Legislature, in the Year 1619*

A large class of craftspeople and artisans grew to provide goods and services to the farmers and to their families, including wagonmakers, blacksmiths, and furniture makers. There were merchants who imported goods from Britain and from the other colonies to sell to the farmers. Slave labor was used not only in farming. It also played a role in the shipbuilding and fishing industries, and in the seaports and sawmills (where the trees were made into lumber to build houses and boats). The enslaved worked as servants in the homes of the wealthy and as caterers, craftspeople, and skilled and unskilled laborers. After the Revolutionary War, many blacks were granted their freedom for having fought in the war. Upon returning home, they became part of the community of free African Americans in New England.

In the mid-Atlantic colonies (Pennsylvania, Delaware, New York, and New Jersey), there were sprawling plantations, thriving seaports, and profitable trading businesses. Enslaved Africans and free blacks worked in the busy ports of New York and Philadelphia as boat pilots, navigators, and seamen; stevedores loading and unloading merchant ships; caulkers repairing ships; shipwrights building ships; sailmakers; and stewards and cooks. Other enslaved people managed the plantations outside of the cities and worked in the households of urban families, where they were sometimes hired out to the local businesses. Wages received by these workers were handed over to their masters in most cases.

In the South (Maryland, Virginia, North and South Carolina, and Georgia), slave labor was the backbone of the plantation system, which produced tobacco, rice, and, later, cotton. These plantations were self-sufficient communities, with the enslaved working as blacksmiths, carpenters, farmers, seamstresses, housekeepers, carriage drivers, and other laborers. The South had the largest slave population. In 1708, the white and slave populations were almost equal in the Carolinas—4,100 blacks and 4,080 whites. By 1715, the slave population in the Carolinas was much greater than the white population, with 10,500 blacks and 6,250 whites.

As the slave population increased, the white slaveholders, especially in the South, became more fearful of slave revolts, during which their families could be harmed. In response to these fears, individual colonies enacted laws known as slave codes to restrict the movements of slaves.

A nineteenth-century wood engraving of Martha Washington, the wife of President George Washington, knitting in her room at their home in Mount Vernon, Virginia, while a house slave cuts cloth to sew for winter clothing. An enslaved child also knits by the fire.

Virginia was the first colony to pass laws restricting the rights of blacks, beginning in 1640. In South Carolina, the Slave Act of 1691 declared "all Negroes, Mulattoes, and Indians" sold into or intended for sale into bondage were slaves.

SLAVE VERSE AND NARRATIVES: IN THEIR OWN WORDS

PHILLIS WHEATLEY, A young slave girl, published a collection of poems titled *Poems on Various Subjects, Religious and Moral* in 1773, when she was around twenty years old, becoming the first enslaved African in America to publish a book of poetry. Phillis had been taken from Africa when she was around eight and sold to the Wheatley family of Boston in 1761. She was taught to read and write and was educated in the classics by the family.

Wheatley eventually began writing poetry. Her first poem, about two men who almost drowned at sea, was published in the *Newport Mercury* in 1767. After publishing her 1773 collection of poems in London, Phillis gained widespread attention in Europe and in America. Phillis Wheatley was freed by her master that same year. In 1774, Phillis married a free black businessman who was arrested for debts. They had three children, all of whom died at very young ages. Phillis died penniless in 1784.

There are many first-person accounts that describe the experience of being enslaved in the American colonies. These autobiographical histories are known as slave narratives.

One of the earliest and more controversial authors to chronicle his kidnapping from Africa was Olaudah Equiano. An abolitionist, Equiano wrote about his experiences in a 1789 best-selling book, *The Interesting Narrative of the Life of Olaudah Equiano, or Gustavus Vassa, the African.* He claimed he was born in 1745 in what is now Nigeria, was the son of an Igbo (Eboe) tribal leader, and was kidnapped at age eleven. However, historian Vincent Carretta, professor of English at the University of Maryland and author of *Equiano, the African: Biography of a Self-Made Man*, discovered documents (a 1759 London baptismal certificate and a 1773 Royal Navy muster roll from the ship *Racehorse*) that indicate Equiano was born in South Carolina rather than Africa. Whether they are his actual experiences or those reported to him by enslaved Africans, researchers are reluctant to completely dismiss the autobiography. The book's thorough account of the transatlantic slave experience and its description of life in an African village are compelling. Based on research, there is convincing evidence that, at the least, the second part of the book is an authentic retelling of Equiano's life story. Since he was an ardent abolitionist, some believe that Equiano's motivation for writing the book may have been to help abolish the slave trade.

In the book, Equiano recounts his kidnapping by Africans:

> One day, when all our people were gone out to their work as usual, and only I and my dear sister were left to mind the house, two men and a woman got over our walls and in a moment seized us both, and, without giving us time to cry out, or make resistance, they stopped our mouths, and ran off with us into the nearest wood. Here they tied our hands, and continued to carry us as far as they could, till night

Phillis Wheatley was the first African American to publish a volume of poetry and the first African American woman to be published. Wheatley's collection, *Poems on Various Subjects, Religious and Moral,* was published in Britain in 1773 while she was still enslaved in America.

LEFT: Olaudah Equiano was an abolitionist in Great Britain who in 1789 published his autobiography, *The Interesting Narrative of the Life of Olaudah Equiano, or Gustavus Vassa, the African*. The bestselling antislavery book has been credited with influencing the abolition of the slave trade in Great Britain in 1807. America abolished the slave trade (but not the owning of slaves) a year later, in 1808.

RIGHT: Harriet Ann Jacobs, 1894. Jacobs authored the slave narrative *Incidents in the Life of a Slave Girl* in 1861, under the pseudonym Linda Brent. Her book was the first to describe the treatment of enslaved females. After hiding for seven years in a small crawl space in her grandmother's home, Harriet escaped by boat to Philadelphia and then went on to New York City, where her freedom was purchased by the sympathetic Cornelia Grinnell Willis, her white employer.

came on, when we reached a small house where the robbers halted for refreshment, and spent the night.

We were then unbound, but were unable to take any food; and, being quite overpowered by fatigue and grief, our only relief was some sleep, which allayed our misfortune for a short time. The next morning we left the house, and continued travelling all the day. For a long time we had kept [to] the woods, but at last we came into a road which I believed I knew. I had now some hopes of being delivered; for we had advanced but a little way before I discovered some people at a distance, on which I began to cry out for their assistance: but my cries had no other effect than to make them tie me faster and stop my mouth, and then they put me into a large sack.

According to his account, Equiano eventually ended up in the hands of white slave traders who shipped him with other captives to the West Indies and then to Virginia, where he was purchased by British naval officer Michael Henry Pascal. As the slave of a British naval lieutenant, and later on as a slave to Robert King, a Quaker merchant, Equiano became a competent sailor and an astute businessman.

Equiano traveled with Lieutenant Pascal during the Seven Years' War to Canada and then to the Mediterranean and to England, and he also traveled to the American colonies, South America, and the Caribbean. Educated in England, Equiano eventually purchased his freedom in 1766 when he was in his early twenties. He settled in London after his career at sea and became a supporter of the abolitionist cause and a successful entrepreneur who campaigned vigorously to bring an end to slavery.

Harriet Ann Jacobs wrote *Incidents in the Life of a Slave Girl,* published in 1861, using the pseudonym Linda Brent to hide her identity. In her groundbreaking book, Jacobs described her enslavement in North Carolina and then her subsequent freedom and reunion with her family in the North. She detailed for readers the sexual abuse and suffering she endured during her captivity and the hard choices she had to make in order to gain her freedom.

Jacobs's story evoked sympathy and support from white female readers in the North not only because it echoed feminist issues of the day, including woman suffrage and the sexism endured, but also because it eloquently described the cruelty and racism that she experienced in bondage. Jacobs escaped her master and moved to Boston, where her son and daughter joined her. Still pursued by her slave mistress and her mistress's husband, Mr. and Mrs. Daniel Dodge, she relocated to Rochester, New York, and then to New York City, where a friend secured her freedom for three hundred dollars. Although grateful for her friend's help, Harriet resented the Dodges and their demands for money, because she believed she did not belong to anyone and her freedom should not be purchased.

> *I had objected to having my freedom bought, yet I must confess that when it was done I felt as if a heavy load had been lifted from my weary shoulders. When I rode home in the cars [horse-drawn streetcars] I was no longer afraid to unveil my face and look at people as they passed. I should have been glad to have met Daniel Dodge himself; to have had him seen me and known me, that he might have mourned over the untoward circumstances which compelled him to sell me for three hundred dollars.*

After Jacobs's book was published, she moved to Alexandria, Virginia, and assisted the freedmen during the Civil War, helping to find them housing and employment and nursing the sick. She also opened the Jacobs Free School to educate black youth.

ANTISLAVERY MILESTONES

The first colony to abolish slavery outright is Vermont, in 1777. During or right after the American Revolution, many of the northern states begin the process of eliminating slavery. Pennsylvania in 1780; Massachusetts in 1783; Connecticut and Rhode Island in 1784; and New York in 1799 adopt laws that allow for the gradual manumission, or freedom, of the enslaved.

The British government passes a law abolishing the importation of slaves in 1807.

America passes a law that ends the importation of slaves, effective January 1, 1808.

Great Britain votes into law the Slave Emancipation Act in 1833, ending slavery in the British Empire.

The Civil War between the Union (the northern states) and the Confederacy (southern states that had seceded from the Union) over slavery begins in 1861 and ends in 1865.

President Abraham Lincoln issues the Emancipation Proclamation on January 1, 1863, which abolishes slavery in the Confederacy, but not in the border states or the southern states that were controlled by the North.

Slave trading across the Atlantic Ocean gradually ends around 1870.

Reverend Josiah Henson, an abolitionist, published his autobiography, *The Life of Josiah Henson, Formerly a Slave, Now an Inhabitant of Canada,* in 1849, detailing his life of slavery with the Riley family in Maryland. It is believed that Henson inspired the main character of Uncle Tom in Harriet Beecher Stowe's controversial antislavery novel, *Uncle Tom's Cabin*.

Other prominent authors of slave narratives included Frederick Douglass, Charles Ball, Josiah Henson, Sojourner Truth, and William Wells Brown. The Library of Congress is the repository for slave narratives written by writers and journalists who were commissioned by the Works Progress Administration from 1936 to 1938 to document the slave experience through interviews with surviving former slaves.

EDUCATING THE ENSLAVED

EACH COLONY AND, later, each state had its own laws or slave codes, particularly in the South, that regulated the behavior of the enslaved, including denying them an education. It was often illegal for enslaved Africans to learn how to read and write, although many learned from their masters' children or from benevolent mistresses or by attending schools run by religious groups.

Slaveholders feared that educated slaves would escape or organize rebellions and revolt. Without slaves to do the work on the plantations and to help care for their families, many planters in the South believed the plantation-based economy would fail. Keeping the Africans ignorant was one way to exert control over a population that was quickly outpacing its white overseers.

Another means of controlling the enslaved was through torture, including physical, sexual, and psychological abuse. Runaway slaves or disobedient slaves were often disfigured or maimed by their owners. As punishment, an ear was chopped off, or a slave was branded with a hot iron or whipped severely, causing lifelong scarring and often permanent disability.

In the northern colonies, the enslaved were not tied to a plantation-based economy and were often trained through apprenticeships as shoemakers, blacksmiths, carpenters, cooks, and seamstresses. Their knowledge of these professions improved the economic standings of their owners. These artisans and craftspeople were loaned out to perform jobs for other slave owners.

Religious groups, abolitionists, and sympathetic white supporters initially founded religious schools and, later, all-black schools that taught enslaved and free blacks reading, writing, arithmetic, grammar, geography, spelling, public speaking, and needlepoint for girls and astronomy and map drawing for boys. Schools were established in New York, Massachusetts, and Pennsylvania. Some religious groups also opened schools for blacks in the South.

The Reverend Alexander Garden, an Anglican minister aided by the church's Society for the Propagation of the Gospel, started a school for enslaved children in South Carolina in 1743, teaching students religion and the basics: reading, writing, and arithmetic.

LEARNING A SKILL

Learning a skill was one of the few avenues open to some black youths. Early in the eighteenth century the St. James Goose Creek parochial school and the Charleston Free School taught white, Indian and black children. In the aftermath of the Stono Rebellion, the Slave Code of 1740 made it illegal to teach blacks to write, but an exception was made for the Reverend Alexander Garden's School.

—Walter B. Edgar, *South Carolina: A History*

New York African Free School Number 2, engraved by student Patrick Reason, at age 13. The school, which opened in 1820, is sometimes referred to as the Mulberry Street School because it was located on Mulberry Street. The school was among seven established by the New York Manumission Society beginning in 1787, to educate African American students in New York City.

The Collegiate School in Manhattan was established by the Reformed Protestant Dutch Church in 1628 to educate Dutch youths and blacks. The school taught black students not only how to read and write, but also instructed them in religion to prepare them for conversion to the Protestant faith.

Elias Neau, a Huguenot missionary, was hired by the Society for the Propagation of the Gospel to establish an Anglican school in New York City in 1704. Colonial governor Robert Hunter praised Neau in a proclamation endorsing his work "to Catechize and Instruct Children, Servants, Negro and Indian Slaves in the Knowledge of Jesus Christ."

Many white New Yorkers were against Neau's mission to educate blacks and Native Americans, and his school was closed briefly after it was thought that some of its black students were involved in the 1712 conspiracy to kill slave owners. The school reopened when it was determined that only one of its students was involved in the plot. The school closed for good in 1722 after Neau's death.

The African Free School, the first in a system of schools for black students sponsored by the New York Manumission Society, opened in Lower

Manhattan in 1787 with twelve students. The school was destroyed in a fire in 1814. With a land grant from New York City, the African Free School Number 1 opened on William Street in January 1815, with a student body of forty. In 1820, the African Free School Number 2, a larger facility with five hundred students, opened on Mulberry Street. The Public School Society of New York, the origin of the public school system, took over the administration of the seven African Free Schools in 1834, which, combined, had an enrollment of over fourteen hundred students, and began integrating them into the larger education system.

Other all-black schools in New York City during the 1800s included the Colored School Number 3, which served the students in the predominantly black community of Seneca Village located in present-day Central Park. The school was housed in the African Union Methodist Church. In Brooklyn, Colored School Number 1 (also known as the African Free School) opened in 1827. Colored School Number 2 was established in 1853, also in Brooklyn, to educate the children of Weeksville, the community founded by freed slaves. Sarah Smith Tompkins, a Weeksville resident, taught at the Colored School Number 3 in 1854 and later went on to become the first African American principal of Grammar School Number 80 in Manhattan in 1863.

In 1798, Primus Hall, an ex-slave and veteran of the American Revolution, opened the first separate school for black students at his home in Boston. The African School was created by members of the black community to educate the children who were not enrolled in the white school system. Two students from Harvard University were hired as teachers. The school moved to the first floor of the African Meeting Room in 1808 and closed in 1835, when a new school, the Abiel Smith School, constructed from money bequeathed from the white businessman, opened.

Bishop Richard Allen, founder of the Mother Bethel African Methodist Episcopal Church in Philadelphia, opened a school in 1795 for black students. In 1804, he founded the Society of Free People of Colour for Promoting the Instruction and School Education of Children of African Descent. By 1811, there were at least eleven schools for African American students in Philadelphia.

EARLY BLACK CHURCHES

RELIGION HAS ALWAYS been an important staple in African American culture. During slavery, Africans were forbidden from practicing their own spiritual beliefs brought with them from Africa. It was against the law, in most of the colonies, for blacks to gather in groups larger than three. As a result, they were not allowed to form their own churches. The enslaved had to worship with their masters at their churches or secretly, in out-of-the-way meeting places.

Religion was one of the ways slaveholders kept the enslaved in bondage. Slaveholders converted thousands of enslaved Africans to Christianity, with the belief that they were saving people they considered "inferior," and they often cited the Bible to validate this idea. They also used the fear of God to enforce a slave's obedience.

At church services attended with their white slaveholders, the enslaved listened to the same sermons and sang the same hymns as the white parishioners, but they were separated during the service. The black worshippers were usually seated in the balcony, in the back of a sanctuary, or in some other area away from the slaveholders. They were also excluded from receiving communion with the rest of the congregation.

Those enslaved who worshipped secretly did so at night, often in forests or swamps, away from their masters and overseers. Individuals would preach from the Bible, sing spirituals, and lead the flock in prayer. Some of these black leaders eventually started their own churches, and, beginning in the eighteenth century, African American religious institutions were established.

THE EARLIEST BLACK CHURCHES

1758
African Baptist (or the Bluestone) Church, founded in 1758 in Mecklenburg, Virginia, and considered the first black church in colonial America.

1773
Silver Bluff Baptist Church in Aiken County, South Carolina, established in 1773. The first "regular pastor was a young slave named David George (c. 1742–1810)." After the outbreak of the American Revolution, many church members fled to freedom in Halifax, Nova Scotia, in Canada. In 1792, George relocated his congregation of twelve hundred to Sierra Leone in Africa.

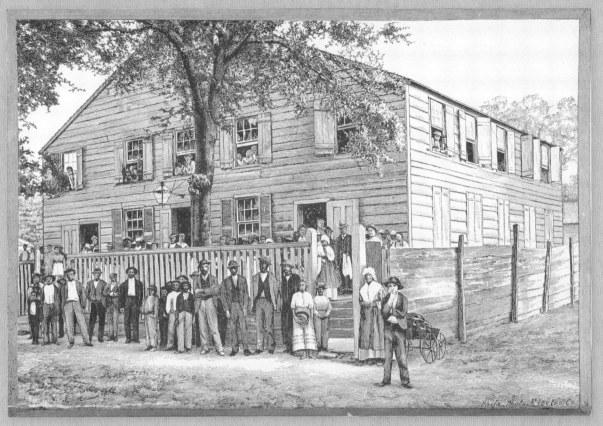

The original caption on this drawing read, "The first colored Baptist church in North America." It appeared as the frontispiece in a book of the same title published by Rev. James M. Simms of Philadelphia. The church was established on January 20, 1788, in Savannah, Georgia, making it one of the earliest African American congregations in America. The First Baptist Church of Petersburg (Virginia), founded in 1774, considers itself the "first" black Baptist church in America. Black churches have played a pivotal role in the social fabric of African American society and are often the central meeting places to discuss and debate issues affecting the black community.

1788
First African Baptist Church of Savannah, Georgia, founded in 1788 by the Reverend Andrew Bryan, a Baptist minister.

1796
African Chapel, which later became Mother African Methodist Episcopal Zion Church (the "Freedom Church"), organized in New York City in 1796.

1816
Mother Bethel African Methodist Episcopal Church, founded in 1816 in Philadelphia, under the leadership of the Bishop Richard Allen.

10 POUND REWARD
FOR RETURN OF RUN AWAY SLAVE

Ran away from his master William Brown of Framingham on the 30th of Sept. last, a mulatto fellow about 27 years of age, named Crispus, 6 feet and 2 inches high, short curl'd hair, his knees nearer together than common; and had on a light colour'd beaver skin coat, plain new buckskin breeches, blue yarn stockings and a checked woolen shirt. Whoever shall take up said runaway and convey him to his aforesaid master shall have 10 pounds old tenor reward, and all necessary charges paid. And all masters of vessels and others are hereby cautioned against concealing or carrying off said servant on penalty of law.

ABOVE: *Boston Massacre*, 1865, by Henry Pelham depicts Crispus Attucks in the Boston Massacre in 1770. Attucks became the first martyr of the American Revolution after a mob attacked a British soldier in front of the Boston Custom House. The soldier was joined by other British soldiers, who fired shots into the unruly crowd, killing four people, including Attucks; a fifth victim would die later. **LEFT**: This notice was published on October 2, 1750, in *The Boston Gazette,* seeking information on Attucks' whereabouts.

BLACKS IN THE REVOLUTIONARY WAR

THE AMERICAN REVOLUTION was a war waged by the American colonists to gain their independence from British rule. The colonies had grown to thirteen distinct and productive geographical areas. Their inhabitants became resentful of laws imposed by a government an ocean away, reaping huge monetary gains that did not benefit the colonists.

The first martyr of the campaign for independence, which occurred five years before the first battles of Lexington and Concord, was a mulatto—part African and part Natick Indian—named Crispus Attucks. An escaped slave and a seaman, Attucks was killed by British soldiers at the Boston Custom House on the evening of March 5, 1770, after confronting a British guard.

Crispus Attucks and his gang of about twenty Irishmen, blacks, and mulattoes taunted the guard at the Custom House because they were frustrated with the restrictions and mounting taxation levied upon them by the British government. Facing a reduction in work because of the Navigation Acts, which limited American trade with foreign countries by prohibiting foreign vessels from entering colonial ports and by limiting the number of American sailors working on British ships, the sailors felt betrayed. The colonists were also incensed by the increased taxation from the British on a wide range of goods, including newspapers, pamphlets, legal documents, advertisements (the Stamp Act of 1765, repealed in 1766), as well as lead, glass, paint, paper, and tea (the Townshend Acts of 1767).

In order to enforce these new laws, the Massachusetts governor requested British troops. Four thousand British soldiers landed in Boston in the fall of 1768, increasing tension in the community and inciting fights, brawls, and riots between the Patriots advocating revolution and the Loyalists who backed the British. With the battle cry of "No taxation without representation," the fervor for freedom rose not only among the white colonists, but also among the free and enslaved blacks. The Revolution was a watershed moment in American history because of the convergence of two social conditions: slavery and colonialism.

When the smoke had cleared from the muskets of the British soldiers who had come to the aid of the guard that night in Boston, Crispus Attucks and three others in the crowd lay dead. A fifth victim would die several days later.

As resentment against the British spread across the thirteen American colonies, the enslaved in Massachusetts petitioned the governor, council, and House of Representatives for their freedom on May 25, 1774. The petitioners did not gain their freedom as a result of their request, but their actions focused attention on the discontentment of the enslaved. Slavery was not officially abolished in Massachusetts until 1783, when the *Quock Walker* case cited the Massachusetts constitution of 1780 as proof that slavery was abolished. The constitution stated that "all men are born free and equal, and have . . . the right of enjoying and defending their lives and liberties."

The Boston Massacre, as the slaying of Crispus Attucks and the others was called, is considered the beginning of the American Revolution. However, it was another five years before the first battles were fought. On April 19, 1775, seven hundred British soldiers attempted to confiscate colonists'

MASSACHUSETTS SLAVES PETITION THE GOVERNOR, COUNCIL, AND HOUSE OF REPRESENTATIVES FOR THEIR FREEDOM

That your Petitioners apprehind we have in common with all other men a naturel right to our freedoms without Being depriv'd of them by our fellow men as we are a freeborn Pepel [people] and have never forfeited this Blessing by aney compact or agreement whatever.

THE BATTLE OF LEXINGTON

"A Poem on the inhuman tragedy perpetrated on the 19th of April 1775 by a number of the British Troops under the command of Thomas Gage . . ."

For Liberty, each Freeman Strives
As it's a gift of God
And for it willing yield their Lives
And Seal it with their Blood

Thrice happy they who thus resign
Into a peacefull grave
Much better there, in Death Confin'd
Than a Surviving Slave . . .

—Lemuel a Young Mollato

Lemuel Haynes (right), wrote the above poem on the battle of Lexington. Freed from his indenture at age twenty-one, joined the militia in 1774 and fought in the Revolutionary War. He was a prolific author of essays, poems, and sermons.

weapons and supplies stored at Concord, Massachusetts. The British Redcoats were met on their way to Concord by seventy-seven armed citizens at Lexington Green. When the militiamen were ordered to put down their weapons, a shot was fired. A skirmish erupted that was later called the Battle of Lexington.

After leaving Lexington, the British arrived in Concord, a short distance away, and started a search for hidden munitions. Although they did not find a significant amount, they destroyed what they found. Patriot militiamen had been warned that the British were coming and had taken up positions at the North Bridge. As British soldiers approached the bridge, several hundred militiamen opened fire, forcing the Redcoats to retreat to Concord, and then to Lexington.

Lemuel Haynes, a twenty-one-year-old former indentured black servant from Massachusetts, joined the militia and fought at Lexington and Concord and later in the Battle of Ticonderoga. Other free and enslaved black militiamen, who fought side by side with their white counterparts, included: Peter Salem of Framingham (who gained his freedom when he enlisted), Samuel Craft of Newton, Caesar Ferrit and his son John of Natick,

Pompy of Braintree, Pomp Blackman, and Prince of Brookline. Prince Estabrook or Easterbrook, a slave from Lexington, who also fought at the Battle of Lexington, was among the first militiamen wounded at Concord.

At the Battle of Bunker Hill (which was actually fought on Breed's Hill) in June 1775, Peter Salem, who also fought at the Battle of Concord, shot and killed British marine Major John Pitcairn, the commander of the British troops at Lexington, forcing the soldiers to retreat. Other black minutemen who fought alongside Salem were Titus Coburn, Grant Cooper, Alexander Ames, Barzillai Lew, Prince Hall (founder of the first black Freemason society in the world), George Middleton (leader of the Bucks of America, an all-black militia), and Caesar Brown. Of special note was Salem Poor, a free black man who shot and killed British lieutenant colonel James Abercrombie, and was recognized as a "brave and gallant soldier" in a petition for his heroic deeds to the General Court of the Massachusetts Bay Colony by his white commanders in December 1775.

On July 3, 1775, when George Washington assumed command of the Continental Army, a fighting force representing all thirteen colonies that was formed after the battles of Lexington and Concord, he bowed to the wishes of the southern colonists to exclude blacks from enlisting. Many

LEFT: Peter Salem, a black Patriot who received his freedom when he enlisted in the Continental Army, fought at the Battle of Bunker Hill in June 1775, at the start of the Revolutionary War. Salem is credited with killing British marine major John Pitcairn during the battle.

RIGHT: *The Flutist*, an oil painting thought to be of Barzillai Lew, attributed to Gilbert Stuart, date unknown. Barzillai Lew was a fifer in the same Patriot regiment as Peter Salem and was with him at the Battle of Bunker Hill, where he played "Yankee Doodle Dandy" to rally the Continental troops against the British.

colonists feared the arming of free and enslaved blacks would result in an insurrection that could not be contained and would in turn destroy their plantation-based economic system. In the North, particularly in the New England states, many free and enslaved Africans had already joined the local white militiamen to fight against the British. Washington's army was assisted by the French, and the British were aided by Hessian mercenaries (German soldiers who were paid to fight).

From the British perspective, the Continental Army's decision not to recruit blacks was to their advantage. They saw a strategic military opportunity and extended an invitation to the free and enslaved blacks to join their side against the American Patriots. The British offered freedom and passage to England or to any of its possessions for any African American who took up arms against the Continental Army.

In December 1775, General George Washington reversed his decision to exclude blacks in the army, because he was in desperate need of more soldiers to fight the war and the British were fortifying their troops by recruiting free and enslaved blacks. To stem the British recruitment and halt the flood of blacks joining the enemy's side, Washington issued an order in January 1776 that allowed free black men to enlist in the Continental Army and the Continental Navy. As the war dragged on, enslaved blacks entered the fight and often served in place of their masters. By the beginning of the American Revolution in 1775, there were five hundred thousand blacks in the thirteen colonies and an estimated five thousand who served in the Continental forces. There were reportedly many more (some accounts estimate more than ten thousand) who served on the British side.

BLACK PATRIOTS WHO FOUGHT FOR INDEPENDENCE

PRINCE HALL

Prince Hall was freed by his owner right after the Boston Massacre in 1770. Hall was one of the many black militiamen who fought on the side of the Patriots during the Revolutionary War. He was a leather craftsman who supplied leather drumheads to the Continental Army. Hall was also a caterer and owned a small home in Boston. Hall was the founder in 1775 of the African Lodge, Number 459, of the Honorable Society of Free and Accepted Masons of Boston, the first lodge of black Freemasonry in the world. The lodge was officially chartered in 1787. It promoted social, political, and economic improvement for African Americans.

On January 13, 1777, Prince Hall was among eight signers of a second petition to the Massachusetts legislature requesting the abolition of slavery in the colony. Although the petition was rejected, Hall, a socially and politically conscious citizen, continued to use his voice for change by petitioning the legislature in 1787 to provide an education for black children.

PRIMUS HALL

Primus Hall, a native Bostonian, was the son of Prince Hall. Primus, a soap-boiler (someone who makes soap), served in the American Revolution and later in the War of 1812, where he helped build fortifications at Castle Island in Boston Harbor. Primus was also a member of the Freemason lodge that Prince Hall founded. He shared Prince's sense of civic responsibility as well, and he established the first separate school for African American children at his home in Boston in 1798.

PRINCE WHIPPLE

Prince Whipple was born in Amabou, Africa, to wealthy parents, and was sent with a cousin to America to further his education. They traveled on board a ship that landed in Baltimore, Maryland. The ship's unscrupulous and greedy captain sold Prince and his cousin, Cuff or Cuffee, into slavery. The Whipple brothers of Portsmouth, New Hampshire, purchased the young boys.

Prince's owner, William Whipple, was an aide to General George Washington, and the young black man is often cited as the rower by Washington's knee in Emanuel Leutze's well-known 1851 painting *Washington Crossing the Delaware*. Although it is not absolutely certain that Prince Whipple is the black man on the boat with Washington, it is certainly true that there was a person of African descent on the boat during the crossing on December 25, 1776, because among the regiments that accompanied Washington was a well-integrated unit of soldiers from Massachusetts.

In this famous 1851 painting, *Washington Crossing the Delaware* by Emanuel Leutze, the African American sitting to the left of General Washington's knee is often identified as Prince Whipple.

The Patriot troops in the mid-Atlantic and southern colonies included in their ranks many African Americans who made significant contributions to the war effort.

CAESAR TARRANT

Caesar Tarrant, a slave from Hampton, Virginia, who gained his freedom after the Revolutionary War, had been commissioned by the Virginia State Navy as a riverboat pilot. Tarrant was at the helm of the schooner *Patriot* in 1777 when it encountered the British naval vessel *Lord Howe*. He resisted the British ship by ramming it and putting up a fierce battle, but despite the crew's and Tarrant's valiant efforts, they were defeated. In another battle, which ended in success, Tarrant's boat captured the British brig *Fanny* and blocked its delivery of supplies to British troops.

On November 14, 1789, the Virginia General Assembly granted freedom to Caesar Tarrant for his meritorious service in the Revolutionary War. Thirty-five years later, the government granted his daughter 2,666 acres of land in the Virginia Military District (in southwestern Ohio) in recognition of her father's service to the Virginia Navy.

JOSEPH RANGER

Joseph Ranger, another Virginian, was a free black man who served in the Virginia Navy on board the *Hero, Dragon, Jefferson,* and *Patriot* during his nine-year stint. While Ranger was on the *Jefferson,* the brig was blown up by enemy fire. On board the *Patriot,* he and the crew were taken prisoner. At the end of his tour of duty, he was given one hundred acres and an annual pension by the Virginia General Assembly.

WILLIAM FLORA

William Flora, a free black man from Portsmouth, Virginia, was among those Patriots who fought and triumphed at the Battle of Great Bridge on December 9, 1775, against Lord Dunmore's Ethiopian Regiment and British soldiers. Flora, one of the soldiers guarding the bridge, was the last man to leave. He took up the plank that slowed the passage of British troops over the bridge. According to an account in the *Virginia Gazette,* December 13, 1775, "[H]e had fired eight times; and after receiving a whole platoon, made his escape over the causeway into our breastwork [barriers]." Flora became a prominent citizen, property owner, and the owner and operator of a successful carting business and livery stable. For his military service, Flora was also given one hundred acres in the Virginia Military District in Ohio.

JAMES FORTEN

Free black Philadelphian James Forten joined the Continental Navy when he was a teenager of fifteen. He had attended the Friends' African School (a Quaker school for black students) up until his father's death. In the navy, he served as a powder boy (bringing gunpowder from below deck to the canons on the upper gun deck) on board the *Royal Louis.*

In a battle with the British frigate *Amphyon,* the *Royal Louis* lost and Forten was taken prisoner with his fellow crew members. While imprisoned on the British ship, he became friends with the captain's son, who was around his age. The captain offered to take Forten to England to live, but he refused and was sent to the British ship *Jersey,* docked at Wallabout Bay in Brooklyn, New York, the site of the Brooklyn Navy Yard. Forten was held on the ship with thousands of other prisoners of war for seven months and was freed during a prisoner exchange.

James Forten returned to Philadelphia, Pennsylvania, where he became

James Forten was a free black man from Philadelphia who joined the Continental Navy. Captured during a battle with the British Navy, Forten became a prisoner of war on the prison ship *Jersey,* docked in Wallabout Bay off the coast of Brooklyn, New York. After the war, he returned to Philadelphia, where he opened a company that made nautical equipment and sails. An inventor and successful businessman, Forten was also an abolitionist.

The Bucks of America flag was presented to the all-black militia by Governor John Hancock of Massachusetts for the group's contributions to the American Revolution.

a wealthy inventor and business owner of a sail-making company. An equal opportunity employer, he hired both blacks and whites. An ardent abolitionist, Forten became very active in the antislavery movement and was an opponent of the American Colonization Society (ACS), which proposed that free blacks return to Africa. Forten helped fund white abolitionist William Lloyd Garrison's newspaper, *The Liberator*, and was also the author of the controversial pamphlet *Letters from a Man of Colour*, published in 1813, which protested the Pennsylvania legislature's proposed law that would require African Americans traveling to the state to register.

THE BUCKS OF AMERICA

The Bucks of America were an all-black militia from New England. Colonel George Middleton, who fought at the Battle of Concord, was the leader of the group and a member of the African Lodge, Number 459, the Masonic Lodge founded by Prince Hall in Boston, and the African Society, another civic organization that assisted blacks. The Bucks of America were presented a silk flag bearing a leaping buck against a pine tree by Massachusetts governor John Hancock "as a tribute to their courage and devotion in the cause of American Liberty."

FIRST RHODE ISLAND REGIMENT

The General Assembly of Rhode Island in its February 1778 session voted to enlist "every able-bodied negro, mulatto, or Indian man-slave in this State ... [and] that every slave so enlisting shall be entitled to and receive all the bounties, wages and encouragements allowed by the Continental Congress to any soldiers enlisting into this service." The resolution also stated that all enlisted slaves would be automatically freed from "the service of his master or mistress, and be absolutely free, as though he had never been encumbered with any kind of servitude of slavery."

On August 29, 1778, the First Rhode Island Regiment distinguished itself at the Battle of Newport. In 1781, under the command of Colonel Christopher Greene, the regiment defended northern Westchester lines in

New York against the British. But during a surprise attack by British Loyalists on Colonel Greene's headquarters in Croton Heights in Yorktown, New York, at the Battle of Pines Bridge on May 13, 1781, Greene was killed.

The First Rhode Island sustained heavy casualties during the massive assault. Fourteen were killed, one hundred wounded, and thirty were taken prisoner (and later sold into slavery in the British West Indies). After Greene's untimely death, the regiment's command was handed over to Lieutenant Colonel Jeremiah Olney. Olney led what was left of the predominately black regiment, which had fought battles at Fort Oswego, Saratoga, and Red Bank. The regiment of white men, free blacks, and Native Americans was disbanded after five years of service.

Many blacks who joined the Continental Army were not necessarily part of a group. Four African American slaves from Plymouth, Massachusetts, fought in the war and were emancipated upon their discharge from service. Cato Howe fought at the Battle of Bunker Hill and served from 1775 to 1780. Howe was given ninety-four acres of land by the town officials of Plymouth for his service. He was joined on the property by the families of Quamony Quash, who, as a teenager, enlisted in 1775 and was discharged in 1782, and Plato Turner, who served from 1776 to 1783. It is also believed that Prince Goodwin, who enlisted in 1777 and served until 1780, also lived on this land. The community of Parting Ways was established in 1794, one of the earliest communities of free blacks in America, and was inhabited by the founders' descendants until 1908, although the town of Plymouth reclaimed the property in 1824.

FIGHTING FOR THE LOYALIST CAUSE

DURING THE AMERICAN Revolution, the British offered emancipation to any enslaved person who fought on their side. This military tactic infuriated the Patriots and caused pandemonium on the southern plantations as thousands of slaves escaped and joined the British Army or sought refuge behind enemy lines.

A black Loyalist soldier is prominently depicted fighting on the British side in this 1782 painting by John Singleton Copley, *The Death of Major Peirson*. The Battle of Jersey in 1781 was an attempt by France, an American ally, to invade Jersey (an island located between the coasts of England and France) and remove the threat the island posed to American shipping in the Revolutionary War.

LORD DUNMORE'S ETHIOPIAN REGIMENT

In Virginia, during the early days of the Revolutionary War, British governor John Murray, the Earl of Dunmore, was unable to get support from British troops in defending the Loyalist position in his colony. Dunmore issued a proclamation in November 1775 that granted freedom to every enslaved person who enlisted in his "Ethiopian Army." As word spread throughout Virginia, hundreds of enslaved African Americans joined Lord Dunmore's regiment, which had its first skirmish with Patriot militiamen at Kemp's Landing on the Elizabeth River. On December 9, 1775, the band of black Loyalists joined with British Redcoats against the Patriots at the Battle of Great Bridge, near present-day Chesapeake, Virginia, and was badly defeated.

Betrayed by an unnamed black spy who told Dunmore that the Patriots' position was weak, the troops advanced unsuspectingly toward the bridge, only to be met by Patriot firepower. The British retreated and some of the survivors of Dunmore's Ethiopian Regiment were reassigned as pilots on small boats that foraged for provisions for British troops in the area. Dunmore and his remaining regiment members along with the British troops retreated to Norfolk, Virginia, where they moved onto his fleet anchored in the Elizabeth River. The fleet retreated to Gwynn's Island near the Chesapeake Bay and sailed to New York. Eventually Dunmore sailed to England. It is believed that the surviving black soldiers from Dunmore's Ethiopian Regiment were taken to Nova Scotia, Canada, by the British and settled near Halifax.

COLONEL TYE AND THE BLACK BRIGADE

One group of Loyalist guerrilla fighters was headed by Titus Cornelius, a slave from Monmouth County, New Jersey. Titus escaped from his owner, Quaker John Corlies, and joined Lord Dunmore's all-black Ethiopian Regiment in Virginia in 1775. After participating in battles in Virginia, Titus returned to New Jersey and formed his own elite group called the Black Brigade. He distinguished himself in the Battle of Monmouth by capturing a captain of a local Patriot militia. The British commanders were impressed with his military skills and Titus became the self-named Colonel Tye, although he did not receive a commission from the British commanders.

The Black Brigade, a group of fearless marauders, kidnapped Patriots, raided military camps and local plantations, and set fire to enemy homes in New Jersey and New York. Colonel Tye's Black Brigade eventually joined up with the Queen's Rangers, a British guerrilla group, and led raids to acquire supplies for troops during the last days of the war.

BLACK PIONEERS AND GUIDES

The Black Pioneers and Guides was a regiment of runaway slaves from North and South Carolina and Georgia who worked for the British as laborers building fortifications, digging trenches, and clearing streets. The Pioneers were stationed in Rhode Island; New York; Philadelphia; Savannah, Georgia; and Charleston, South Carolina. British general Henry Clinton, the commander of the group, led a contingent of Black Pioneers to New York City at the end of the war, where many boarded British ships and sailed to freedom in Canada.

PATRIOT SPIES

BEING A SPY during the American Revolution was a role that a black person was well suited for. As the "invisible race," it was easy for blacks to gain access to information that would help either the Patriots or the Loyalists, because many on both sides did not believe that a black person had the cunning or intellect to be a spy. Black housekeepers, servants, cooks, and maids were often present when valuable information about troop positions, troop movements, and artillery and supply routes was discussed.

JAMES ARMISTEAD LAFAYETTE

James Armistead, a slave from Williamsburg, Virginia, enlisted in the Continental Army under the Marquis de Lafayette's command in 1781. Lafayette, a young Frenchman who volunteered to help the Americans against the British, immediately asked Armistead to spy on the enemy.

Armistead infiltrated the camp of American traitor Benedict Arnold, who was now a brigadier general in the British Army. Arnold, an ambitious soldier, had served with distinction on the American side until a series of incidents with his superiors, including insubordination and mismanagement of funds, caused him to be nearly court-martialed. It was at this point that Arnold, seeing that his fortunes were changing, came up with the plan to help the British gain West Point, where he was the commander, for the sum of twenty thousand pounds. The plan failed when his British co-conspirator was captured and revealed the plot. Arnold fled to the British.

Armistead volunteered as a servant and a guide to Arnold, since he was familiar with the area where the troops were located in Virginia. Unsuspecting of Armistead's real agenda, Arnold gave him the job. Armistead sent back secret reports to Lafayette by messenger.

After Benedict Arnold and his troops left Virginia for the North,

James Armistead Lafayette was a Patriot double agent who infiltrated the British command in Virginia and reported on troop movements that enabled the Continental Army to win a decisive victory at Yorktown.

Armistead moved to British general Lord Cornwallis's headquarters, where he became a waiter. In this key position, Armistead was able to learn about strategic plans and the movements of the British troops.

When Cornwallis shifted his troops to Portsmouth, near the Chesapeake Bay, the Americans were puzzled. Armistead reported to Lafayette that a fleet of ships had anchored in the harbor to carry the troops to some other location. When the British sailed, Armistead made his report to Lafayette of their departure. Lafayette was then informed that Cornwallis and his troops were unloading at Yorktown, located on the York River. James Armistead was sent by Cornwallis to the American camp of Lafayette to spy, which made Armistead a double agent, though his loyalty was with the Patriots. He continued to provide Lafayette with information about Cornwallis, which helped the Americans win the final major battle of the Revolutionary War at Yorktown, Virginia, by cutting off Cornwallis by land and by sea.

Armistead received a certificate from Lafayette praising the intelligence

Fraunces Tavern, located at Broad and Pearl streets in Lower Manhattan, was owned by Samuel Fraunces, a free black man from the Caribbean. The tavern was the setting for General George Washington's Farewell Address to his troops at the end of the American Revolution, in 1783. Samuel Fraunces became the first steward of the White House when Washington became the first president of the United States of America.

work that he had done. In turn, Armistead sent the certificate to the Virginia General Assembly and requested his emancipation. The legislature granted him his freedom after reimbursing his master, William Armistead, for his services. Armistead, in tribute to the Marquis de Lafayette, changed his name to James Lafayette.

SAUL MATTHEWS

Another Virginian who helped the Continental Army by passing on valuable information about enemy troops was Saul Matthews. He worked at the British camps in Portsmouth, Virginia, as a guide and smuggled plans about their troop movements to the Continental Army's colonel Josiah Parker. Although praised by officers Baron Friedrich von Steuben and Peter Muhlenberg and General Nathaniel Greene for his exemplary service as a Patriot guide and a spy, Matthews remained enslaved after the war, until he petitioned the Virginia General Assembly for his freedom in 1792. He was finally granted full liberty.

SAMUEL FRAUNCES

General George Washington's Continental Army fought several battles in New York City and the surrounding area. The Battle of Harlem Heights, the Battle of Long Island, and the Battle of White Plains were important fights in the struggle for independence, and at different points in the conflict, modern-day Manhattan was overrun by British troops.

One of General Washington's chief New York supporters was Samuel Fraunces, a free black man from the West Indies, who was the owner and proprietor of Fraunces Tavern, at 54 Pearl Street in New York City. Originally called the Queen's Head, the restaurant and pub opened in 1762, and it was frequented at different times by American Patriots and British Loyalists. The Sons of Liberty, a secret group of Patriots that rebelled against the Stamp Act and the Townshend Acts that taxed tea and other goods imported to the colonies, met at Fraunces Tavern frequently and planned their own historic tea party. The Sons of Liberty dumped a shipment of tea in New York Harbor on April 22, 1774, a rebellious act that was inspired by the Boston Tea Party, which had occurred months earlier on December 16, 1773. Other tea party protests were held in New Jersey and Maryland.

Samuel Fraunces not only ran a pub that was a watering hole for troops; during the war, he was also in the unique position of receiving information that was helpful to Washington and the Patriots' campaign. When New York was occupied by the British in September 1776, Fraunces became a cook for the British soldiers. In that position, he spied for General Washington, providing him with valuable information. Fraunces's daughter Phoebe worked with her mother, Elizabeth, as a housekeeper at Washington's temporary headquarters at Richmond Hill, a mansion located in Greenwich Village, at what is now Varick and Charlton streets.

Phoebe was the companion of George Washington's Irish bodyguard, Thomas Hickey. A British sympathizer, Hickey was recruited to assassinate Washington and enlisted Phoebe's help in carrying out his plan to poison George Washington's peas. Phoebe appeared to go along with the plot, but she informed General Washington, who when served the poisoned peas, threw them out the window, where chickens hungrily ate them and died. Hickey was arrested, tried, and hanged.

Fraunces Tavern was also the site of General George Washington's Farewell Address to his officers on December 4, 1783, at the end of the Revolutionary War. When Washington became the first president of the United States of America, Samuel Fraunces became his steward at the New York White House. When the capital was moved to Philadelphia in 1790, Fraunces became the steward at the new presidential residence.

THE END OF THE REVOLUTIONARY WAR

IN 1783, WHEN the British troops withdrew from the colonies, according to the National Park Service, "an estimated 75,000 to 100,000 black Americans left the 13 states." The emancipated were resettled in Nova Scotia, New Brunswick, and Ontario, Canada; Great Britain; Florida; and Africa.

> One corps of black drummers, who served in Baron Friedrich von Redesel's Brunswick forces [German soldiers hired by the British], chose to go to Germany . . . Some three thousand former slaves chose to emigrate to Nova Scotia. The British had promised ex-slaves farms in Nova Scotia after the war, but when they arrived there were no farms, only wretched hovels, barely adequate to protect them against the harsh winters, and slave-like work for refugees.
>
> British abolitionists, led by William Wilberforce and Thomas Clarkson, established the Sierra Leone Company to enable destitute blacks [in Canada] to settle in West Africa. They persuaded the British secretary of state to order the governor of Nova Scotia to either give land to some two hundred black families, or send them to Sierra Leone at government expense. In January 1792, David George led about twelve hundred black settlers from Halifax, Nova Scotia, to Freetown to start the Sierra Leone colony.

Upset by the exodus of blacks fleeing America after the war with the British, General George Washington, still commander of the Continental Army, issued an order that the names, ages, physical descriptions, and status (free or enslaved) of all black Loyalists leaving the country be recorded in the *Book of Negroes*. The listing was created to compensate American slave owners for their lost property. When completed, the *Book of Negroes* was a three-volume, handwritten listing that included the identities of more than three thousand men, women, and children who migrated to lands under British rule on British ships disembarking from New York City. The original *Book of Negroes* is located in the National Archives in Washington, D.C.

For the African Americans who remained in America, many in the New England states were freed as a result of their military service, while others gained their freedom through legislation enacted in the 1780s. In New York, New Jersey, and Pennsylvania, the process of gradual manumission, or freedom, began after the war's end. Full freedom was granted to the enslaved in New York in 1827, in New Jersey in 1846, and in Pennsylvania in 1847. In the South, although some slaves were freed during the war, many remained enslaved to work on the plantations.

BLACKS IN THE WAR OF 1812

SOON AFTER THE American Revolution was won by the colonists, Britain began raiding American ships in search of British sailors who worked on American vessels. The British needed more sailors to fight against France, led by Napoleon Bonaparte, in the Napoleonic Wars. During these raids, American sailors were also taken by the British Navy and impressed into service. The Americans objected to Britain's aggressive behavior and declared war.

The War of 1812 was another campaign in which enslaved and free blacks showed their patriotism. Although they were officially banned from serving in the American military—army and navy—they volunteered anyway.

In March 1813, the U.S. Navy officially permitted blacks to enlist. The British also recruited American blacks, offering freedom to the enslaved, just as they had in the American Revolution.

> One-sixth of the U.S. Navy seamen who fought in the War of 1812, serving on warships and privateers, were black. They fought conspicuously in the only two American naval victories that directly affected the course of the war . . . [the] Battle of Lake Erie on September 10, 1813, and the Battle of Lake Champlain on September 11, 1814.

Both victories helped the Americans move into Canada and furthered the American quest to annex Canada, a British possession. Free and enslaved blacks also fought at the Battle of New Orleans. Three African American officers in the Louisiana Battalion of Free Men of Color included

H. CHARLES McBARRON JR.

"black second lieutenants Isidore Honoré, Vincent Populus, and Joseph Savary, who had been an officer in the Santo Domingo army." The War of 1812 ended in a stalemate, with neither side gaining their objectives.

SLAVE REBELLIONS, REVOLTS, AND INSURRECTIONS

THE ENSLAVED AFRICANS brought to the British colonies against their will did not acquiesce during their bondage in America. There were many revolts, rebellions, and insurrections in which hundreds of whites and blacks were killed in the North and in the South. One of the earliest and bloodiest, the Slave Revolt of 1712, occurred in New York on April 6.

A group of black men and women armed with knives, hatchets, guns, and swords waited as their co-conspirators set fire to a building on Maiden Lane, which is located in Lower Manhattan near current-day Wall Street. When the white colonists came out of their homes to fight the fire, they were attacked. At least nine whites were killed and seven were wounded. The attackers ran into the woods, but many were eventually captured. Six committed suicide before capture; twenty-seven were brought to trial and condemned to death. Twenty-one were executed, except a mother and child whose sentences were suspended. The remaining were acquitted for lack of evidence.

The rebellion was an indication of how volatile the situation was among the enslaved and their owners in colonial New York. With the black population increasing, the white citizens of New York were ever more fearful that another rebellion would take place and enacted extremely harsh and restrictive laws called the slave codes, which regulated virtually all of the movements of the enslaved population in the colony.

More revolts followed. There were several factors in South Carolina that inspired the Stono Rebellion. The Spanish had settled the neighboring colony of St. Augustine in Florida. In 1738, they offered escaped slaves from the British colonies of mainly Georgia and the Carolinas freedom and land.

OPPOSITE: *Free Men of Colour and Choctaw Indian Volunteers at New Orleans, Louisiana, 1814.* During the War of 1812, free African American soldiers helped wage war against the British in the Battle of New Orleans, making significant contributions in the defeat of Great Britain. The First and Second Battalions of Free Men of Color fought bravely with the U.S. Army. The black militias joined the fighting because of provisions in the Louisiana Purchase, which had no restrictions on separate black units entering the conflict, unlike the U.S. Army, which did not officially allow blacks to enlist until 1862.

At the same time, laws were put in place in the British colonies to restrict the few privileges that the enslaved had in an attempt to prevent rebellions.

On the morning of September 9, 1739, a disgruntled band of slaves, which grew to more than sixty rebels, roamed the countryside outside of Charleston, South Carolina, killing white families and setting fire to homes. They were stopped by a group of armed whites, who shot and killed nearly half of the group and executed the remaining rebels over a period of time.

The Great Negro Plot, or the Great New York Conspiracy of 1741, began with a series of fires set in different locations around Manhattan during a three-week period, causing terror among the white citizenry. With the population of black slaves continuing to grow and the mounting hysteria of the white community over rumors of a rebellion, the government launched an investigation and offered a reward for information leading to the arsonists.

Through a tip from Mary Burton, a white teenage indentured servant who worked at a local pub, the authorities focused their attention on members of the slave population and the poor white working-class community. They rounded up suspects identified by Mary Burton, but many of the accused whites were released. But of those convicted by the courts, four whites, including the pub owner and his wife, and thirty-five blacks were executed. Seventy blacks and seven whites were transported out of the colony.

Gabriel Prosser, a slave from Richmond, Virginia, planned one of the most elaborate and extensive slave revolts in August 1800. As a hired-out blacksmith, Gabriel traveled freely and made his own money through his trade. He met and talked with other slaves who had been hired out, and with working-class whites as well. Gabriel was literate and was not only aware of his condition as a slave, but also of conditions of other slaves in places like the French colony of Saint Domingue (Haiti) on the island of Hispaniola. The first recorded slave revolt in the New World had taken place there in the Spanish colony of Santo Domingo (Dominican Republic) on December 27, 1522. Another revolt occurred in Saint Domingue in 1791, led by Toussaint L'Ouverture.

Gabriel was aware of the 1791 revolt in Haiti, and he, too, wanted freedom and a prosperous life. He believed the only way to get that freedom

An 1831 woodcut from the book *Authentic and Impartial Narrative of the Tragical Scene Which Was Witnessed in Southampton County* of the Nat Turner Rebellion on Sunday, August 21, 1831, in Virginia. The revolt was crushed by state militia and armed services, backed by federal troops from nearby Fort Monroe.

was through conflict. Gabriel recruited free black men, the enslaved, and working-class whites to join his cause for freedom. His plan was to kidnap Virginia governor James Monroe and use him to bargain for freedom of the enslaved. The plan began to unravel when a rainstorm postponed the band's assault on Richmond's Capitol Square. Rumors of their plan spread, alerting authorities, who then captured many of the conspirators. Gabriel was eventually caught and hanged along with twenty-six fellow conspirators. About sixty-five others were tried, transported to other states, or pardoned.

Other important uprisings took place. New Orleans, Louisiana, in 1811, is considered the site of the largest rebellion with more than three hundred slaves led by Charles Deslondes, a former Saint Domingue slave. In Southampton County, Virginia, in 1831, the Nat Turner Rebellion was inspired by David Walker's fiery *Appeal*, which implored the enslaved to shun the return-to-Africa plan promoted by the American Colonization Society, and, instead, stay on American soil and fight for their freedom and their rights. On board the Spanish slave ship *Amistad* in 1839, slaves mutinied and then sailed up the eastern coast of America, where they were captured and detained by the U.S. Navy. With the help of American abolitionists, who presented the Africans' case before the U.S. Supreme Court, the slaves won their freedom.

✿ ✿ ✿

John Brown's raid on Harper's Ferry in Virginia (now West Virginia) was a unique rebellion because Brown was white and only five of the twenty-one men who accompanied him were black. John Brown was an abolitionist who fought passionately for the end of slavery and had enlisted the support of a network of prominent abolitionists, known as the "Secret Six," to fund his elaborate raid. Black abolitionist and former slave Frederick Douglass knew about the plan, but he did not think it would succeed and did not join up with Brown. However, Harriet Tubman did support John Brown's effort, but she was not present at the Harper's Ferry raid because of illness.

John Brown and his rebels captured the federal arsenal at Harper's Ferry on October 16, 1859, to arm themselves in order to free local slaves. Their hope was that their rebellion would spread and create a movement of insurrection among the enslaved population. John Brown and his raiders were captured and hanged, but not without leaving an indelible mark on the abolition movement and the world.

They were hailed as martyrs by supporters at home and abroad, including Victor Hugo, the famous French novelist, poet, playwright, and essayist, who wrote a letter protesting Brown's execution to the *London News* on December 2, 1859. Hugo ended his letter with these words to America, comparing John Brown's execution to the slaying of Spartacus, the leader of a slave revolt against the Roman Empire in ancient times.

> [Y]es, let America know it and ponder on it well—there is something more terrible than Cain slaying Abel: It is Washington slaying Spartacus!

John Brown and his raiders are credited by some with having started the Civil War. Frederick Douglass echoed this sentiment in a May 30, 1881, speech at Storer College, a historically black college in Harper's Ferry:

> If John Brown did not end the war that ended slavery, he did at least begin the war that ended slavery . . . Until this blow was struck, the prospect for freedom was dim, shadowy, and uncertain. The irrepressible conflict was one of words, votes and compromises. When John Brown stretched forth his arm the sky was cleared. The time for compromises was gone—the armed hosts of freedom stood face to face over the chasm of a broken Union—and the clash of arms was at hand.

June 13th 1859
Your Affectionate Father
John Brown

John Brown, a white revolutionary abolitionist, and twenty-one of his followers raided the federal arsenal at Harper's Ferry, Virginia (now West Virginia), in 1859, to seize weapons and arm the enslaved for an insurrection. Brown and his group were captured; some were killed during the raid, and seven were hanged for treason, including John Brown.

 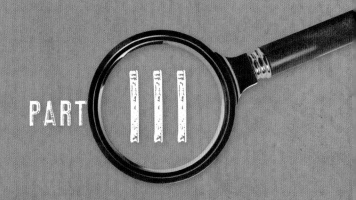

THE ROAD TO THE CIVIL WAR

THIS PAGE: Battle of Olustee, February 20, 1864, the largest Civil War conflict in Florida. Three African American regiments fought in this battle, including the 8th U.S. Colored Troops, the 54th Massachusetts, and the First North Carolina Colored Volunteers. The Confederates won the battle.

PREVIOUS PAGE: Contraband who served with the 13th Massachusetts Infantry circa 1863–1865. Fugitive slaves worked for the Union Army as nurses, cooks, laundresses, and laborers.

THE DECLARATION OF Independence adopted by the Second Continental Congress on July 4, 1776, states in its preamble, "We hold these truths to be self-evident, that all men are created equal, that they are endowed by their Creator with certain unalienable Rights, that among these are Life, Liberty and the pursuit of Happiness." However, when the Revolutionary War officially ended on September 3, 1783, with the signing of the Treaty of Paris, the plight of African Americans, many of whom had played pivotal roles in the pursuit of the colonies' independence, and many of whom were free, were conspicuously ignored. The United States Constitution was adopted by members of the Constitutional Convention on September 17, 1787, and ratified by the states, creating the new federal government in 1789. Nowhere in the original documents of the Declaration of Independence or the Constitution was there mention of freedoms or rights for blacks, Negroes, or African Americans.

The resulting Constitution did not end slavery or change it in any way; it accommodated the existing institution and made it legal in the United States of America. The compromise between the northern and southern states concerned the issues of how to count slaves in the population formula for state representation in Congress, the importation of slaves, and upholding the fugitive slave laws.

In Article I, Section 2 of the Constitution, the process of representation by population is described. States would count enslaved individuals as three-fifths of a person in the census, not as a whole person. In Section 9 of Article I, the importation of slavery is allowed for another twenty years until 1808, which was the year that the slave trade was finally outlawed in the United States. The Constitution states: "The Migration or Importation of such Persons" shall be permitted, "but a tax or duty may be imposed on such Importation." In Article IV, Section 2, the institution of slavery is upheld from state to state, with the provision that "No Person held to Service or Labour in one State . . . escaping into another, shall . . . be discharged from such Service or Labour" but be delivered back to his or her owner from whom they escaped.

The Constitution ignored the push for freedom by African Americans, both enslaved and free, and became a major factor in the escalation of the abolition movement in the late 1820s and early 1830s. The movement was fueled by antislavery activists, black and white, and the growing discontent among the enslaved and free black men who were petitioning unsuccessfully in their state legislatures and in the U.S. Supreme Court for freedom and civil rights. Slave petitions were not unusual and had been submitted to the courts by free and enslaved blacks starting in 1773 and 1774 in Massachusetts and in 1788 in Connecticut. In Missouri, in 1846, enslaved Dred Scott first petitioned the Missouri lower court for freedom for him and his wife.

THE AMERICAN COLONIZATION SOCIETY AND *THE LIBERATOR*

THE AMERICAN COLONIZATION Society (ACS) was founded by a group of white men in 1817 for the resettlement of free blacks in Africa. In 1822, a group of free blacks emigrated to the west coast of Africa to a colony established by the ACS, and settled in what would become the nation of Liberia. By 1867, the Society had sent thirteen thousand African Americans to Liberia.

David Walker published his seventy-six-page *Appeal to the Coloured Citizens of the World* in 1829 to demand the abolition of slavery. Some believed that Walker's *Appeal* inspired the Nat Turner Rebellion in 1831.

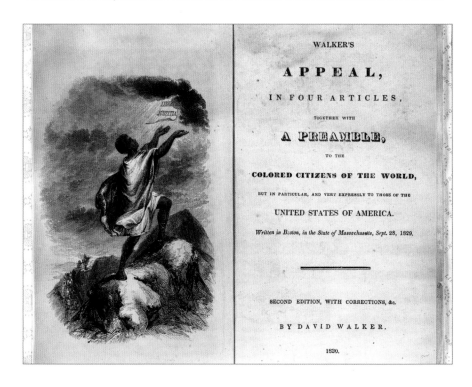

WALKER'S

APPEAL,

IN FOUR ARTICLES,

TOGETHER WITH

A PREAMBLE,

TO THE

COLORED CITIZENS OF THE WORLD,

BUT IN PARTICULAR, AND VERY EXPRESSLY TO THOSE OF THE

UNITED STATES OF AMERICA.

Written in Boston, in the State of Massachusetts, Sept. 28, 1829.

SECOND EDITION, WITH CORRECTIONS, &c.

BY DAVID WALKER.

1830.

David Walker, a free black man from Wilmington, North Carolina, took up the cause of emancipation with his pen but he differed in opinion from the ACS. He wrote a series of articles promoting the abolition of slavery, which he used in presentations and lectures he made in Boston and around the New England region. In his 1829 series entitled *Appeal to the Coloured Citizens of the World,* Walker exhorted black Americans to not embrace the colonization movement, which advocated sending free men and women back to Africa:

> *Let no man of us budge one step, and let slave-holders come to beat us from our country. America is more our country, than it is the whites—we have enriched it with our* blood and tears*. The greatest riches in all America have arisen from our blood and tears:—and will they drive us from our property and homes, which we have earned with our* blood?

White abolitionist William Lloyd Garrison, publisher of the abolitionist weekly newspaper *The Liberator* (1831), was at first in support of the ACS because he believed in freedom for black Americans. But he later opposed the colonization movement when he realized that supporters were merely trying to rid America of free blacks. He also had become aware of the poor living conditions in Liberia, where many of the repatriated blacks died. He wrote about it in his paper. Garrison was also a founding member of the American Anti-Slavery Society in 1833, which demanded emancipation and equal rights for blacks.

LEFT: William Lloyd Garrison was an abolitionist and the publisher of the weekly antislavery newspaper *The Liberator*. A friend and colleague to Frederick Douglass, Garrison encouraged Douglass to tell his story of enslavement and freedom at anti-slavery conventions.

RIGHT: Banner of *The Liberator*, which was first published on January 1, 1831. Garrison published his newspaper for more than three decades, ceasing only after the Civil War ended in 1865.

FUGITIVE SLAVE LAWS AND THE COMPROMISE OF 1850

BY 1846, THE free states and the slave states were evenly matched: fourteen to fourteen. The free states in the North included Maine, Massachusetts, New Hampshire, Vermont, Connecticut, Rhode Island, New York, New Jersey, Pennsylvania, Ohio, Indiana, Illinois, Michigan, and Iowa. The slave states located in the South were Delaware, Maryland, Virginia, North Carolina, South Carolina, Missouri, Kentucky, Tennessee, Georgia, Alabama, Louisiana, Arkansas, Mississippi, and Texas. At the time, the estimated number of slaves in the United States was approximately three million, or one-sixth of the total population. Between 1830 and 1865, the free black population was between three hundred thousand and five hundred thousand.

The Compromise of 1850 was a series of laws enacted to quell a crisis between the North and the South, when California petitioned Congress to join the Union as a free state. Representatives from the southern states were upset because the balance of power in Congress—the number of representatives from free and slave states—would be tipped in favor of the free states.

A compromise was reached to appease the southern states, which were threatening to secede from the Union. It included the Fugitive Slave Act of 1850, which strengthened the Fugitive Slave Law of 1793, and gave any citizen the authority to capture and deliver fugitive slaves back into slavery. It denied captured African Americans access to a jury trial, fined federal marshals who did not arrest or return fugitive slaves to their owners, and threatened imprisonment to anyone aiding in the escape of a fugitive.

California joined the Union as a free state; the slave trade (not slavery) was abolished in Washington, D.C.; the boundary dispute between Texas and New Mexico was settled; and the territories of New Mexico and Utah (which included the present-day states of Nevada and Arizona) agreed to declare their designation as a slave or a free state when they applied for statehood, although as territories they were allowed to have slaves.

$150 REWARD

RANAWAY from the subscriber, on the night of the 2d instant, a negro man, who calls himself *Henry May*, about 22 years old, 5 feet 6 or 8 inches high, ordinary color, rather chunky built, bushy head, and has it divided mostly on one side, and keeps it very nicely combed; has been raised in the house, and is a first rate dining-room servant, and was in a tavern in Louisville for 18 months. I expect he is now in Louisville trying to make his escape to a free state, (in all probability to Cincinnati, Ohio.) Perhaps he may try to get employment on a steamboat. He is a good cook, and is handy in any capacity as a house servant. Had on when he left, a dark cassinett coatee, and dark striped cassinett pantaloons, new—he had other clothing. I will give $50 reward if taken in Louisvill; 100 dollars if taken one hundred miles from Louisville in this State, and 150 dollars if taken out of this State, and delivered to me, or secured in any jail so that I can get him again. WILLIAM BURKE.

Bardstown, Ky., September 3d, 1838.

This 1838 advertisement requesting the return of a runaway slave for a reward was typical of ads placed in newspapers during that period. Descriptions included height, weight, complexion, birthmarks, clothing, and sometimes a profile detailing special skills of the individual.

THE UNDERGROUND RAILROAD

AS CRIES FOR freedom grew louder, many enslaved pursued routes to their own freedom. They escaped by "railroad." Not a traditional railroad, the Underground Railroad (U.G.R.R.) was a network of people, places, and modes of transportation that helped fugitive slaves escape to freedom. The U.G.R.R. reached its peak between 1820 and 1865. In the early stages of the U.G.R.R., the northern states were the primary destination for runaways from the South, but after legislation was passed that authorized the capture and return of fugitive slaves to their owners, Canada, America's northern neighbor, became the most desirable destination. Many of the escaped slaves settled in Canada West (known today as Ontario), but New Brunswick; Halifax, Nova Scotia; and Montreal were also places to which slaves fled.

Passengers on the Underground Railroad were part of an elaborate production that required disguises, scripts, signals hidden in song lyrics,

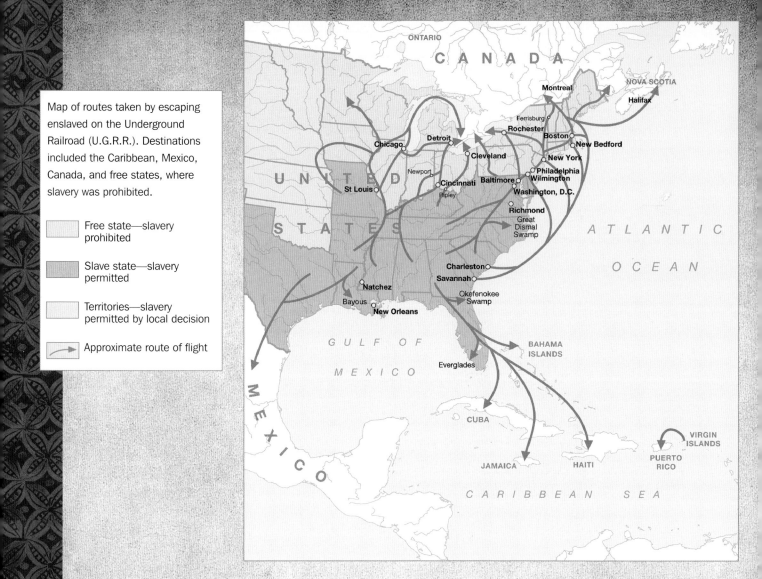

Map of routes taken by escaping enslaved on the Underground Railroad (U.G.R.R.). Destinations included the Caribbean, Mexico, Canada, and free states, where slavery was prohibited.

- Free state—slavery prohibited
- Slave state—slavery permitted
- Territories—slavery permitted by local decision
- Approximate route of flight

and role playing. The U.G.R.R. was a system of secret stations and depots consisting of homes, churches, and other places to hide from slave catchers; station masters who ran the stations and depots; ticket agents who helped the fugitives set up their escapes; dispatchers who helped with the routes; and conductors who coordinated and supervised trips by moving passengers from one station to the next. The system stretched throughout the South, from Florida to Texas, with many routes leading to Canada. The Underground Railroad branched out through the Midwest to Ohio, Illinois, Michigan, Indiana, Wisconsin, Iowa, and Kansas. There were routes to Mexico and the Caribbean as well.

The fugitives were transported from one station to another by railroad, in carriages, by boat, and on foot. They were led by blacks and by white sympathizers, who also provided food and lodging.

Travelers moving on foot under the protection of the night sky were instructed by conductors to follow the North Star to freedom or to look for the Drinking Gourd (the Big Dipper), which included the North Star. Lanterns were lit at the hitching posts or in the windows of safe houses, and markers were left on routes. Some researchers claim that quilts with symbolic patterns containing coded messages were hung on clotheslines outside of sympathetic homes to signal to fugitives that here was a safe place to seek food and shelter.

In part, as a reaction to the U.G.R.R., the Fugitive Slave Law of 1850 legalized the pursuit and capture of runaway slaves who crossed state lines. Captured fugitives would be returned to their masters. Many times, though, slave catchers would kidnap free blacks and sell them into slavery at auctions in the South. Not protected by the law, there was very little that the kidnapped victims could do.

Shadrach Minkins was a fugitive slave who fought reenslavement with the help of the abolitionist community in Boston. Minkins had escaped from Virginia and worked as a waiter in a coffeehouse in Boston. One morning in February 1851, two slave catchers posing as customers seized Minkins and took him to court. Minkins's defense lawyers, financed by white abolitionist and wealthy industrialist Amos A. Lawrence, sought his release through a writ of habeas corpus, demanding that the court show cause for detaining Minkins or release him.

The Supreme Judicial Court of Massachusetts refused to consider the writ because the Fugitive Slave Law of 1850 said it did not have to comply. Meanwhile, a group of black abolitionists, including businessmen Lewis Hayden, an ex-slave, and John J. Smith, who had heard of Minkins's detention, stormed the court and forcibly took Minkins out of the courtroom and hid him until he escaped to Canada on the Underground Railroad. U.S. president Millard Fillmore (1850–1853) intervened and ordered the arrest of the nine abolitionists who participated in the escape. The final result was that charges were dropped against some of the abolitionists and the others who stood trial were acquitted.

In another runaway case, Anthony Burns, a slave from Richmond, Virginia, made his escape as a stowaway on a ship and landed in Boston, where

Anthony Burns was a fugitive slave who escaped from Virginia to Boston, Massachusetts, where he was captured by a slave catcher. Because of the Fugitive Slave Law of 1850, Burns had to be returned to his master, even though he had fled to a free state.

he found work in a clothing store owned by Lewis Hayden. On May 24, 1854, three months after he arrived, Burns was captured by his owner and arrested under the Fugitive Slave Law. Black and white abolitionists met separately to discuss how they could help Burns. The group led once again by Hayden stormed the courthouse to rescue Burns while he was in custody. In the melee, thirteen people were arrested and a marshal was killed.

Burns was returned to his master in Virginia under heavy guard. Two thousand federal troops were called to Boston to quell the unrest and to escort the shackled Burns to an awaiting government ship. "Protesters suspended a coffin across State Street with the word 'Liberty' painted on its side" to protest Burns's reenslavement. They gathered along the route, which was draped in black with American flags hung upside down. By February 1855, Reverend Leonard A. Grimes, with the help of the Boston community, raised enough money to purchase Anthony Burns's freedom. Burns returned to Boston a free man and later attended Oberlin College in Ohio.

BLACK ABOLITIONISTS

FREDERICK DOUGLASS

One of the most outspoken African American abolitionists was Frederick Douglass. Born into slavery on the eastern shore of Maryland, Douglass was taken from his mother, Harriet Bailey, when he was an infant. His mother was a field-worker and his father was, it is believed, the white plantation owner.

Douglass was raised by his grandparents, Betsey and Isaac Bailey, on a farm twelve miles away from the plantation where his mother lived. Douglass wrote in his autobiography, *The Life and Times of Frederick Douglass*, published in 1881:

> *The practice of separating mothers from their children and hiring them out at distances too great to admit to their meeting, save at long intervals, was a marked feature of the cruelty and barbarity of the slave system; but it was in harmony with the grand aim of the system, which always and everywhere sought to reduce man to the level of the brute. It had no interest in recognizing or preserving any of the ties that bind families together or to their homes.*

While in his teens, Frederick Douglass was sent to Baltimore to live with the Auld family. In this urban setting, Douglass was treated kindly at first by the young, white Mrs. Auld, who taught him to read. Her attitude changed when her husband explained the necessity of keeping the slaves illiterate in order to maintain control over them. This did not stop young Frederick, who enlisted his white friends to help him learn how to write. Literacy, he realized, was his ticket to freedom. In 1838, Douglass escaped to New York.

Underground Railroad conductor David Ruggles

One of the men who assisted Frederick Douglass in his escape to freedom was abolitionist and Underground Railroad conductor David Ruggles. A free black man in New York City, Ruggles owned a house and a reading room on Lispenard Street in Lower Manhattan.

Douglass described the first meeting with Ruggles:

> A sailor named Stuart, a warm-hearted and generous fellow . . . saw me standing on the opposite sidewalk near "The Tombs." As he approached me I ventured a remark to him which at once enlisted his interest in me. He took me to his home to spend the night and in the morning went with me to Mr. David Ruggles, the secretary of the New York vigilance committee, a co-worker with Isaac T. Hopper, Lewis and Arthur Tappan, Theodore S. Wright, Samuel Cornish, Thomas Downing, Philip A. Bell and other men of their time.
>
> Once in the hands of these brave men, I felt comparatively safe. With Mr. Ruggles, on the corner of Lispenard and Church streets, I was hidden for several days, during which time my intended wife [who was already free] came from Baltimore at my call, to share the burdens of life with me.

Douglass and Anna Murray were married. At the suggestion of David Ruggles, they moved to Bedford, Massachusetts, where Douglass's skill as a caulker (sealing the wood planks of the ship to make it watertight) helped him get work at a shipyard.

Frederick Douglass attended abolition meetings in Massachusetts and was a subscriber to William Lloyd Garrison's weekly abolitionist paper, *The Liberator*. When Garrison learned of Douglass's life as a slave and his escape to freedom, he encouraged him to share his experiences. Frederick Douglass spoke at antislavery conventions and became known as an eloquent orator. His *Narrative of the Life of Frederick Douglass, an American Slave*, published in 1845, became a national and international success. He then embarked on a trip to Ireland and Great Britain, where he spent two

Masthead of Douglass's *The North Star* newspaper, which he began publishing in Rochester, New York, in 1847

THE NORTH STAR.

FREDERICK DOUGLASS, } Editors.
M. R. DELANY,

RIGHT IS OF NO SEX—TRUTH IS OF NO COLOR—GOD IS THE FATHER OF US ALL, AND ALL WE ARE BRETHREN

WILLIAM C. NELL, Publisher.
JOHN DICK, Printer.

VOL. I. NO. 1.   ROCHESTER, N. Y. FRIDAY, DECEMBER 3, 1847.   WHOLE

years, and lectured at churches about his life as a slave in America. While in Europe, Douglass raised money to pay for his freedom from Hugh Auld in America.

When Douglass returned to America, he published his first newspaper, *The North Star*, an abolitionist publication. He later renamed it the *Frederick Douglass' Paper*, when it merged with white abolitionist Gerrit Smith's *Liberty Party Paper*.

Because of the city's proximity to the Canadian border, Douglass's home in Rochester became an important station on the Underground Railroad. Hundreds of escaped black people passed through his doors to freedom.

Frederick Douglass was also an adviser to President Abraham Lincoln on the treatment of black soldiers during the Civil War, as well as a recruiter of black troops. He also campaigned for Ulysses S. Grant for president in 1868 and lobbied for the passage of the Fifteenth Amendment, which gave blacks the right to vote. It became law in 1870. President James Garfield (1881) appointed Douglass recorder of deeds for Washington, D.C., in 1881.

SOJOURNER TRUTH

She was born Isabella Baumfree, but took the name Sojourner Truth in 1843 after experiencing a religious vision that inspired her to speak out

LEFT: Frederick Douglass, orator, publisher, and writer, was a major figure in the abolition movement. Douglass escaped slavery in Maryland and traveled to New York City using forged documents. He went on to become an adviser to President Abraham Lincoln during the Civil War and the publisher of *The North Star* newspaper.

RIGHT: Anna Murray Douglass was the wife of Frederick. They married in New York City and moved to Massachusetts, at the suggestion of Underground Railroad conductor David Ruggles, to avoid Frederick's recapture.

about slavery's injustices. Sojourner became a prominent voice in the abolition movement and in the woman suffrage movement (the campaign for a woman's right to vote). She delivered her most moving speech, "Ain't I a Woman?," which summarized the plight of women and blacks in America, at the 1851 Women's Rights Convention in Akron, Ohio.

Truth was born around 1797 in Ulster County, New York, and was a slave in the Johannes Hardenbergh household, a Dutch family in the upstate New York community. At around nine years old, Isabella was sold to an English family, who owned a store near Kingston, New York. They beat her severely because she spoke only Dutch and did not understand their commands. Truth was sold several more times and eventually ran away with her baby daughter, Sophia, after much abuse and promises of freedom from her owner. Truth, the mother of five children, four of whom she left behind when she escaped, spread the word of freedom and equality through her travels, and this brought her recognition as an activist. Truth used the legal system to free her son, Peter, when he was taken by slave catchers and sold into slavery in the South after he had been emancipated in New York in 1827.

Sojourner also assisted the black soldiers in the Union Army during the Civil War by collecting food and clothing for them. A constant voice for the equality of blacks and the rights of women, Sojourner Truth became a champion for resettlement of free blacks in the western territories, away from the violence and racism in the post–Civil War South. Sojourner Truth met with presidents Abraham Lincoln (1861–1865) and Ulysses S. Grant (1869–1877) to press her case of equality for blacks. She died in 1883.

REV. HENRY HIGHLAND GARNET

When he was nine years old, in 1824, Henry Highland Garnet and his family escaped from Maryland on the Underground Railroad. They settled in New Hope, Pennsylvania, and then moved to New York City, where Garnet attended the African Free School Number 2 on Mulberry Street, founded by the New York Manumission Society. Among Garnet's classmates were many notables. Alexander Crummell attended Queens College in Cambridge, England, and then became a minister. James McCune Smith was the first African American to receive a medical degree from Glasgow University in Scotland. Smith opened a medical practice and a pharmacy when

he returned to New York. George T. Downing was an abolitionist and restaurateur whose father, Thomas, owned the famous Oyster House in Lower Manhattan. Other well-known classmates were the Reason brothers—Elmer, Patrick, and Charles L.; the latter was the first black college professor in the United States—and Peter Guignon, a Brooklyn pharmacist.

Garnet attended the Noyes Academy in Canaan, New Hampshire, where he was forced to leave because of racism, and then the Oneida Institute in upstate New York. He became a Presbyterian minister and abolitionist and toured England promoting the antislavery movement in America. Garnet was one of eight black founding members of the American and Foreign Anti-Slavery Society in 1840 and the African Civilization Society in 1859, which promoted the emigration of blacks to Africa. This was an unpopular notion with abolitionists, who wanted equality and freedom for blacks in America. Garnet was appointed by President James Garfield to the post of United States Minister and as Consul General to Liberia, Africa. Garnet died in Monrovia in 1882.

WILLIAM STILL

William Still lived in Philadelphia, Pennsylvania, during the height of the Underground Railroad movement. His home was a station on this intricate escape network, and it is estimated that he helped hundreds of fugitives

LEFT: Sojourner Truth was an evangelist, abolitionist, reformer, and women's rights activist.

RIGHT: William Still was the first secretary of the Pennsylvania Abolition Society and an active member of the U.G.R.R. In his book, *The Underground Rail Road*, Still documented the experiences of the fugitive slaves who passed through Philadelphia on their way to Canada.

escape from slavery in the South to freedom in the North. Like the many people he assisted, Still's parents had also been enslaved in Maryland. His father purchased his own freedom and his mother eventually escaped slavery. The reunited family settled in New Jersey, where William was born.

When he was around twenty years old, Still moved to Philadelphia, where he found work at the Pennsylvania Society for the Abolition of Slavery as a janitor and an office worker. While there, he began helping escaped slaves on their journey to Canada.

In the preface of his book, *The Underground Rail Road*, Still begins by describing the circumstances from which the fugitives were fleeing:

> *In these Records will be found interesting narratives of the escapes of many men, women and children, from the prison-house of bondage; from cities and plantations; from rice swamps and cotton fields; from kitchens and mechanic shops; from Border States and Gulf States; from cruel masters and mild masters; some guided by the north star alone, penniless, braving the perils of land and sea, eluding the keen scent of the blood-hound as well as the more dangerous pursuit of the savage slave-hunter; some from secluded dens and caves of the earth, where for months and years they had been hidden away waiting for the chance to escape; from mountains and swamps, where indescribable suffering from hunger and other privations had patiently been endured . . .*
>
> *Passes have been written and used by fugitives, with their masters' and mistresses' names boldly attached thereto, and have answered admirably as a protection, when passing through ignorant country districts of slave regions, where but few, either white or colored, knew how to read or write correctly . . . They were determined to have liberty even at the cost of life.*

Still was committed to helping the fugitives. He was the corresponding secretary and chairman of a subcommittee of the Philadelphia Vigilance Committee, another very important antislavery organization that defended blacks against the activities of slave catchers and provided shelter for fugitive slaves. Thomas Garrett, a white Quaker of Wilmington, Delaware, was one of Still's colleagues as well as Harriet Tubman's. Garrett corresponded with Still frequently, sharing information on the challenges he faced helping the many fugitive slaves on their journey north to freedom.

Ann Maria Weems escaped via the Underground Railroad, disguised as a man. Fugitive slaves often used such methods, as well as forged documents, to reach the North undetected.

WILLIAM STILL DESCRIBES "SOME OF THE INGENIOUS METHODS FUGITIVES USED TO ESCAPE TO FREEDOM":

Occasionally fugitives came in boxes and chests, and not infrequently some were secreted in steamers and vessels, and in some instances journeyed hundreds of miles in skiffs [small boats]. Men disguised in female attire and women dressed in the garb of men have under very trying circumstances triumphed in thus making their way to freedom. And here and there when all other modes of escape seemed cut off, some, whose fair complexions have rendered them indistinguishable from their Anglo-Saxon brethren, feeling that they could endure the yoke no longer, with assumed airs of importance, such as they had been accustomed to see their masters show when traveling, have taken the usual modes of conveyance and have even braved the most scrutinizing inspection of slave-holders, slave-catchers and car conductors, who were ever on the alert to catch those who were considered base and white enough to practice such deception.

As a respected businessman in Philadelphia, Still was dedicated to the abolitionist movement, and he continued to work for the equality of African Americans throughout his life. He was one of the founders of the Mission School and an organizer of the Colored YMCA in Philadelphia. Still was president of the Pennsylvania Anti-Slavery Society, which assisted free blacks, until 1901, a year before his death.

HARRIET TUBMAN

Harriet Tubman was born around 1820 and is thought to have escaped to freedom when she was around twenty-five. Harriet had been enslaved on the eastern shore of Maryland and made her way to Philadelphia, Pennsylvania, on foot, where she worked in hotels, and later in establishments in Cape May on the New Jersey shore.

Harriet Tubman was considered the "Moses" of her people because of her role of leading hundreds of African Americans to freedom in the North. Tubman had escaped slavery from Maryland and returned repeatedly to the area to bring friends, family, and strangers to Canada on the Underground Railroad.

Harriet used her wages from her work in hotels to help others escape the bondage of slavery. She went back and forth to Maryland from her northern base nineteen times. Known as "Moses" for leading her people to the Promised Land of freedom, Harriet was so successful that Maryland slaveholders posted a reward of twelve thousand dollars (and there were some reports of a forty-thousand-dollar reward) "for the head of the woman who was constantly appearing and enticing away parties of slaves from their masters." After the Fugitive Slave Law of 1850 was passed, Harriet guided groups of escaped slaves eleven times to Canada using the Underground Railroad.

In a letter written in June 1868, Quaker abolitionist Thomas Garrett of Wilmington, Delaware, describes the time period and the number of people Harriet helped to freedom who passed through his home, a station on the Underground Railroad. "The date of the commencement of her labors, I cannot certainly give; but I think it must have been about 1845; from that time till 1860, I think she must have brought from the neighborhood where she had been held as a slave, from 60 to 80 persons, from Maryland, some 80 miles from here."

Tubman traveled many different routes on the Underground Railroad, and it is estimated that she helped more than three hundred people reach freedom. On Harriet's last trip from Maryland to Ontario, Canada, she brought her parents, Benjamin Ross and Harriet Greene, out of bondage. In 1857, they moved to Harriet's home in Auburn, New York, which she had purchased from William H. Seward, who at the time was the U.S. senator from New York and who later became the secretary of state (1861–1869) during the Abraham Lincoln and Andrew Johnson administrations.

Along with her freedom raids during the Civil War, Harriet Tubman cleaned and dressed wounds, and she cured the soldiers of the Union Army who contracted dysentery by administering her homemade remedy. She also nursed hundreds of soldiers with fevers and smallpox. Harriet accompanied Colonel James Montgomery up the Combahee River in South Carolina on expeditions to clear the "torpedoes placed by the rebels in the river, destroy railroads and bridges and cut off supplies to the rebel troops."

Seemingly fearless, Harriet was also a spy for the Union Army, bringing back "valuable information on [rebel] troop and battery positions." A woman of many talents, she also baked gingerbread and made root beer, which she sold to the troops. After the war, the United States Congress granted Tubman a monthly pension for her remarkable work leading her people out of slavery and as a guide, nurse, and spy for the Union Army during the Civil War.

NEW YORK CITY: A DESTINATION FOR FUGITIVE SLAVES

MANHATTAN HAD A thriving community of free blacks in the 1800s, and by 1810 the free black population was around 7,400 and the slave population was a little more than 1,400. Beginning in 1785, the New York State Legislature passed laws on the gradual manumission (freedom) of the enslaved, authorizing the freedom of "all slaves under age 50." This was followed by a statute in 1799 that "freed all slaves born after 1799." And in 1827, New York State abolished slavery for all the enslaved, regardless of age or birth date.

The large community of educated and free blacks in New York City owned businesses and homes, worshipped at their own churches, created social institutions to assist former slaves, and educated their children at black schools. The city was also a major hub for fugitive slaves, and many churches, with both black and white congregations, became important stations on the Underground Railroad. Some significant churches on the U.G.R.R. inside and outside of New York City were Mother A.M.E. Zion in Lower Manhattan, Rossville A.M.E. Zion on Staten Island, St. David A.M.E. Zion in Sag Harbor on Long Island, and Foster Memorial A.M.E. Zion in Tarrytown.

Plymouth Church of the Pilgrims, a white Congregational church located in Brooklyn, became known as the "Grand Central Depot" of the U.G.R.R. because of the many fugitive slaves that hid in the basement and escaped to freedom through a secret passageway.

The minister, Reverend Henry Ward Beecher, was the brother of Harriet Beecher Stowe, the author of the controversial antislavery book *Uncle Tom's Cabin*, published in 1852. It was adapted into a 1903 silent film,

The Colored Sailors' Home at 330 Pearl Street was a refuge for the African American sailors who stopped over in New York City. Under the direction of the American Seamens' Friend Society, the boardinghouse was located in Lower Manhattan, by the seaport, and was operated by William Powell in the 1840s.

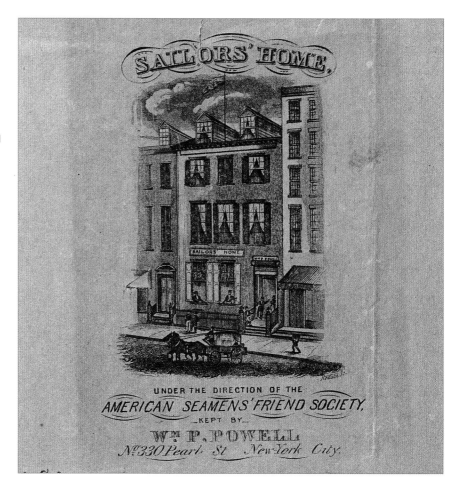

which by today's standards would be considered demeaning because of the stereotypical portrayal of the characters, especially the black characters.

Before he announced his run for president, Abraham Lincoln visited the Plymouth Church in February 1860 to hear Reverend Beecher speak. Beecher also invited "famous antislavery advocates . . . including William Lloyd Garrison, Sojourner Truth, Wendell Phillips, Charles Sumner and Frederick Douglass" to address his congregation. Other guest speakers over the years "included Booker T. Washington . . . [and] Charles Dickens—who read 'A Christmas Carol' to capacity crowds for three nights running in 1868."

In the 1800s, among New York's African American business owners were seamstresses, candlemakers, tailors, bookstore owners, pharmacists, pickle makers, newspaper publishers, caterers, restaurateurs, hairdressers and barbers, tobacconists, and jewelers. A number of their establishments were located in Lower Manhattan.

James Brown, a veteran of the American Revolution, opened a tobacco shop at 326 Spring Street sometime around 1812. William Alexander Brown established a pleasure garden in his backyard on Thomas Street in Greenwich Village about 1820 or 1821. The outdoor café was named the African Grove and served patrons cold drinks and ice cream while they enjoyed poetry readings and theatrical recitations by black performers.

Complaints from his neighbors caused Brown to close the backyard garden. Undeterred from his goal to provide a place for African Americans to relax and mingle with other free blacks, Brown and his friend, actor James Hewlett, opened a theater on Mercer Street in 1821 and formed an all-black theater company that performed Shakespearean plays as well as productions written by Brown. He and Hewlett named their theater the African Grove after the backyard café.

Another businessman who operated in Lower Manhattan was abolitionist William Powell, a former seaman, who opened the Colored Sailors' Home at John and Gold streets in 1839. Powell's boardinghouse catered to black sailors who worked on the ships that traveled in and out of the busy seaport. He not only provided meals, but also a reading room and an employment agency to help sailors find work. Powell did not allow sailors to consume alcohol at the home and created an environment of learning and gentility, the opposite of the rowdier boardinghouses sailors frequented. At some point, Powell moved the Colored Sailors' Home to 330 Pearl Street.

The sailors also participated in Powell's abolitionist activities and carried messages to the enslaved in the South and the Caribbean about free black communities in the North. Powell and his family left New York for Europe after the enactment of the Fugitive Slave Law of 1850, turning his business over to Albros Lyons Sr. In the mid-1850s, Lyons, also a black abolitionist, moved the Colored Sailors' Home to his own home at 20 Vandewater Street near the East River. Lyons aided fugitives on the Underground Railroad by providing them with food and a place to stop on their journey to Canada.

Other black-owned businesses in Manhattan in 1855 included W. F. Brown and W. I. Scott's ice cream parlor at 70 Bleecker Street; B. A. Burgalew's watchmaker establishment at 352 Canal Street; Thomas A. Downing's

Oyster House at 3–5 Broad Street, which had been in business since 1825; Stephen Lawrence's engineering and steam pressure gauge business at 35 William Street; Patrick H. Reason's engraving shop at 56 Bond Street; and James McCune Smith's medical practice and pharmacy at 55 West Broadway.

These early business owners were politically involved and civic-minded individuals who worked for the freedom of the enslaved. They shared their wealth with the less fortunate, in addition to providing funds for abolitionist causes.

❀   ❀   ❀

Thomas Downing's Oyster House became well known for its delicious oysters and plush interior. From the 1830s to 1860s, the restaurant was frequented by elite white New Yorkers, including merchants, politicians, and bankers. Downing's reputation for the finest oysters was so renowned that he shipped orders to Europe. He sent British monarch Queen Victoria his famous oysters, and she was so impressed with the tasty morsels that she sent Downing a gold chronometer watch as a thank-you.

Both white and black citizens in the New York City community respected Downing, a free black from Virginia, who worked tirelessly in the abolition movement for equality in the education of black children and for voting rights for blacks. Downing's son George T. Downing, before opening up his own restaurant, worked in his father's establishment, which was near the Hudson River, and hid fugitive slaves, on their way to freedom in Canada, in the basement.

❀   ❀   ❀

David Ruggles, a prominent abolitionist and a free black man originally from Connecticut, opened the first African American reading room and print shop at 36 Lispenard Street at Church Street in 1834. A stop on the Underground Railroad, the building was also the headquarters for the New York Vigilance Committee, which helped provide food and shelter to fugitive slaves and protect free blacks and fugitives from being kidnapped by slave catchers. Ruggles was a leading member of that organization.

Another building owned by Ruggles, at 67 Lispenard Street at Broadway, housed a boardinghouse and was used for abolition meetings. Ruggles wrote and printed pamphlets protesting slavery and articles for the *Emancipator*, an abolitionist weekly newspaper, which he sold subscriptions for in the Northeast. The paper was started in 1837 by the American Anti-Slavery Society. Ruggles used journalism to focus on the slavery issue in his own publication, *Mirror of Liberty*, the first African American magazine to document slave kidnappings and court cases as well as antislavery speeches given by members of black organizations. *Mirror of Liberty* was published sporadically from 1838 to 1841.

Pierre Toussaint, an enslaved Haitian, established a lucrative business as a hairdresser in New York, with the blessing of his owners. Although Toussaint was very successful and could have purchased his freedom, he remained enslaved until the death of his widowed and destitute mistress in 1807. As a wealthy, free businessman, Toussaint purchased the freedom of his relatives and provided an education for his orphaned niece. A devout Roman Catholic, Toussaint and his wife provided housing for homeless black youth, assistance to the poor, job training and jobs for free blacks, and money and support to a variety of charitable organizations, the Catholic Church among them.

EARLY BLACK NEWSPAPERS

THE FIRST NEWSPAPERS written, edited, and published by African Americans appeared in the northern United States and Canada beginning in the early 1800s. They focused primarily on issues that were important to the black community, including the abolition of slavery and the rights of free blacks. Many of these early newspapers were underfunded and did not have the circulation necessary to sustain them, and some of them went out of business a year or two after their initial publication.

FREEDOM'S JOURNAL, NEW YORK CITY, MARCH 16, 1827–MARCH 28, 1829

Samuel E. Cornish and John B. Russwurm published the first black-owned and operated newspaper in America for African Americans. *Freedom's*

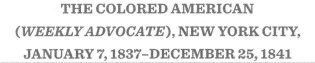

FREEDOM'S JOURNAL.

"*RIGHTEOUSNESS EXALTETH A NATION.*"

CORNISH & RUSSWURM,
Editors & Proprietors.

NEW-YORK, FRIDAY. MARCH 30, 1827.

[VOL. I. No. 3.

MEMOIRS OF CAPT. PAUL CUFFEE.

Being now master of a small covered boat of about 12 tons burthen, he hired a person to assist as a seaman, and made many advantageous voyages to different parts of the state of Connecticut and when about 25 years old married a native of the country, a descendant of the tribe to which his mother belonged.— For some time after his marriage he attended chiefly to his agricultural concerns, but from an increase of family he at length deemed it necessary to pursue his commercial plans more extensively than he had before done.— He arranged his affairs for a new expedition

ral good. It is not so much a right of property, as it is a legal relation; and it ought to be treated as such.

The second object was, to relieve slaveholders from a charge, or an apprehension of criminality, where in fact, there is no offence. There can be no palliation for the conduct of those who first brought the curse of slavery upon poor Africa, and poor America too.— But the body of the present generation are not liable to this charge. Posterity are not answerable for the sins of their fathers, unless they approve, their deeds. They found the blacks among them, in a degraded state,

ance. We may hope to enjoy the favor of our merciful heavenly Father, But this is not done. I think I may venture to assert, that most of the slave-holding states, neither the laws, nor public opinion, secure to the slaves any of the privileges of humanity. Nothing more is done for them, in kind, than is done for the domestic beasts; and nothing more in degree, except as they are a more valuable species of property, and are recognised, to some extent, as possessing rational faculties. Let the contrary be shown. I say that of all that kind of provision, which goes to purify and elevate the character, and

retarded; and that the same prejudice will continue to have a similar operation, so long as it shall continue to exist. Not that they are wanting men of humanity among our West Indian legislators. Their humanity discernable enough when it is to be applied to the *whites*; but such is the system of slavery, and the degradation attached to slaver that their humanity seems to be lost or gone when it is to be applied to the *blacks*. No again that there are wanting men of sense among the same body. They are shrewd and clever enough in the affairs of life, when they maintain an intercourse with the *whites*

In 1827, John B. Russwurm (middle) and Samuel E. Cornish (bottom) established *Freedom's Journal*, the first African American newspaper published in the United States (top).

Journal covered international, national, and regional news and provided its readership with useful information. The paper made its debut in 1827, the same year slavery was abolished in New York. The editors wrote editorials on the abolition of slavery and black colonization in Africa, as well as articles about important African Americans of the day. Cornish left *Freedom's Journal* in September 1827 because of philosophical differences with Russwurm. A supporter of the colonization movement, Russwurm emigrated to Liberia after the paper ceased publication in March 1829.

THE COLORED AMERICAN (*WEEKLY ADVOCATE*), NEW YORK CITY, JANUARY 7, 1837–DECEMBER 25, 1841

Phillip A. Bell published the *Weekly Advocate* from January 7, 1837, to March 4, 1837, when he changed the name of the newspaper to *The Colored American*. The latter was published from March 4, 1837, to December 25, 1841, with Samuel E. Cornish as the editor. The newspaper's editorial content focused on informing newly freed African Americans about the abolition movement, the colonization movement, and equal rights. The paper also published articles about self-improvement and speeches delivered at national and local black conventions. *The Colored American* also printed requests for financial support of black institutions in the community, including orphanages for black children, local churches, and the newspaper itself.

THE NORTH STAR, ROCHESTER, NEW YORK, DECEMBER 3, 1847–APRIL 17, 1851; FREDERICK DOUGLASS' PAPER, ROCHESTER, NEW YORK, 1851–1860

Frederick Douglass published his first newspaper, *The North Star,* an abolitionist publication, on December 3, 1847. The Rochester, New York–based paper was published until April 17, 1851, when Douglass changed the name to *Frederick Douglass' Paper,* after it merged with white abolitionist Gerrit Smith's *Liberty Party Paper* based in Syracuse, New York. The new abolitionist paper, which also supported the woman suffrage movement, was active until 1860.

THE PROVINCIAL FREEMAN, WINDSOR AND CHATHAM, CANADA WEST (ONTARIO), MARCH 24, 1853–SEPTEMBER 20, 1857

The Provincial Freeman was published by founder Mary Ann Shadd Cary, the first black woman publisher in North America and the first woman publisher in Canada. Samuel A. Ward, the editor, wrote articles that focused on the equality, integration, and self-education of blacks. *The Provincial Freeman* was read by the large community of fugitive slaves and free blacks who had settled in Canada and by African Americans living in the United States.

THE CHRISTIAN RECORDER, PHILADELPHIA, PENNSYLVANIA, 1852–PRESENT

The Christian Recorder is published by the African Methodist Episcopal Church, founded in 1816 after black worshippers left the white-dominated Methodist churches because of discrimination. *The Christian Recorder* was established to unify the various black congregations through providing news about the churches. With the Civil War raging, the newspaper became a bridge between black Union soldiers at war and family and friends at home. *The Christian Recorder* published letters from the soldiers detailing their lives in the army, including the racism they experienced and the unequal pay they received from the government. Black soldiers received seven dollars per month, while their white counterparts received thirteen. This discrepancy was corrected when the United States Congress passed a law in 1864 that mandated equal salaries for black and white soldiers.

BLACK INVENTORS

GREEK PHILOSOPHER PLATO once wrote, "Necessity . . . is the mother of invention." And the need to make their lives easier is exactly what inspired the African American inventors in the eighteenth and nineteenth centuries. Their inventiveness flew in the face of the campaign to slander their intelligence and work ethic waged by the white slaveholders and others who felt blacks were not equal to whites.

Eli Whitney, the holder of the 1794 patent for the cotton gin (a mechanical comb) that revolutionized removing the seeds from cotton efficiently, was given the idea, according to anecdotal reports, by a slave named Sam whose father had used a comb to clean the cotton. A patent is a grant from the government that gives a person the right to manufacture and sell their invention.

It is generally acknowledged that other enslaved individuals came up with inventions, and because they were not citizens and were not legally allowed to patent their ideas, it is speculated that some slave owners patented the inventions of their enslaved and reaped the rewards and recognition.

While some freed African Americans were creating and patenting inventions to make their lives and others' easier and often better, groups of antislavery protesters and newspaper publishers were pressing for the abolition of the "peculiar institution" known as slavery. The conflict between the North and the South was escalating, setting the stage for war.

Here is a small sample of the free African American inventors who contributed to the growth and success of America, including those who received patents for their inventions.

Granville T. Woods was an African American inventor who created the process called telegraphony (combined telegraph and telephone technology) that enabled operators to send and receive messages more quickly. Woods also developed a telegraph device that allowed trains to communicate with each other.

BENJAMIN BANNEKER, a free black man, was an inventor, astronomer, and mathematician who created the first wooden striking clock in 1761. He did not receive a patent for his clock. Banneker was also the publisher and author of six farmers' almanacs, published from 1792 to 1797. Banneker, a surveyor, was part of the team that laid out the ten-mile-square area that would become the nation's capital, Washington, D.C., in 1791.

Benjamin Banneker was an inventor, astronomer, and mathematician. The cover of the 1795 almanac he published features a woodcut of his portrait.

THOMAS L. JENNINGS, a free tradesman in New York City, was the first African American to receive a patent, in 1821, for his dry-cleaning process.

NORBERT RILLIEUX, born free in New Orleans, invented the sugarcane evaporator, which was used in refining sugar from sugarcane juice. He patented his invention in 1843.

LEWIS LATIMER invented the method of making carbon filaments for the electric incandescent lamp, and created the patent drawings for Alexander Graham Bell's application for the telephone in 1876. He also invented the toilet designed for use in railroad cars, for which he received a patent in 1874.

JAN MATZELIGER invented the shoe lasting machine, which he patented in 1883. The machine streamlined the shoemaking process by attaching the sole to the shoe mechanically instead of sewing the pieces together by hand.

JUDY W. REED was the first African American woman to receive a patent, in 1884, for a hand-operated kneading and dough-rolling machine for the production of bread.

SARAH E. GOODE was the second African American woman to receive a patent, in 1885, for her invention of the cabinet bed, which folded into a desk and was designed to make space in small apartments.

GRANVILLE T. WOODS was known as the "Black Edison." Woods received patents for a steam-boiler furnace in 1884; a telephone transmitter in 1885, which he sold to (Alexander Graham) Bell Telephone; a system that allowed trains to communicate with each other and between stations in 1887; the overhead electric-conducting wire system for electric railroads in 1888; and the automatic brake in 1902.

GEORGE GRANT patented the improved golf tee, which stabilized the ball on the green, in 1899. Grant graduated from Harvard Dental School, where he also later taught. Grant invented an appliance to repair a cleft palate, a birth defect in which the roof of the mouth is not developed.

❁ ❁ ❁

L'Union, considered the first black newspaper in the South, was published during the Civil War in New Orleans from 1862 to 1864. After *L'Union* folded, it was followed in July 1864 by *The New Orleans Tribune*, the first black daily published in French and English, which lasted until 1870. The current *New Orleans Tribune* was reestablished in 1985.

During Reconstruction, the period after the Civil War from 1865 to 1877, several black newspapers began appearing in the South. These publications emphasized political equality, protested laws restricting the rights of the enslaved, and denounced racial violence against blacks. *The Colored Tribune* was started in Savannah, Georgia, in 1875. The *Jackson Index* was established in Tennessee in 1870 and published until 1937.

DRED SCOTT DECISION OF 1857: PRELUDE TO A WAR

Dred Scott sued for his and his wife's freedom because they lived in areas where slavery was illegal. Scott lost his case, which went all the way to the Supreme Court, where it was ruled that slaves were property and could not sue for their freedom.

AS MORE AND more new states joined the Union as free states, the southern states' influence on Congress was threatened. Plantation owners and other southerners became increasingly alarmed that their way of life was going to end. The Dred Scott decision of 1857 validated the institution of slavery for the South, but it simultaneously increased the anger and determination of the abolitionists and antislavery supporters in the northern states.

Dred Scott was a slave who sued for his and his wife Harriet's freedom because, for part of their enslavement, they had lived in the free state of Illinois and the free territory of Wisconsin, where slavery was illegal. After losing their cases in the lower courts, Dred Scott took his case to the Supreme Court of the United States, where Chief Justice Roger B. Taney delivered a ruling for the court's majority, in 1857. The Dred Scott decision stated that slaves were not citizens of the United States; they were private property, and therefore could not sue for their freedom. Dred Scott and his family were freed in 1857 by his original owners, the Blow family. Scott died of tuberculosis in 1858.

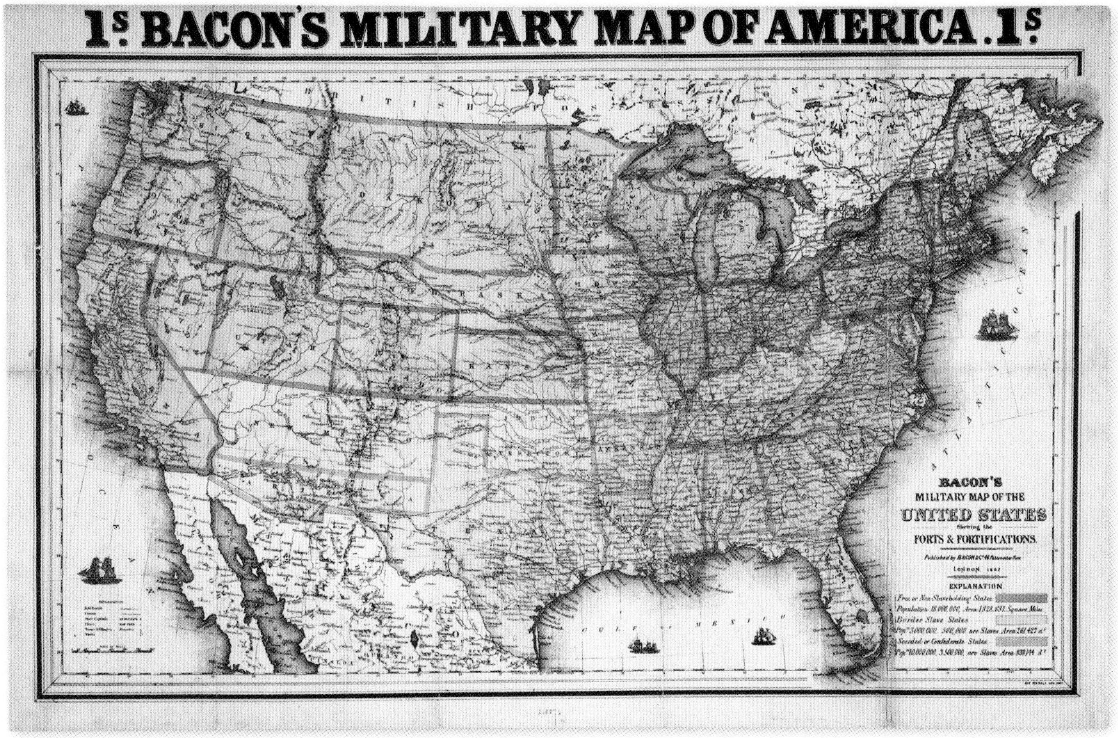

1S BACON'S MILITARY MAP OF AMERICA.1S

BACON'S
MILITARY MAP OF THE
UNITED STATES
Showing the
FORTS & FORTIFICATIONS.

Slavery was euphemistically referred to as the "peculiar institution" by southerners, because it was a contradiction to hold a group of people in bondage in a country that had fought and won its freedom from the British. The phrase, used in conversation, was a way to talk about a horrific institution in polite terms. The rationale for slavery's existence for southerners was that the system was the foundation of their economy. The end of slavery would be the end of their prosperous and genteel lifestyle facilitated by a large enslaved black population that performed every imaginable service. It was this conflict of interest, enslaved or free, between the southern and northern states that led to the Civil War.

This 1862 map of the United States shows the Union's free states and territories in blue-green, the states and territories that seceded from the Union in pink, and the border states and slaveholding territories that did not secede in yellow.

THE CIVIL WAR: BATTLE FOR FREEDOM

THE AMERICAN CIVIL War began on April 12, 1861, with the attack by Confederate soldiers (southern) on the United States facility at Fort Sumter in South Carolina. The Confederate States of America consisted of seven southern states—South Carolina, Mississippi, Florida, Alabama, Georgia,

Abraham Lincoln was the sixteenth president of the United States, who worked to keep the nation intact.

Louisiana, and Texas—that had seceded (created their own separate government) from the Union, as the United States was called as of February 1861. These states left the Union after the 1860 presidential election of Abraham Lincoln. Lincoln had campaigned to end the spread of slavery, and his election, as far as the South was concerned, was the death knell that signaled the end of their peculiar institution. Jefferson Davis became the president of the Confederacy. Four more states—Virginia, Arkansas, Tennessee, and North Carolina—joined the Confederacy in the spring of 1861, bringing the southern total to eleven.

The Union consisted of twenty-three free states that supported the abolition of slavery. There were four border states—Delaware, Maryland, Missouri, and Kentucky—slave states that shared a border with the free states and supported the Union. These states would be joined by the new state of West Virginia in June 1863.

ALL-BLACK UNION REGIMENTS

BLACK TROOPS HAD seen battle in the Revolutionary War. They also had fought in the War of 1812, although African Americans were prohibited from bearing arms by federal law through the Second Amendment of the 1792 Uniform Militia Act. Just like these earlier wars fought in America, African Americans were on the front lines on both sides of the Civil War conflict. According to the National Park Service, "approximately 180,000 African Americans comprising 163 units served in the Union Army during the Civil War, and many more African Americans served in the Union Navy. Both free African Americans and runaway slaves joined the fight."

All-black Union regiments included the 1st South Carolina Volunteers, a regiment of enslaved soldiers from South Carolina, Georgia, and Florida that formed in March 1862. Later, the regiment became the 33rd U.S. Colored Troops. Another was the 1st Kansas Colored Volunteer Infantry Regiment, which officially joined the fight in January 1863. The 1st Kansas fought gallantly during the Battle of Island Mound, Missouri, in October

1862, successfully holding off the Confederates. In July 1863, at the Battle of Honey Springs, in current-day Oklahoma, the regiment waged a fierce fight capturing the flag of the Texas regiment. The Commanding "General James Blunt wrote after the battle, 'I never saw such fighting as was done by the Negro regiment. . . . The question that Negroes will fight is settled; besides, they make better soldiers in every respect than any troops I have ever had under my command.'"

1ST LOUISIANA NATIVE GUARDS

The 1st Louisiana Native Guards, a regiment of free men of color, was originally formed in 1861 to assist the Confederate Army. It was disbanded a year later because southern army authorities did not trust the military ability or the allegiance of the black men. After the fall of Louisiana in the summer of 1862, three thousand black soldiers were enlisted in the Union Army's new Louisiana Native Guards, which consisted of three regiments with a few black officers who held the rank of major.

The Louisiana Native Guards did not have it easy under the Union command, either. They faced prejudice, suspicion, and mistrust from their white counterparts who believed that black soldiers could not perform militarily in the face of battle. However, the Native Guards distinguished themselves in the Battle of Port Hudson, near Baton Rouge, Louisiana, on the Mississippi River, in May 1863. Here they lent support to Union major general Nathaniel P. Bank's troops in a brave attack on the Confederate garrison over open ground. Some of the criticism from the southern army authorities was put to rest.

In June 1863, the Louisiana Native Guards was renamed the Corps d'Afrique. In April 1864, the Corps became part of the 73rd and 74th Regiments of the United States Colored Troops of the U.S. Army.

54TH MASSACHUSETTS VOLUNTEER INFANTRY

The 54th Massachusetts Volunteer Infantry was organized by Governor John A. Andrew in March 1863. Two sons of abolitionist Frederick Douglass, Lewis and Charles, were members of this regiment, as were free blacks from New York and Pennsylvania. Lewis Douglass was among the black troops who fought the courageous battle at Fort Wagner, South Carolina, on July 18, 1863.

Sergeant Major Lewis Douglass, a son of Frederick Douglass, was a member of the famed 54th Massachusetts Volunteer Infantry with his younger brother, Charles R. Douglass.

Fort Wagner was a Confederate fortification on Morris Island near Charleston, South Carolina. The men of the 54th stormed the fort but were met with heavy artillery fire and were overwhelmed. The Union continued shelling the fort for two months and eventually the Confederate troops abandoned it.

The 54th Massachusetts distinguished itself in this historic battle, and although the regiment suffered heavy losses, their heroism became legendary. For his bravery during the battle, Sergeant William Carney was the first African American to be awarded a Medal of Honor. Sergeant Carney was rewarded for his heroism, because he picked up the American flag after the flag bearer was wounded. Despite being wounded himself several times, he held on to the flag, never letting it touch the ground. "After being shot in the thigh, Carney crawled uphill on his knees bearing the Union flag and urging his troops to follow." However, Carney did not receive his Medal of Honor until May 23, 1900.

The Bureau of United States Colored Troops (USCT) was established in May 1863 by the War Department to recruit free African Americans into the Union Army and organize the all-black state militias under one bureau. The soldiers came from all over and were a major factor in securing the Union victory, although they were not officially allowed in the army until two years before the end of the war. The exceptions were the 1st South Carolina Volunteers and the Louisiana Native Guards regiment, which unofficially joined the Union effort under Major General Benjamin Butler's command before the formation of the USCT.

The USCT was also responsible for regiment assignments and paying black soldiers, but black soldiers did not receive the same pay as the white troops and faced racism from within the army rank and file. Black soldiers were paid ten dollars per month, minus three dollars for clothing, while white soldiers were paid thirteen dollars with no clothing allowance deducted. The African American recruits were placed in cavalry, infantry, and artillery units led by white officers. With the exception of black surgeons and chaplains, blacks were not commissioned as officers. On June 15, 1864, Congress passed a law guaranteeing equal pay to *all* black and white soldiers. The black soldiers were paid at the higher rate retroactively.

African Americans also served in the Confederate Army, but it is not clear how many were actual soldiers. The vast majority of the enslaved and free blacks that assisted the army were teamsters (wagon drivers), cooks, hospital workers, or musicians. Several Confederate states allowed free African Americans to enlist in their state militias, such as Tennessee, which authorized the recruitment of free blacks in June 1861, and Louisiana, which initially authorized the formation of the 1st Louisiana Native Guards, shortly after Tennessee's commissioning of black troops.

A recruitment poster for "colored men" from the United States War Department

ABOVE: "The effects of the Emancipation Proclamation—freed negroes coming into our lines at Newbern, North Carolina" read the caption of this drawing published in *Harper's Weekly*, February 21, 1863. These ex-slaves were "contrabands" who chose to relocate after the Emancipation Proclamation.

OPPOSITE: The draft lottery was held on July 13, 1863, at the provost marshal's office on Third Avenue in New York City. Members of a volunteer firefighting company, incensed over not being exempt from the draft, set fire to the marshal's office. The fire spread to stores and other buildings.

EMANCIPATION PROCLAMATION

IN JANUARY 1863, in the middle of the Civil War, President Lincoln issued his Emancipation Proclamation. It abolished slavery in the Confederate states, but not in the border states of Delaware, Maryland, Kentucky, and Missouri or the southern states of Tennessee, southern Louisiana, parts of Virginia, and the soon-to-be-formed West Virginia that were under Union control. Since the onset of the war, President Lincoln had been careful to emphasize he was fighting to preserve the Union, not to end slavery. He knew it was of great importance strategically to keep the loyalty of the slave-owning border states.

During the war, men both white and black were eager to serve the Union and signed up. Beginning in 1863, however, many more were drafted by the government. Wealthy citizens eligible for military service were able to avoid fighting by paying a fee or by presenting a suitable substitute to fight in their place. This "privilege" was made possible by the Conscription Act of 1863 and caused a division between the wealthy and the poor, and riots broke out across the country. One of the most serious disturbances was in New York City.

DRAFT RIOTS OF 1863 IN NEW YORK CITY

THE NEW YORK City Draft Riots began on July 13, 1863, and for four days mobs of mostly Irish immigrants roamed the streets of Manhattan, killing, looting, setting fires, and destroying the homes and businesses of black New Yorkers and institutions that supported the war, the Republican Party, or the wealthy. The Conscription Act was at the root of the rebellion; many rioters believed the war was for the freedom of the blacks, who they feared would compete for employment and housing.

Race relations between free blacks and the Irish immigrants were historically very tense in the city. In the 1840s, many Irish came to America and settled in the same community where the free African Americans had lived since 1827—the Five Points section of Lower Manhattan. When novelist Charles Dickens visited America in 1842, he toured the Five Points district and described the slum and its denizens in his travelogue, *American Notes for General Circulation*:

> This is the place: these narrow ways diverging to the right and left, and reeking everywhere with dirt and filth. Such lives as are led here bear the same fruit here as elsewhere. The coarse and bloated faces at the doors have counterparts at home and all the world over. Debauchery has made the very houses prematurely old. See how the rotten beams are tumbling down, and how the patched and broken windows seem to scowl dimly, like eyes that have been hurt in drunken frays. ... Where dogs would howl to lie, women, and men, and boys slink off to sleep, forcing the dislodged rats to move away in quest of better lodgings. Here, too, are lanes and alleys paved with mud knee-deep; underground chambers where they dance and game...

Dickens sums up Five Points with the remark: "All that is loathsome, drooping, and decayed is here."

Competing for the same cheap housing and low-paying jobs as waiters, domestic servants, and laborers, the free blacks and Irish were at conflict with each other from the start. So, it was not a surprise that the Irish strongly protested the Civil War draft, a war they felt would benefit blacks, but be fought by poor whites.

Six thousand Union soldiers were summoned to restore peace and quell the roaming bands of agitators consisting of men, women, and children. Rioters set fire to the Colored Orphan Asylum on Fifth Avenue, between 43rd and 44th streets, burning it to the ground. The young charges barely escaped the raging inferno and the riotous mob with their lives. Two black men were lynched and mutilated. This made an indelible mark on the psyche of the black citizens of New York City.

The exact number of casualties, both black and white, is not really known. Some estimates have at least 119 killed, with more than 300 rioters, policemen, and soldiers injured. Reportedly, 19 African Americans were beaten and murdered.

Fearing the violence would continue after the draft riots, many African Americans fled Lower Manhattan to all-black communities in Brooklyn (Weeksville) and Staten Island (Sandy Ground), and some also moved north and west to Connecticut, Massachusetts, Rhode Island, and New Jersey. Other African Americans had already left New York City because of the slave catchers, for areas as far away as California, Canada, and the West Indies and Africa.

BLACK DISPATCHES

FOR THOSE AFRICAN Americans who answered the call to war, some were on the front lines, as soldiers and sailors. Others helped feed the soldiers, nurse the sick, and transport supplies. Still others provided information about the enemy. Just as they did in the American Revolution, enslaved and free blacks supplied valuable intelligence that was used to plot strategies for battles, identify battery locations, interrupt enemy supply lines, and monitor troop movements.

The term "Black Dispatches" was used by the Union military to describe the information gathered by the black agents or spies who worked behind enemy lines of the Confederate Army as servants or menial workers. Much of the information also came from fugitive slaves traveling from the South to the North. The information was handed over to Union officers by escaping slaves who would encounter Confederate activity on their way to freedom.

"One of the first large-scale Civil War battles was the result of information provided by George Scott, a runaway slave. He furnished intelligence on Confederate fortifications and troop movements to Gen. Benjamin F. Butler, commander of Fort Monroe [in Virginia] . . . Butler determined that Confederate forces were planning an attack on Newport News [Virginia], which would isolate Fort Monroe from Union re-supply." Butler ordered a preemptive attack on the Confederate troops, but lost the battle.

Allan Pinkerton, a white Chicago detective and the chief of intelligence under Union major general George B. McClellan, was responsible for

ABOVE: A Civil War sailor holding portraits of two Confederate soldiers, c. 1865

RIGHT: Robert Smalls, in his sprint to freedom, commandeered a Confederate boat, the *Planter*, during the Civil War, and delivered the steamer to Union troops.

gathering information on the southern states and the Confederate Army during the war. Pinkerton, an abolitionist, used all kinds of informants, including merchants, deserters, prisoners of war, refugees fleeing the fighting, and former slaves.

John Scobell, a former enslaved person from Mississippi who was well educated, became an important Pinkerton operative. "An accomplished role player," Scobell would assume "different identities on various missions, including food vendor, cook, or laborer" to infiltrate enemy ranks. He also used his membership in the clandestine Legal League, a group of African Americans in the South who supported freedom for the enslaved, to gain information on "local conditions, fortifications, and troop dispositions." League members also acted as couriers carrying information to Union lines.

Another Pinkerton agent was riverboat worker W. H. Ringgold. After being forced to help Confederates move troop supplies on the York River in

Virginia, Ringgold made his way to Pinkerton. He was able to give Pinkerton information about Confederate fortifications, the number of troops, and artillery locations.

African American women also helped the Union effort through their heroic deeds. Harriet Tubman became well known not only for her work on the Underground Railroad, but also for her work as a guide and spy with Union troops in South Carolina. Mary Touvestre, a freed slave, worked as a housekeeper for the engineer who designed the first ironclad warship for the Confederate Navy, the retrofitted *Merrimac*—known as the *Virginia* to Confederates—that had been damaged by fire. She stole the plans that helped the Union speed up construction of its own ironclad warship, the *Monitor*.

There are many more black men and women who risked their lives for the Union cause, including Charlie Wright, Mary Elizabeth Bowser, and William A. Jackson. One outstanding African American who performed a major feat was Robert Smalls, a slave from South Carolina. As a pilot on the Confederate steamer the *Planter*, Smalls commandeered the ship loaded with armaments. With his wife and children and twelve other enslaved persons on board, he piloted the ship through a Union blockade and turned it over to the Union Navy. Hailed as a hero and written about in newspaper accounts, Smalls became a major general in the Union's South Carolina militia and later a state legislator. During Reconstruction, Smalls served five terms as a U.S. congressman.

The Civil War ended on April 9, 1865, with the surrender of Confederate general Robert E. Lee to Union lieutenant general Ulysses S. Grant at McLean House, near the town of Appomattox Court House, Virginia. News of the Emancipation Proclamation of 1863 had been received by the enslaved in the South with joy. Now at the end of the Civil War all of the enslaved were freed. Many in bondage, however, were not told of their freedom by their white plantation owners and found out through word-of-mouth. And in Galveston, Texas, the enslaved did not learn about their emancipation until June 19, 1865, more than two years after it went into effect and two months after the end of the war. Union soldiers rode through town and told them the war was over and that they were free. Juneteenth is now a celebration that many African Americans hold annually on June 19, in remembrance of this historic event.

Entered according to act of Congress in the year 1872 by Currier & Ives, in the Office of the Librarian of Congress at Wa

ROBERT C. DE LARGE, M.C. of S. Carolina.   JEFFERSON H. LONG, M.C. of Georgi

U.S. Senator, H.R. REVELS, of Mississippi   BENJ. S. TURNER, M.C. of Alabama.   JOSIAH T. WALLS, M.C. of Florida.   JOSEPH H. RA

THE FIRST COLORED SENATOR AND REP

In the 41st and 42nd Congress of the United

NEW YORK, PUBLISHED BY CURRIER & IVES, 125 NASSAU STREET.

rolina.   R. BROWN ELLIOT, M.C. of S. Carolina.

ENTATIVES.

PART **IV**

RECONSTRUCTION
AND
JIM CROW

THIS PAGE: Fugitive slaves in Cumberland County, Virginia, escaped to Union lines in 1862 for protection and shelter from Confederate troops. Known as "contrabands," the displaced individuals would be settled on confiscated property or travel with Union troops. When the war ended, contrabands were provided aid by the newly formed Freedmen's Bureau.

PREVIOUS PAGE: The original caption on this lithograph read, "The first colored senator and representatives in the 41st and 42nd Congress of the United States," elected during Reconstruction.

THE CIVIL WAR ended on April 9, 1865, with the surrender of the Confederacy to the Union. Six days later, on April 15, President Abraham Lincoln died from wounds inflicted by an assassin's bullet. There were two major issues facing the United States after the war: assimilating the newly freed enslaved into society, and rebuilding and reuniting the war-torn South with the rest of the United States. This was called Reconstruction.

President Lincoln was shot on April 14, 1865, by John Wilkes Booth, an actor, in Washington, D.C., while watching a performance at Ford's Theatre with his wife, Mary Todd Lincoln. Booth vehemently opposed Lincoln's policies regarding the emancipation of African Americans, and he supported the Confederacy. Booth's original plan was to kidnap Lincoln and exchange him for Confederate prisoners.

When that plot failed, Booth made a more elaborate and lethal plan and conspired with eight co-conspirators to assassinate Lincoln, Vice President Andrew Johnson, Secretary of State William H. Seward, and General Ulysses S. Grant. Booth believed that the death of these key members of Lincoln's administration would cause a major disruption of the U.S. government and the result would be the Confederacy gaining control of the United States. Booth was killed near Bowling Green, Virginia, on April 26, while trying to escape capture. His eight co-conspirators were caught and arrested days after the assassination. Four were hanged, one died in jail, and three were pardoned.

After Lincoln's death, Andrew Johnson, a Democrat who had supported the Civil War and who had survived the attack, became president of the United States. Once he assumed office, Johnson received resistance from the Radical Republicans, a faction within the Republican party, when he attempted to implement a policy of Reconstruction that favored the southern states. The Radical Republicans wanted to reorganize the South into a society where everyone would be paid for their labor, where African Americans would have equal rights, and where the states would adhere to the U.S. Constitution.

The marriage of a colored soldier at Vicksburg, Virginia, officiated by Chaplain Warren of the Freedmen's Bureau. The illustration appeared in the June 30, 1866 issue of *Harper's Weekly*.

THE FREEDMEN'S BUREAU

ALTHOUGH IT GAVE hope and a new meaning to life to millions of people, emancipation was a disaster. Four million freed black people, many of whom were illiterate and who did not have jobs, food, or shelter, had to be assimilated into American society. This massive task was undertaken, in part, by the Freedmen's Bureau, whose official name was the Bureau of Refugees, Freedmen, and Abandoned Lands, established in 1865 under the jurisdiction of the United States War Department. Major General Oliver O. Howard, a Medal of Honor recipient, was appointed commissioner of the bureau. He later became the third president of the historically black university Howard University in Washington, D.C., established in 1867 during Reconstruction and named after Howard.

Prior to the formation of the Freedmen's Bureau, a combination of aid societies, church organizations, and relief associations sprung up in the South during the Civil War to handle the contraband, a term used to describe the African Americans freed by the Emancipation Proclamation and the other homeless refugees. With no clear plan and no place to live, many of the former enslaved settled in contraband camps, where they worked on crews and received government food rations and some medical care. Still others traveled with Union troops, performing jobs as servants, cooks, nurses, laundresses, and teamsters.

The Freedmen's Bureau was responsible for managing the eight hundred thousand acres of land in the South that had been abandoned by the fleeing plantation owners and other southerners during the war. The bureau was also charged with providing medical support and housing as well as educational, employment, and financial services to the newly freed and the displaced white southerners. Some of the abandoned or confiscated plantations were put back into operation, and black workers were hired to work on the farms; these grew into large communities of freed black people. After emancipation, many of the freedmen became tenant farmers or sharecroppers, some of whom remained on the very same plantations where they were enslaved, working for their former owners.

FORTY ACRES AND A MULE

TO HELP IN the resettlement of the thousands of freedmen who joined Major General William Tecumseh Sherman's "march to the sea" from Atlanta to Savannah, Georgia, in November 1864, Sherman issued Special Field Orders, No. 15, on January 16, 1865. The march to the sea had been Sherman's scorched-earth campaign during which his troops destroyed transportation routes, communication equipment, factories, farms, and plantations from Atlanta to Savannah to impede the South in fighting the war.

The Special Field Orders, No. 15, approved by President Lincoln, divided up more than four hundred thousand acres of confiscated land in South Carolina, Georgia, and Florida into forty-acre tracts to be distributed among forty thousand freedmen and their families, who received "possessory" titles to the land. Sherman also provided the freedmen with livestock that his troops had confiscated during the march to the sea. This act was what many blacks have referred to today as "reparations"—payment of "forty acres and a mule" for their years of enslavement and to begin their new lives of freedom. The freedmen's land ownership was short-lived, as Special Orders, No. 15, was rescinded by president Andrew Johnson. In February 1866, the freedmen were ordered to leave the land, and the property was returned to the white plantation owners.

Meanwhile, Congress, led by the Radical Republicans, including Senator Charles Sumner and Representative Thaddeus Stevens, enacted the Reconstruction Acts of 1867 and 1868 to nullify Democratic president Johnson's Reconstruction program. Sumner, Stevens, and other Republican legislators felt the president's plan readmitted states to the Union too easily, was too conciliatory, and did not go far enough to punish the southern states for seceding from the Union. The Radical Republicans were outraged that states that had been readmitted under Johnson's program were now creating laws called Black Codes, which limited the civil rights of blacks as citizens, guaranteed to them under the Fourteenth Amendment, and denied the newly freed economic opportunities.

The Reconstruction Acts divided the rebel states of Virginia, North Carolina, South Carolina, Georgia, Mississippi, Alabama, Louisiana, Florida, Texas, and Arkansas into five military districts and put the states under martial law. Tennessee had already been readmitted to the Union.

Assistant commissioners were appointed to head each district and were given the responsibility of protecting the rights and property of all citizens through the help of federal troops, maintaining the peace, punishing lawbreakers, and establishing a court system. The southern states also had to ratify the Fourteenth Amendment, which gave all citizens, including the recently freed, equal protection under the law and due process (the protection of an individual's rights). The states also had to rewrite their state constitutions to reflect black male suffrage, which gave black men the right to vote, and hold elections for new governors and legislators before being readmitted to the Union.

Through the assistance of the wartime commissioners and the Freedmen's Bureau, the formerly enslaved received other benefits as well. These included the issuing of marriage certificates, negotiating work contracts, and providing an education for all refugees and freed persons.

The Freedmen's Bureau established forty hospitals, including the

Freedmen's Hospital in Washington, D.C. The bureau also started the Freedman's Savings and Trust Company, which opened in 1865 and grew to thirty-seven offices in seventeen states. By 1872, it had more than seventy thousand African American depositors whose funds totaled more than $3.7 million in assets. At one point, the bank's deposits reached $55 million, but it closed in 1874 due to mismanagement.

Legislation passed by Congress to help freed blacks assimilate and combat the Black Codes enacted by southern legislatures included the Civil Rights Act of 1866, passed on April 9, despite President Andrew Johnson's veto. The law stated that all persons born in the United States, regardless of race, color, or previous condition of servitude, were citizens. It also guaranteed citizens the ability to make and enforce contracts; to sue or be sued; testify in court; and inherit, buy, sell, lease, hold, or convey property. Anyone denying these rights to former enslaved would face a fine or imprisonment. The Fourteenth Amendment to the Constitution was adopted, in part, to ensure that the rights granted in the Civil Rights Act of 1866 would be adhered to in the event the act was repealed.

In 1868 Ulysses S. Grant was elected president. He did not initiate any great reforms or advancement during Reconstruction, but he did aid it at times with the use of the military.

FREED MEN AND WOMEN ADVANCE IN EDUCATION AND POLITICS

A NUMBER OF historically black colleges and universities (HBCUs), about four thousand institutions of higher learning, were founded during this time. They offered technical, agricultural, and basic education courses to prepare the newly freed as teachers and to provide them with vocational skills. The schools included: Fisk University, Nashville, Tennessee (1866); Morehouse College, Atlanta, Georgia (1867); Morgan State University, Baltimore, Maryland (1867); Hampton University, Hampton, Virginia, founded as Hampton Normal and Agricultural Institute (1868); and Tuskegee Institute in Alabama (1881).

Politics changed dramatically in the South during Reconstruction. Previously, the representatives to Congress were all white. With Confederate states (Democrats) not represented in Congress because they had seceded from the Union, African Americans who had joined the Republican Party, the party of Lincoln, were elected to political office by the many black voters who had recently gained the right to vote. In the Senate and the House of Representatives starting in the 1870s, there were two African American senators and twenty African American representatives.

African Americans in the Reconstruction U.S. House of Representatives:

John W. Menard (1868; the first African American elected to Congress but denied a seat because his opponent challenged the election results), Louisiana; **Joseph H. Rainey** (1870–1879), South Carolina; **Jefferson F. Long** (1870–1871), Georgia; **Robert C. DeLarge** (1871–1873), South Carolina; **Robert B. Elliott** (1871–1875), South Carolina; **Benjamin S. Turner** (1871–1873), Alabama; **Josiah T. Walls** (1871–1877), Florida; **Richard H. Cain** (1873–1875 and 1877–1879), South Carolina; **John R. Lynch** (1873–1877 and 1882–1883), Mississippi; **James T. Rapier** (1873–1875), Alabama; **Alonzo J. Ransier** (1873–1875), South Carolina; **Jeremiah Haralson** (1875–1877), Alabama; **John A. Hyman** (1875–1877), North Carolina; **Charles E. Nash** (1875–1877), Louisiana; **Robert Smalls** (1875–1879, 1881–1883, and 1884–1887), South Carolina; **James E. O'Hara** (1882–1884 and 1884–1886), North Carolina; **Henry Cheatham** (1888–1890 and 1890–1892), North Carolina; **John M. Langston** (1890–1891), Virginia; **Thomas E. Miller** (1888–1890), South Carolina; **George W. Murray** (1892–1894), South Carolina; and **George H. White** (1897–1901), North Carolina, who was the last African American elected to Congress during this period.

African Americans in the Reconstruction U.S. Senate:

Hiram R. Revels (1870–1871), Mississippi; and **Blanche K. Bruce** (1875–1881), Mississippi.

Among African Americans elected to local legislatures and appointed to local and federal government positions:

P. B. S. Pinchback, the African American lieutenant governor of Louisiana, became acting governor in 1872. **Oscar J. Dunn** and **Cesar C. Antoine**, former officers of the Louisiana Native Guards (also known as the Corps d'Afrique), served as lieutenant governor in Louisiana in 1868 and 1872, respectively. A person of particular note was **Richard Greener**, the first black graduate of Harvard University, in 1870, who was appointed to the diplomatic corps as a U.S. consul in Vladivostok, Russia, in 1898.

The Compromise of 1877 ended the contested presidential election of 1876 between Republican Rutherford B. Hayes and Democrat Samuel J. Tilden, in which Tilden won the popular vote and Hayes won the electoral vote. To end the dispute, both parties agreed to a compromise that called for the appointment of one Democrat to Hayes's administration; the withdrawal of Union troops from South Carolina, Louisiana, and Florida, and effectively giving back control of the southern state legislatures to the white Democratic lawmakers; and help industrializing the southern economy through federal legislation. The southern state legislatures passed laws called Black Codes, which substantially weakened the Fourteenth Amendment that granted equal rights to all citizens and the Fifteenth Amendment that gave black males the right to vote. These discriminating Black Codes denied blacks employment, housing, and due process and required them to pay poll taxes and take literacy tests in order to qualify to vote. The Compromise of 1877 ended Reconstruction and ushered in the era of Jim Crow and the white supremacy movement. Members of the movement believed that they were superior to blacks and other people from different ethnic backgrounds and that blacks were not entitled to equal rights.

An 1870 lithograph by James C. Beard portraying a parade held in Baltimore, Maryland, to celebrate the passing of the Fifteenth Amendment on May 19, 1870. The other images depict African American heroes and leaders and their accomplishments after slavery was abolished.

THE BIRTH OF JIM CROW

An image of "Jim Crow"

THERE WAS ENORMOUS resentment from the white southerners who lost the war, especially the wealthy ones who also lost their plantations and their slaves. During the Civil War there were 630,000 troops killed and more than one million injured during the Civil War on the Confederate and Union sides. Mothers, wives, sisters, and older male relatives who did not fight in the war were left in the South to deal with burned-out, ransacked, and gutted homes. In addition to this, there were acres of ravaged farmland, damaged roads, blown-up bridges, and destroyed railway tracks. These southerners also faced starvation and had few amenities of their previous life or the resources to resume a normal one. Their economy, which was based on cash crops of cotton, rice, and tobacco and the work of slave labor, had been demolished. A new society would need to develop that was unlike any that had existed before in the South. To make matters worse, the white southerners had to deal with four million freed blacks whom they now feared because of how they previously tortured and abused them, but whom they now needed to employ, reluctantly, to run their farms and plantations.

After Reconstruction, the southern states regained their power. Through their newly elected state legislatures, the states of the abolished Confederacy passed Jim Crow laws that in effect rolled back the civil rights advances that blacks had made during Reconstruction. Essentially, the free blacks were reenslaved. These new laws were named for a white minstrel who wore blackface and called himself "Jim Crow" and acted like a buffoon. The cartoonish stereotype cast the black man as intellectually inferior, lazy, and shiftless, and the image was published and distributed widely by white southerners in cartoons placed in newspapers, magazines, and books. The purpose of these caricatures was to demean blacks and undermine their drive for equal rights. A major goal of Jim Crow laws was to legalize the segregation of the white race and the black race and to prevent blacks from participating in the democratic process.

To further intimidate blacks and to enforce the Jim Crow laws, white supremacist groups were founded. One of these was the Ku Klux Klan, originally formed in 1866 by ex-Confederate soldiers in Tennessee. The Klan used torture, lynchings (in which victims were hanged from a tree), murders, cross burnings, and arson to intimidate freed blacks and white supporters of Reconstruction. Dressed in white sheets to hide their identity from federal troops, the Klan's reign of terror included not only killing blacks, but also destroying black institutions by burning churches and schools to halt the political and social advances African Americans had made during Reconstruction. These Klan groups did not just focus their hatred and vendettas on African Americans and their white sympathizers; they also terrorized other groups that were different from them, including immigrants, Jews, and Catholics.

As white hatred for blacks grew in the South and in other parts of America, the violence became more lethal. Lynchings continued, as well as riots and massacres that killed thousands of blacks throughout the South and, in the early 1900s, in some northern and midwestern cities, too. From the late 1880s through the 1930s, approximately 3,700 African Americans had been lynched, mostly in the South.

Attacks against blacks by whites began erupting in the 1860s during Reconstruction. In Memphis, in May 1866, white citizens and local police killed forty-six blacks and burned ninety homes, twelve schools, and four churches. In New Orleans on July 30, 1866, police stormed a meeting of black and white Republicans, killing more than forty and wounding more

Riots in Memphis, Tennessee, on May 2, 1866, killed forty-six African Americans and burned down ninety homes.

than one hundred and fifty. In Opelousas, Louisiana, on September 28, 1868, between two hundred and three hundred African Americans were massacred. During the Clinton Massacre of 1875 in Mississippi, more than twenty African Americans were killed from September 4 to September 6. In Carrollton, Mississippi, on March 17, 1886, twenty African Americans were murdered. Racial disturbances in Danville, Virginia; Wilmington, North Carolina; Atlanta, Georgia; and Brownsville, Texas, also claimed the lives of many African Americans.

A wood engraving of an enlisted man of the 10th (Colored) Cavalry, known as the Buffalo Soldiers, on maneuvers in Arizona. The engraving, created in 1888, is by Frederick Remington.

As whites resoundingly rejected integration and political equality for blacks, their outrage and resistance was marked by the increased violence that rocked the South from the 1860s through the 1900s. In 1883, the U.S. Supreme Court overturned the Civil Rights Act of 1875 that gave blacks equal rights to use public accommodations and the right to be called as jurors. This set the stage at the state level to further restrict the rights of African Americans and further disenfranchise them.

WESTWARD EXPANSION: THE BUFFALO SOLDIERS

AFTER THE UNION Army won the Civil War, many African Americans fled the violence of the South to settle in towns on the western frontier. There, they would be able to stake a claim on property, farm the land, raise their families, and most of all be safe. The United States government offered homesteaders the opportunity to own land for a nominal amount of money if the settlers lived on it for a period of time.

The goal of the government was to clear the land of Native Americans—among them the Sioux, Apache, Kiowa, Comanche, and Cheyenne—and to enable primarily white homesteaders to develop communities on land west of the Mississippi River extending to the coast of California. To accomplish this, the new military formed in 1866 was a leaner, but a still-segregated, corps of black and white soldiers.

Among the United States Army recruits were the all-black 9th and 10th cavalries and the 24th and 25th infantries. The Native people named them the Buffalo Soldiers "because of the likeness in appearance to the buffalo [a sacred animal to the Native people]" and for their bravery, tenacity, and combat ability. Their ranks were made up of 12,500 former slaves, some of whom had served in the Civil War, and free men. The Buffalo Soldiers fought successfully in the battles of the Indian Wars (1817–1898) and in the Spanish-American War (1898–1902). Later, black troops would also participate in World Wars I and II, as laborers and service troops, and in the Korean War, where the segregated troops saw combat. The Buffalo Soldiers, the 27th and 28th calvary units, were disbanded in December 1951.

By 1875 the U.S. Army had twenty-five thousand troops of which one in five soldiers was black. Despite the racism and contemptuous treatment by the white soldiers, the Buffalo Soldiers, throughout their distinguished careers, consistently performed at a higher level than many of their white counterparts. The army's best horsemen and the best marksmen, the Buffalo soldiers were awarded eighteen Medals of Honor during the western campaigns between 1866 and 1891.

BLACKS MIGRATE WEST TO KANSAS AND BEYOND

BEGINNING IN THE 1830s, black migration westward escalated as thousands escaped slavery on the Underground Railroad and, after Reconstruction, the racist Jim Crow laws and terroristic violence in the South. These black migrants sought cheap land, political autonomy, and safety in Kansas, Oklahoma, Nebraska, and Indian Territory (between the Missouri River and the Rocky Mountains). The earliest black towns were established and settled in Upper Canada (Ontario) beginning in 1829 by fugitive slaves during the abolition movement. By the late nineteenth and early twentieth centuries, at least eighty-eight, and by some estimates as many as two hundred, black towns were established throughout the United States.

During California's gold rush, "between 1850 and 1860, four thousand African Americans reached the Golden State. Half of that number settled in San Francisco and Sacramento, creating the first English-speaking black urban communities in the Far West."

Freed blacks also migrated to Texas because of the abundant jobs and good pay. During the late nineteenth century, "the number of black Texans increased from 393,384 in 1880 to 620,722 in 1900." They worked "as sharecroppers, but some herded cattle and others worked on railroads, in lumber camps, on seaport docks, or as skilled craftsmen."

The Homestead Act of 1862 allowed any adult citizen or intended citizen who had never borne arms against the U.S. government to claim 160 acres of government-surveyed land in the western United States. After improving the land, building a dwelling, and cultivating the land for five years, the claimant was entitled to the property, free and clear, for a small registration fee. Ownership could also be acquired after living on the property six months, making improvements, and paying the government $1.25 per acre.

Benjamin "Pap" Singleton—an escaped slave who fled to Canada—returned to work in Union-occupied Nashville, Tennessee, as a carpenter during the Civil War. Singleton and other freedmen in Nashville became disillusioned after the war with the violence and poverty experienced by the former enslaved. In April 1875, they convened to discuss black migration to the west and formed the Tennessee Emigration Society. The society distributed flyers titled "The Advantage of Living in a Free State," encouraging blacks to leave the South and touting the benefits of living in Kansas. In 1875, Singleton and his associates established the Edgefield Real Estate and Homestead Association to facilitate the exodus of 2,400 blacks from Tennessee to Kansas. By 1890, approximately ten thousand African Americans had migrated there. The Exodusters, blacks who settled in Kansas, were at the forefront of this westward movement. The migration to Kansas continued with black farmers moving farther west and settling in Iowa, Nebraska, Oklahoma, Missouri, and Colorado.

In 1877, white developer W. R. Hill and black minister Reverend W.

Benjamin "Pap" Singleton was the leader of the Exoduster movement, in which thousands of African American families relocated to the Midwest to homestead.

All Colored People

THAT WANT TO

GO TO KANSAS,

On September 5th, 1877,

Can do so for $5.00

H. Smith founded the town of Nicodemus, Kansas. The first arrivals faced many challenges, including harsh weather, barren land, and very few resources. With the help of the Osage, the native people of the region, the homesteaders survived the winter and established their own government in 1878.

By 1886, the settlement population grew to two hundred. The town included a bank, three grocery stores, four general stores, four hotels, three pharmacies, two millineries (hat makers), two liveries (stables where horses were boarded and carriages were rented out), and two barbershops. The town declined when the hoped-for railroad line bypassed it. Nicodemus exists today and is a National Historic Site, with five of its original buildings intact.

Other major black towns established during this period include Langston City, Oklahoma Territory; Boley, Indian Territory; Mound Bayou, Mississippi; Dearfield, Colorado; and Allensworth, California.

As African Americans moved westward, many pursued work on farms and ranches as cowhands and as performers on the rodeo circuit. Black women opened businesses in frontier towns as innkeepers, seamstresses, and laundresses. They were also school teachers, cooks, and farmworkers. To make sure that there was protection for these new citizens, a group of white and black marshals and sheriffs roamed the range. Their job was to arrest the horse thieves, train and stagecoach robbers, and murderers.

Nat "Deadwood Dick" Love was a black cowboy who was born in Tennessee. After the Civil War, he moved to Dodge City, Kansas, where he made his living on cattle drives—roping, branding, and breeding the animals. In 1876, Love, an expert horseman, earned the nickname "Deadwood Dick" when he entered a rodeo competition and was able to stay mounted on a bucking mustang for, as the legend goes, twelve minutes and thirty seconds. Love's autobiography, *The Life and Adventures of Nat Love, Better Known in the Cattle Country as "Deadwood Dick,"* was published in 1907.

Bill Pickett was born in Taylor, Texas, and became known as the "Greatest Cowboy" of his day. He was an extraordinary horseman and could immobilize a longhorn steer by wrestling it to the ground and biting the animal's upper lip, temporarily paralyzing it. He went on to perform at rodeos. He and his brothers formed the Pickett Brothers Bronco Busters and Rough Riders Association, which traveled to Texas, Arizona, Wyoming, and Oklahoma. Known as "the Bulldogger," for his unique way of taming the steers, Pickett was killed in 1932 by a kick in the head from a horse.

Women played an important role in the settlement of the West as well. "Stagecoach Mary" Fields was an ex-slave from Tennessee who in 1881 went to Montana to assist Mother Amadeus, a member of the Ursuline Sisters, in setting up a Catholic mission school for Blackfeet Indian women and girls. Fields, an imposing woman of six feet, knew how to shoot and ride a horse. An independent woman, she opened several businesses out west, including a restaurant and a laundry. She is best known, though, for her job as a mail carrier who drove her stagecoach between the mission school and Cascade, Montana. Fields wore a man's coat and hat and smoked a cigar as she traveled her mail route. She had the reputation as someone not to cross.

Another prominent woman in the history of the black West was Mary Ellen Pleasant. She had a mysterious past with numerous twists and turns, but it is generally agreed that she was a former slave born in Virginia around 1814 to a white father and black mother. She was raised by a white abolitionist family named Hussey in Nantucket, Massachusetts, where she developed her commitment for helping the enslaved. Pleasant married several times, and her first husband, James Smith, a wealthy mulatto, helped to transport fugitive slaves to freedom on the Underground Railroad. When he died, Pleasant continued his work.

Pleasant moved to San Francisco, California, in 1852 to escape the Fugitive Slave Law of 1850. There she worked as the champion of the enslaved, and provided shelter and jobs to fugitives. She also contributed

Mary Fields, or "Stagecoach Mary" as she was known, was an African American frontier woman. In 1895, she became the first African American mail carrier, and delivered the mail by stagecoach in Cascade, Montana.

money to John Brown's effort to raid the Harper's Ferry arsenal in pre–Civil War Virginia. An activist determined to test the judicial system, Pleasant went to court in 1868 and sued for blacks to have the right to ride the trolley in San Francisco without discrimination. She won her case and became known as the "Mother of Civil Rights in California."

Bill Pickett was an African American cowboy during the late 1800s, who gained fame for his technique of "bulldogging" (grabbing the horns of a bull and pulling its head to the ground), which rendered the bull helpless.

BOOKER T. WASHINGTON AND W. E. B. DU BOIS

TWO PROMINENT AFRICAN American activists working for the improvement of blacks after Reconstruction were Booker T. Washington and W. E. B. Du Bois. These men had very different approaches to how the race should advance in post-slavery America.

BOOKER T. WASHINGTON

Booker T. Washington, a former slave, was born in Virginia and graduated as a teacher from Hampton Normal and Agricultural Institute, now Hampton University. Washington talked about his education in his 1901 autobiography, *Up from Slavery*, and how he paid for tuition and his room and board by taking a job as a janitor on campus. Inspired by his white mentor, General Samuel Chapman Armstrong, a founder of Hampton Institute, Washington developed a strong work ethic, a belief in self-reliance, high moral standards, and discipline. He would go on to become the first principal, based on Armstrong's recommendation, of Tuskegee Institute, founded in 1881 in Tuskegee, Alabama, and home of the future Tuskegee Airmen.

Washington's philosophy, to educate the newly freed with an emphasis on a curriculum of industrial or vocational education, evolved over time as a means to prepare students to immediately earn a living upon graduation from school and pull themselves up socially and economically. Although Washington also believed in teaching academics, he felt it was paramount that blacks learn a trade to become self-sufficient members of American society. He did not advocate forced integration of the white and black races, but rather a slow and gradual coming together. This was illustrated in his "Atlanta Compromise" speech of 1895, when he was invited to speak to a predominantly white audience attending the Cotton States and International Exposition in Atlanta, Georgia. The speech made him very controversial in the black community. Some felt that Washington was kowtowing to whites and assuring them that blacks would not be aggressive and demand an equal place in society. He outlined his philosophy of racial accommodation and gradualism in his speech.

Our greatest danger is that in the great leap from slavery to freedom we may overlook the fact that the masses of us are to live by the productions of our hands, and fail to keep in mind that we shall prosper in proportion as we learn to dignify and glorify common labour, and put brains and skill into the common occupations of life; shall prosper in proportion as we learn to draw the line between the superficial and the substantial, the ornamental gewgaws of life and the useful. No race can prosper till it learns that there is as much dignity in tilling a field as in writing a poem. It is at the bottom of life we must begin, and not at the top.

Tuskegee Institute flourished under Booker T. Washington, an apt fund-raiser whose nonthreatening educational philosophy and strategy of accommodation for blacks appealed to white industrialists such as John D. Rockefeller and Andrew Carnegie, who were investing in the institute's vocationally trained blacks as future employees. These businessmen hoped the Tuskegee graduates would not strike or cause problems in their factories, unlike white trade unionists.

One of Tuskegee Institute's most famous teachers was agricultural scientist George Washington Carver, who was hired by Washington to run the new agricultural school. Carver carried out many experiments at Tuskegee,

LEFT: Booker T. Washington was an educator who believed that African Americans needed to prepare for life after slavery by learning skills and trades that would put them to work immediately. He was the first principal of the historical black university Tuskegee Institute in Alabama.

RIGHT: George Washington Carver was an agricultural scientist who invented over three hundred uses for peanuts and other vegetables. As director of agriculture at Tuskegee Institute, he changed the way farmers grew crops by introducing crop rotation.

introducing peanuts, soybeans, and sweet potatoes as crops to restore the soil that was no longer fertile after growing cotton. This method of farming was called crop rotation.

Washington was widely supported across racial lines for his work in educating the freedmen and attracted funding from philanthropists for projects such as building rural schools for blacks. He also became a confidante of President Theodore Roosevelt and was the first African American to dine at the White House as a guest, amid much controversy.

W. E. B. DU BOIS

Unlike Booker T. Washington, W. E. B. Du Bois was born free in Great Barrington, Massachusetts. A Harvard-educated civil rights activist, Pan-Africanist, historian, author, editor, and scholar, Du Bois held vastly different views from Booker T. Washington about educating the African American for inclusion in American society, post-Reconstruction. He believed African Americans were equal to whites and must not accept being less than a full citizen. Du Bois also believed that blacks should seek an academic education and be groomed as future leaders, and this was how the race would be elevated.

In a 1963 interview published in the November 1965 issue of the *Atlantic Monthly* magazine, Du Bois, who at ninety-five years old was living in self-exile in Ghana on the African continent, talked with journalist Ralph McGill about Booker T. Washington and their differences:

> *I never thought Washington was a bad man. I believed him to be sincere, though wrong. He and I came from different backgrounds. I was born free. Washington was born a slave. He felt the lash of an overseer across his back. I was born in Massachusetts, he on a slave plantation in the South. My great-grandfather fought with the Colonial Army in New England in the American Revolution. [This earned the grandfather his freedom.] I had a happy childhood and acceptance in the community. Washington's childhood was hard. I had many more advantages: Fisk University, Harvard, and graduate years in Europe. Washington had little formal schooling. I admired much about him.*

Du Bois was a founding member of the National Association for the Advancement of Colored People (NAACP) and an outspoken critic of

W. E. B. Du Bois, a historian, educator, and civil rights advocate, was the first African American to earn a PhD from Harvard University. Du Bois believed that African Americans should pursue an academic education to excel in American society.

accepting unequal treatment of the races. Du Bois was a prolific writer. He opposed a vocational education for blacks and, instead, proposed that a Talented Tenth of college-educated African Americans take the lead in the campaign for racial equality and equal rights for American blacks.

Delegates of the Niagara Movement, the precursor to the National Association for the Advancement of Colored People (NAACP), at their first meeting in the United States, at Storer College, Harper's Ferry, West Virginia, August 15–19, 1906. W. E. B. Du Bois is pictured front row, fifth from right.

In his article titled "The Talented Tenth," from the 1903 book *The Negro Problem: A Series of Articles by Representative Negroes To-day*, Du Bois detailed his strategy for uplifting black people:

> *Men of America, the problem is plain before you. Here is a race [the Negro] transplanted through the criminal foolishness of your fathers. Whether you like it or not the millions are here, and here they will remain. If you do not lift them up, they will pull you down. Education and work are the levers to uplift a people. Work alone will not do it unless inspired by the right ideals and guided by intelligence. Education must not simply teach work—it must teach Life. The Talented Tenth of the Negro race must be made leaders of thought and missionaries of culture among their people. No others can do this and Negro colleges must train men for it. The Negro race, like all other races, is going to be saved by its exceptional men.*

Du Bois published his *Souls of Black Folks: Essays and Sketches* in 1903. This book was considered a groundbreaking work on the sociology of being black in America. Du Bois believed, according to the 1965 *Atlantic Monthly* article, that Booker T. Washington's Atlanta Compromise Speech of 1895 "bartered away much that was not his to barter . . . it seemed to me he was giving up essential ground that would be hard to win back." Du Bois was referring to this passage in Washington's Atlanta Compromise Speech:

As we have proved our loyalty to you in the past, in nursing your children, watching by the sick-bed of your mothers and fathers, and often following them with tear-dimmed eyes to their graves, so in the future, in our humble way, we shall stand by you with a devotion that no foreigner can approach, ready to lay down our lives, if need be, in defense of yours, interlacing our industrial, commercial, civil, and religious life with yours in a way that shall make the interests of both races one. In all things that are purely social, we can be as separate as the fingers, yet one as the hand in all things essential to mutual progress.

Du Bois pointed out to interviewer Ralph McGill how this part of Washington's speech defined the Negro as a separate, lesser citizen. He explained:

I also have talked with men who saw and heard him [Washington] deliver it. They've told me of the tremendous drama of that day. They said that when he came to his key paragraph, he began it by holding up both arms, the fingers of each hand spread wide, and said "In all things that are purely social we can be as separate as the fingers, yet as the hand"—and here Washington quickly clinched each hand—"in all things essential to mutual progress."

According to McGill, "There was no doubt in Du Bois's mind. He was sure, he said, that without Washington's position there would have been no Plessy-Ferguson decision in 1896," which legislated separate but equal accommodations for blacks and whites throughout the United States. Disillusioned with the United States, Du Bois joined the Communist Party, renounced his American citizenship, and moved to Ghana. He died on August 27, 1963, on the eve of the historic March on Washington for Jobs and Freedom, nearly one hundred years after his birth.

The Supreme Court ruling in the 1896 *Plessy v. Ferguson* case was a tremendous setback for African Americans at a national level. The ruling made it legal to have separate but equal accommodations for blacks and whites, codifying the Jim Crow laws of the South and the policy of segregation throughout the United States. This landmark decision permitted every state to have separate but equal facilities that served "Whites Only" and "Coloreds Only," such as restaurants, hotels, schools, libraries, bathrooms, movie theaters, parks, playgrounds, hospitals, prisons, and transportation. There were even separate water fountains for whites and blacks.

The migrants arrived in great numbers, 1940–41, a painting by Jacob Lawrence, an artist of the Harlem Renaissance

THE GREAT MIGRATION NORTH

AT THE TURN of the twentieth century, African Americans migrated by the thousands from southern communities to large urban cities in the North. Primarily, they moved to Detroit, Cleveland, St. Louis, Pittsburgh, Baltimore, Philadelphia, New York, Boston, and Chicago, to escape the South's racism and violence and in search of jobs and housing. This period is referred to as the Great Migration, with the influx of African Americans increasing after the outbreak of World War I.

When the United States entered the war in 1917, many white males went to fight, leaving factory jobs open in the North that employers filled with white women and black men. The railroads and the automotive, steel, and meatpacking industries were major employers for the black migrants. Black women also moved to the North and were employed as domestics, earning a higher salary than they would have in the South. Between 1914 and 1919, a half million to one million blacks left the South. During the next ten years, another one million migrated from the rural South to the urban North and Midwest.

Recruitment of young African American men and women in the South for good-paying jobs up North was spread by word of mouth, by the black press, and through letters home from relatives who had already relocated. Churches also played a role in passing along information about jobs and housing and what was waiting for migrants who wanted to leave the South. Labor agents were employed by the railroads and other large corporations to recruit black workers, offering free railroad passes, which were sometimes deducted from their first paychecks. Many young African American men and women traveled on their own, using money they had saved up or funds borrowed from family members who hoped that they would be brought North once the young people were settled in a job and had a place to live.

With this massive migration of African Americans to northern cities, tensions increased within the white communities already there. Angry because blacks were competing for jobs in the factories and moving into the neighborhoods where they lived, whites started attacking blacks. Fueling the rage was also the use by some northern manufacturing companies of black strikebreakers, which infuriated the white union members. Race riots erupted throughout the United States in the South and in the North.

By the summer of 1919, called the Red Summer by NAACP investigator James Weldon Johnson because so much blood flowed in the streets from the violence, twenty-five American cities were in the throes of violent race riots. Blacks responded to white aggression in Charleston; Knoxville; Washington, D.C.; Omaha; and Elaine, Arkansas. One of the largest riots was in Chicago. It lasted five days, and hundreds of people were injured or killed.

Various incidents sparked these riots. Reasons ranged from the killing of a black swimmer who wandered into the waters at a whites-only beach to rumors of black men assaulting white women. But the principal underlying

Soldiers on guard at 24th and Lake streets following the 1919 Omaha riot

reason for all this discontentment was that whites in the North were react-
ing to the influx of African Americans into the whites' communities and
the perceived threat the African Americans posed to the whites' way of life.
In the South, whites rebelled against blacks' new freedoms and the whites'
inability to control a race of people they had formerly enslaved.

One of the worst riots began on May 31, 1921, and ended with the arrival
of the Oklahoma National Guard the following day in the Greenwood Community of Tulsa. It began after a young black man was accused of assaulting
a white woman on an elevator and was subsequently arrested. Fearing the
accused would be lynched, blacks armed with guns offered to protect the
black prisoner from the steadily growing white mob in front of the Tulsa
courthouse. The two groups confronted each other, a shot was fired, and the
riot erupted. Mobs of whites burned and destroyed more than a thousand
homes, businesses, and churches in the black community of Greenwood.

Walter F. White, who went on to become the executive secretary of the
NAACP, wrote in a June 29, 1921, article titled "The Eruption of Tulsa,"
published in *The Nation* magazine, that:

> *[A] mob of 100-per-cent Americans set forth on a wild rampage
> that cost the lives of fifty white men; of between 150 and 200 col-
> ored men, women and children; the destruction by fire of $1,500,000
> worth of property; the looting of many homes; and everlasting dam-
> age to the reputation of the city of Tulsa and the State of Oklahoma
> . . . Machine-guns were brought into use; eight aeroplanes were
> employed to spy on the movements of the Negroes and according to
> some were used in bombing the colored section.*

The number of African Americans who died or were injured in the Tulsa riot was estimated by the American Red Cross to have been three hundred, while other reports list over eight hundred injured.

Before the riot, Greenwood was an African American community with an impressive commercial district. It was known as the Negro Wall Street because of its large and prosperous business district. In the 2001 report commissioned by the City of Tulsa, eighty years after the riot, the Greenwood section was described as a vibrant black community:

> The backbone of the community . . . was Greenwood Avenue. Running north for more than a mile—from Archer Street and the Frisco yards all the way past Pine—it was not only black Tulsa's primary thoroughfare, but also possessed considerable symbolic meaning as well. Unlike other streets and avenues in Tulsa, which crisscrossed both white and black neighborhoods, Greenwood Avenue was essentially confined to the African American community.

According to the report, the district included dozens of "black-owned and operated grocery stores and meat markets, clothing and dry goods stores, billiard halls, beauty parlors and barber shops, as well as the Economy Drug Company, William Anderson's jewelry store, Henry Lilly's upholstery shop, and A. S. Newkirk's photography studio." There was also a public library, a post office, a YMCA, and two black newspapers—the *Tulsa Star* and the *Oklahoma Sun*. Also located in the Greenwood district were two black-owned theaters; restaurants; business and professional office buildings housing the offices of black lawyers, black doctors, black realtors, and other business people; a dozen churches; and two black-owned and operated hotels.

African American business owners, doctors, lawyers, and educators lived in the neighborhoods off Greenwood in beautiful, modern homes, while other black Tulsans who were domestic workers lived in the homes of their white employers outside of the Greenwood community. They would come to shop, eat, and enjoy the entertainments of the African American enclave.

The Tulsa riot is emblematic of the mood in America in the early decades of the twentieth century. White resentment against black achievement was at the center of this conflict, which was as much about race as it was about class. Tulsa was experiencing boom times as a result of an oil discovery. Walter White explains, in his article "The Eruption of Tulsa," the impact that the economic and racial changes had on creating a climate for the riot:

> First, the Negro in Oklahoma has shared in the sudden prosperity that has come to many of his white brothers, and there are some colored men there who are wealthy. This fact has caused a bitter resentment on the part of the lower order of whites, who feel that these colored men, members of an "inferior race," are exceedingly presumptuous in achieving greater economic prosperity than they who are members of a divinely ordered superior race.

The Tulsa riot changed the Greenwood community forever. Many black Tulsans whose homes and businesses had been destroyed moved away. In June, the Tulsa City Commission passed a fire ordinance preventing black businessmen from rebuilding where their businesses previously stood before the riot. The ordinance was overturned, and by "early July 1921, the city of Tulsa began granting building permits to African American residents in North Tulsa . . . This happened amidst the efforts of white Tulsa to industrialize this sector with various codes to prevent black rebuilding." Despite these challenges, Greenwood was rebuilt but not to the extent that it resembled the original community.

Man with camera surveys the rubble and devastation in Greenwood after the Tulsa Riots

TWO WORLD WARS AND THE BLACK CULTURAL AWAKENING

WHILE MANY BLACK men stayed at home, migrating to new jobs in the North or remaining in the South, others enlisted or were drafted into the military. They hoped that by joining in the fight with America and her allies of Great Britain, France, and Russia against Germany, Austria-Hungary, and Turkey, they would be regarded as patriotic and worthy of equal treatment at home.

WORLD WAR I: BLACK SOLDIERS FIGHT ON TWO FRONTS

THE UNITED STATES entered World War I on April 6, 1917, three years after the global conflict had started. About 380,000 African American soldiers were in the U.S. Army at the time. Approximately 200,000 were deployed to Europe, with around 42,000 seeing combat. The black soldiers, who were segregated from the white soldiers, were assigned to all-black labor, supply, and service battalions led by white officers. The discrimination experienced by the black soldiers was pervasive and sanctioned by the highest echelons of the military. When black U.S. troops shipped out to France, the racist policies of the military followed them.

General John J. Pershing's secret directive to the French military summed up the attitude of the white military toward black soldiers at that time:

> Although a citizen of the United States, the black man is regarded by the white American as an inferior being with whom relations of business or service only are possible. The black is constantly being censured for his want of intelligence and discretion, his lack of civic and professional conscience, and for his tendency toward undue familiarity. The vices of the Negro are a constant menace to the American who has to repress them sternly . . . We must prevent the rise of any pronounced degree of intimacy between French officers and black officers.

Neither black nor white women served in combat, but they volunteered in service organizations, including the American Red Cross, as nurses (whites only) who were mobilized into medical units that served the U.S. Army and the navy; and the YMCA, as canteen workers and Y secretaries who were deployed overseas to provide educational and recreational activities for soldiers fighting the war. Addie D. Hunton and Kathryn M. Johnson were two African American women who worked as Y secretaries in France in a recreational center for black soldiers. They wrote about their experiences in a 1920 book, *Two Colored Women with the American Expeditionary Forces*, which can be found at the Library of Congress. Black women were not allowed to work as nurses until after World War I was over, when they were assigned to work on military bases in the United States taking care of prisoners of war.

One unit of black soldiers that rose above the prejudice and performed gallantly was the 15th New York National Guard Regiment from Harlem, which became the 369th Infantry Regiment, or the "Harlem Hellfighters." This group of African American soldiers fought on the front lines in France for more than six months and was recognized for its efforts in the liberation of the village of Séchault during the Meuse-Argonne Offensive on September 29, 1918. The Harlem Hellfighters received more than 170 awards from the French, including the Croix de Guerre and the Medal of Honor, for their valiant combat work. They did not receive any awards from the American military for their achievements.

The Hellfighters were recognized not only for their fighting by the Europeans. They were also celebrated for their band, headed by African American bandleader James Reese Europe, who introduced ragtime and jazz to the continent. Before the war, James Reese Europe was already a famous bandleader who had established the Clef Club, a union and booking agency for African American musicians in New York City. In 1912, Europe's Clef Club Symphony Orchestra of 125 musicians became the first African American band to perform at Carnegie Hall, where they presented a concert of all "Negro" music composed by African Americans. Europe founded the Tempo Club in 1914, similar to the Clef Club, which booked African American musicians for the dances that were so popular during the era. He also partnered with the dance team of Vernon and Irene Castle, with whom he invented the turkey trot and the fox-trot dances.

The Harlem Hellfighters Band and its success and popularity in France during World War I introduced Europeans to African American music. The world also gained a glimpse into the artistic and creative abilities of the black musicians, artists, and writers at the center of what came to be known as the Harlem Renaissance.

BLACK CULTURAL AWAKENING

THE HARLEM RENAISSANCE, a cultural, social, and political movement that celebrated African American literature, art, and music as well as African American self-determination and independence, began around the conclusion of World War I in 1919 and ended roughly around the start of the Great Depression after the stock market crash of 1929. A combination of factors contributed to this exciting period in African American history—the Great Migration of southern blacks and West Indians from the Caribbean to New York City; the end of World War I and a renewed optimism among African Americans; and, most important, the move of thousands of African Americans from neighborhoods in Midtown, New York City, in the 1900s to the northern neighborhood of Harlem, making it the "Black Capital" of the world.

Before Harlem became the "Black Capital" of the world, it had been home to a population of middle-class white residents, mostly English, German, and later Jewish and Italian immigrants. These groups moved to the northern suburb to escape the overcrowded conditions in Midtown Manhattan from commercial development and the Lower East Side from the increase in new immigrants.

The construction of elevated trains in 1878 and 1880 along New York's Second, Third, and Eighth avenues was a key factor in driving the development of single-family dwellings and multifamily apartment buildings in a community with acres of undeveloped land. The new residents commuted by train to their offices in Lower Manhattan.

The IRT, the first continuously operated subway system in New York City, opened in 1904, with a route from City Hall in Lower Manhattan to Broadway and 145th Street in Harlem on the Upper West Side. Subway service subsequently extended to the other boroughs: the Bronx in 1905, Brooklyn in 1908, and Queens in 1915.

By the early 1900s, the real estate boom had declined and black real estate entrepreneur Philip A. Payton, Jr., proposed to white developers that he become their agent and fill the empty apartment buildings with black tenants. Rebuffed initially by the real estate companies, Payton formed his

James Weldon Johnson was an author, teacher, civil rights activist, and diplomat. He wrote the words to "Lift Every Voice and Sing," which is recognized as the Negro National Anthem and the Negro National Hymn. When hearing it sung in public, the audience rises to its feet, out of respect.

Real estate brokers initially developed the Harlem community for middle-class whites who commuted downtown to work. However, the builders were overly ambitious and soon had a large inventory of housing in Harlem but not enough prospective white tenants. In fact, African Americans were moving to the area as white residents moved away. By the 1920s the realtors opened up the market to African Americans.

own company. As it became harder and harder for the developers to fill the vacant apartments, they finally began renting to blacks.

Through his investor-funded company, the Afro-American Realty Company, Payton purchased five apartment buildings on West 135th Street, evicted the white tenants, and rented the apartments to black renters who wanted to move from run-down tenements in the Tenderloin and San Juan Hill sections of Manhattan. Blacks and Irish immigrants in these districts were at constant odds with each other as they competed for the same jobs and apartments. Payton's company became a major provider of housing for African Americans in Harlem before the Renaissance.

Along with apartments, the housing stock in Harlem was some of the best in New York City. The wide, tree-lined streets and the attached houses, called limestones and brownstones, with intricate architectural details, had been built to accommodate the influx of middle-class white residents. They were now being offered to blacks.

When the Afro-American Realty Company folded after two years because of financial mismanagement, former Afro-American Realty agents John E. Nail and Henry C. Parker started their own successful real estate company, Nail & Parker Realty. They became the agents for the homes on Strivers' Row, which had been owned previously by the Equitable Life Assurance Company. The historic properties, also known as the King Model Houses, on West 138th and West 139th streets between 7th and 8th avenues, were designed by the influential white architectural firm of McKim, Mead & White. African American residents on Strivers' Row during the Harlem Renaissance included the movers and shakers of the period, such as architect Vertner Tandy; musicians W. C. Handy, Eubie Blake, and Noble Sissle; and bandleader Fletcher Henderson.

For African Americans, moving from the tenements on the West Side of Manhattan to Harlem was heaven. James Weldon Johnson captured the feelings of black Harlemites in his book *Black Manhattan*, when he described these beautiful new apartments as "better, cleaner, more airy, more sunny houses than they [African Americans] ever lived in before."

The neighborhood of Harlem attracted not only people looking for a better life for their families. Artists, writers, singers, actors, and political activists moved in as well. Black social, political, and religious organizations also came to Harlem, providing the residents with a wide range of

Founded in 1796, Mother A.M.E. Zion Church on West 137th Street in Harlem was known as the "Freedom Church" because of its history of activism in the struggle for equality for African Americans.

churches, community organizations, and businesses to choose from. This made Harlem a city within a city.

Churches established in Lower Manhattan relocated uptown to Harlem. Mother A. M. E. Zion, known as the "Freedom Church" for its activism during the abolition movement, was at Leonard and Church streets. It moved to Greenwich Village and then opened a church on West 137th Street in Harlem. St. Philip's Episcopal Church, a black offshoot of Trinity Church at Wall Street, was previously at Centre Street between Worth and Leonard streets. After a move from their West 25th Street site, the parishioners relocated to a new church on West 134th Street, built in 1910 and designed by the black architectural firm of (Vertner) Tandy & (George W.) Foster. The church purchased a block of buildings at 107–145 West 135th Street to provide housing for blacks moving to Harlem. Abyssinian Baptist Church, formerly located at Anthony Street (now Worth Street), moved from the West Village to West 40th Street. In 1923, the church relocated to West 138th Street.

Many of the nation's most influential African American political and social institutions were located in Harlem. Among them were the National Association for the Advancement of Colored People (NAACP), founded in 1909; the National Urban League (NUL), established in 1910; and Marcus Garvey's Universal Negro Improvement Association (UNIA), founded in 1916. Activist A. Philip Randolph founded the labor union the Brotherhood of Sleeping Car Porters (BSCP) in 1925, and opened an office in Harlem. All of these organizations had at the heart of their mission the equal rights—political, economic, educational, and social—of African Americans and the elimination of racial discrimination.

Harlem-based black newspapers and magazines kept the local and national African American community informed of the pressing issues of the day surrounding race relations. Topics included the continued violence against and the lynching of blacks in the South, as well as the achievements of black people. These publications also showcased black literary talent. The *Amsterdam News*, first published in 1909 by James H. Anderson, was a community newspaper. The paper's reach expanded after its purchase by C. B. Powell, a Harlem physician, in 1936. *The Crisis Magazine*, the official voice of the NAACP, edited by W. E. B. Du Bois, first appeared in 1910 and was a major outlet for Harlem Renaissance writers, publishing their works

Vol. II. No. 7   JULY, 1918

THE
MESSENGER
"ONLY RADICAL NEGRO MAGAZINE IN AMERICA"

Edited by
Chandler Owen — A. Philip Randolph

LIBERTY NUMBER

15c. per Copy $1.50 per Year

The Messenger was founded in 1917 by writer Chandler Owen and political activist A. Philip Randolph. The magazine published up-and-coming political and literary writers during the Harlem Renaissance.

Marcus Garvey was a political activist, publisher, and entrepreneur who founded the Universal Negro Improvement Association, which promoted the "Back to Africa" movement to African Americans in the 1920s. Garvey would amass a fortune from his followers, called Garveyites, to resettle them in Africa.

from 1919 to 1926. The magazine also sponsored contests for aspiring writers. Other black publications that supported the work of the Renaissance artists through publication and literary cash prizes or that published articles about the struggle for equality were the *Opportunity* magazine, published by the Urban League; *The Messenger*, a magazine established by A. Philip Randolph, the founder of the Brotherhood of Sleeping Car Porters; and *The Negro World*, published by Marcus Garvey.

Marcus Garvey was also instrumental in creating black businesses and in helping supporters establish their companies in Harlem and in other black communities in the United States, in keeping with his mission of black self-determination and economic independence. In 1920, he formed the Negro Factories Corporation to provide loans and technical assistance to African Americans who wanted to start their own businesses. By selling stock at five dollars per share, Garvey's corporation helped develop a chain of grocery stores, a restaurant, a laundry, a tailor and dressmaking store, a millinery shop, and a publishing company.

In 1917, Herbert Pace founded Pace and Handy Music, with musician W. C. Handy. The company published sheet music, including Handy's popular "St. Louis Blues." In 1921, Pace established the Pace Phonograph Corporation in Harlem at 257 West 138th Street. It was the first black-owned record company and it produced "race records," recordings made exclusively by black artists for black audiences, on its label, Black Swan Records. African Americans also owned and operated businesses in the fields of health and beauty, banking, and insurance.

In 1901, one of the first black street vendors, "Pigfoot Mary," set up her jerry-rigged steam table on 61st Street and Amsterdam Avenue and sold the popular southern dish—hot pig's feet—to the residents of what was then the black community. Mary later moved her successful pushcart business to Harlem, and eventually invested her considerable earnings in real estate.

Wealthy black female entrepreneur Madam C. J. Walker also made Harlem her home. She invented a hair care formula that nourished hair and aided in its growth. Her formula was patented in 1905, and Walker became the first black female millionaire in the United States. Walker's national sales force of all women, who sold her products door-to-door, predated the Avon cosmetics sales model and the popular Mary Kay sales campaigns of today. In 1914, Walker built a luxurious townhouse at 108–110 West 136th Street that housed a fully equipped beauty salon for black patrons. On the second floor, her daughter A'Lelia Walker, a patron of the arts, created a literary salon named the "Dark Tower," after poet Countee Cullen's column in *Opportunity* magazine. The salon became the meeting place of Renaissance writers, artists, and musicians, and of black and white patrons who wanted to be part of the scene of the Harlem Renaissance.

Madam C. J. Walker, an inventor and businesswoman, created a hair care product company that amassed a fortune in the early 1900s. Pictured are: Madam C. J. Walker (at wheel of car) with her niece Anjetta Breedlove. Alice Kelby and Lucy Flint, forewoman secretary of Walker's company, are seated in the rear.

Hughes's Iconic 1922 Poem "Mother to Son"

Well, son, I'll tell you:
Life for me ain't been no crystal stair.
It's had tacks in it,
And splinters,
And boards torn up,
And places with no carpet on the floor—
Bare.
But all the time
I'se been a-climbin' on,
And reachin' landin's,
And turnin' corners,
And sometimes goin' in the dark
Where there ain't been no light.
So, boy, don't you turn back.
Don't you set down on the steps
'Cause you finds it's kinder hard.
Don't you fall now—
For I'se still goin', honey,
I'se still climbin'
And life for me ain't been no crystal stair.

Langston Hughes was a leading poet and author of the Harlem Renaissance.

Madam Walker also had Vertner Tandy design and build a thirty-four-room mansion, which she named Villa Lewaro, in the upscale Westchester County community of Irvington, north of New York City. Villa Lewaro became a cultural weekend retreat during the Renaissance, where daughter A'Lelia entertained national and international artists and writers, singers, and dancers, as well as European royalty and near-royalty. Poet Langston Hughes called A'Lelia the "Joy Goddess" of the Harlem Renaissance because of her lavish parties and her generous support of Renaissance artists by providing them with a place where they could mingle and share ideas. The community of creative African Americans attracted African American supporters, wealthy white patrons, and foundations and publications that provided funding so the artists could concentrate on their art.

The literature of the Harlem Renaissance was a major component of the movement, and some of the poets and writers who defined the movement were Langston Hughes, Claude McKay, Jean Toomer, Wallace Thurman, Countee Cullen, Alain Locke, Arna Bontemps, Zora Neale Hurston, and Jessie Redmon Fauset. This avalanche of black literary thought was embodied in the term the "New Negro," which was also the title of Alain

Zora Neale Hurston, in a photograph by celebrated photographer Carl Van Vechten, was a novelist and anthropologist of the Harlem Renaissance. Her research on various cultures found its way into her novels.

Locke's anthology, that described a spirit of self-respect, pride, and independence for African Americans of the period who reveled in their racial awakening. Langston Hughes, one of the most recognized members of the Renaissance writers, wrote about life around him using the speech patterns and language of everyday black people. His poem "The Negro Speaks of Rivers" was published in *The Crisis* magazine in 1921 and was later included in his 1926 volume of poetry, *The Weary Blues*.

Poet Claude McKay's militant poem "If We Must Die" was a profound statement about inequality, and it was written in response to the riots of the Red Summer of 1919. His 1922 volume of poetry, *Harlem Shadows*, was the first major book of the Harlem Renaissance. Jean Toomer's 1923 book, *Cane*, in which he explored race and identity, was also considered a major work of the period.

Among the artists at the time were painter Aaron Douglas and sculptors Richmond Barthé and Augusta Savage, who interpreted African American experiences. Douglas included African and African American themes and designs in his paintings and murals. This is illustrated in his four-panel 1934 work, *Aspects of Negro Life*, created for the 135th Street library in New York City. Barthé's sculptures reflected images of blacks as well as other subjects. An example of his work, a sculpture of an American eagle, is in front of the Social Security Administration Building in Washington, D.C. Augusta Savage created a sculpture entitled *The Harp*, which was commissioned for the 1939 World's Fair and was inspired by the poetic words of James Weldon Johnson and the music of his brother J. Rosamond Johnson in their anthem "Lift Every Voice and Sing," also referred to as the Negro National Anthem.

Black theater also thrived during this period. Productions depicting African Americans in non-stereotypical roles were an important goal of the Harlem Renaissance in combating negative images not just in America

A scene from the play *Porgy* at the Guild Theatre in New York City in 1927. Actors Wesley Hill, Rose MacClendon, and Georgette Harvey are pictured, left to right.

but in Europe as well. Plays by and about African Americans presented on Broadway during this era included *Shuffle Along* (1921), *Porgy* (1927), and the *Blackbirds of 1928*, with dancer Bill "Bojangles" Robinson. Dancer and singer Florence Mills starred in the European production of *Blackbirds of 1926*, and was to appear in the Broadway production but died suddenly of appendicitis in 1927. Her funeral was said to have been the largest ever in Harlem at that time. It was estimated that five thousand attended the service at Mother A. M. E. Zion Church and more than one hundred thousand mourners watched the funeral procession move down 145th Street as an airplane released a flock of blackbirds.

Charles Gilpin starred in the 1920 New York stage production of *The Emperor Jones* but was replaced by Paul Robeson, a graduate of the London production. Gilpin was instrumental in the development of the Lafayette Players, the first black acting company in Harlem. Robeson, a political activist, singer, and actor, returned to the stage after quitting the practice of law. He starred in two plays by Eugene O'Neill—*The Emperor Jones* (May 5, 1924) and *All God's Chillun Got Wings* (May 15, 1924). Robeson's most famous role was in *Showboat*, where he performed the song "Ol' Man River." Later in his career, Robeson would be blacklisted (prevented from working and traveling outside of the United States) and investigated by the House Un-American Activities Committee (HUAC), which tracked and questioned American citizens they believed were either Communist Party members or sympathizers or were spying for the Soviet government.

There were also productions at Harlem theaters, the Lafayette and the Lincoln among them. Activist and scholar W. E. B. Du Bois founded the Krigwa Little Theatre, as part of the nationwide Krigwa Little Negro Theatre Movement in 1925, which promoted the writing and production of black plays that employed and nurtured black playwrights, composers, musicians, and actors.

Harlem was the center of black artistic creativity, and it was an entertainment mecca. To white New Yorkers, coming uptown to Harlem was a mysterious and exotic adventure. It was the place where they could experience excitement and freedom from the social rules that governed their behavior downtown in Manhattan. Known as slummers, this group of white partygoers would come to Harlem to let their hair down.

Paul Robeson, activist, actor, and singer, appeared in a number of stage productions, most notably *Showboat*.

Ethel Waters was a jazz and blues singer who performed at the Cotton Club in the 1930s, as well as acted in several plays on Broadway.

The trip might include a stop at a speakeasy, a nightclub, or a private establishment that sold bootleg (illegal) liquor during Prohibition—the period from 1920 to 1933 when it was against the law in the United States to sell or buy alcoholic beverages. An excursion might take partygoers to the mob-run Cotton Club. This famed Harlem club sold illegal liquor and excluded blacks. It entertained the whites-only audience with elaborate stage productions featuring black chorus girls backed by black orchestras led by Cab Calloway, Duke Ellington, and Jimmie Lunceford. Ethel Waters and Lena Horne, who got her start at the Cotton Club when she was just sixteen, starred in extravagant musical reviews featuring jungle themes.

Connie's Inn, next to the Lafayette Theater on 7th Avenue, was another club with an exclusionary policy, which catered to gangsters and white slummers looking for a good time. The white-owned basement club featured slide piano player Fats Waller. Clubgoers from downtown came uptown to party after hours at Small's Paradise, a black-owned club known for its dancing waiters who sometimes served patrons on roller skates. Located on 7th Avenue (near 135th Street), the club catered to white patrons and black Harlemites. Black musicians gathered at Small's Paradise after their regular gigs and held jam sessions, entertaining mixed audiences until the wee hours of the morning.

Trumpeter Louis Armstrong also performed at Connie's Inn. *Hot Chocolates*, a review staged originally at Connie's, opened on Broadway in June 1929 with music by Fats Waller and a cast that included Louis Armstrong. Two of the most famous songs from the production were "Ain't Misbehavin'" and "What Did I Do to Be So Black and Blue?"

Two popular venues for dancing during the 1920s and 1930s were the Renaissance Ballroom and Casino, home to Fletcher Henderson's band, and the Savoy Ballroom, the scene of a legendary battle between the swing bands of Chick Webb and Benny Goodman in 1936. In January 1938 during another battle of the bands, the Chick Webb and the Count Basie bands, assisted by jazz singers Ella Fitzgerald and Billie Holiday, played to a record crowd of supporters in a historic contest.

The Savoy, an integrated dance hall called "the house of happy feet," was where patrons would show off their moves as they danced the popular Lindy Hop, an enthusiastic swing dance characterized by acrobatic leaps, improvised moves, and tosses of female partners in the air. The Lindy Hop, also known as the jitterbug, was named after the aviator Charles Lindbergh, nicknamed "Lindy," whose cross-Atlantic flight to Europe in 1927 was the first solo nonstop flight.

By the early 1930s, the Harlem Renaissance was winding down. Because of the 1929 stock market crash and the beginning of the Great Depression, Renaissance patrons and supporters of the publishing, theater, music, and art worlds did not have the money to invest any longer. During the Depression, the people of Harlem turned their attention to the rising crime rate, unemployment, poverty, deteriorating housing conditions, and other social problems.

DUKE
ELLINGTON
AND HIS FAMOUS Cotton Club
Orchestra
Management
IRVING MILLS
150 WEST 46th ST.
NEW YORK CITY

ABOVE: Duke Ellington was a composer, musician, and bandleader whose orchestra performed at the Cotton Club in Harlem. Duke's jazz orchestra was full of talented musicians who went on to make jazz history on their own, including saxophonist Ben Webster and bassist Jimmy Blanton. Composer Billy Strayhorn penned Ellington's signature song "Take the A Train," about taking the subway to Harlem.

LEFT: The Savoy Ballroom was the place to go to show off your dancing skills. Called "the house of happy feet," it was where black and white dancers would perform the latest dance moves.

THE GREAT DEPRESSION AND THE NEW DEAL

THE STOCK MARKET crash of 1929 marked the beginning of the Great Depression in the United States, and the financial crisis spread to other industrialized nations of the world. Banks failed, businesses folded, homes went into foreclosure, jobs were lost, and the U.S. economy came to a standstill. The number of unemployed, homeless, and starving Americans swelled to record numbers, especially among African Americans who had migrated to northern cities during the Great Migration to work in plants and factories, on the railroads, and in private homes as domestic workers. Many black factory workers, who were not protected by labor unions, lost their jobs and were quickly replaced by white workers.

In the South, the black farmworkers and tenant farmers also lost their jobs as it became harder to pay for seeds to plant crops, demand for crops decreased because people could not afford to buy food, and farmers could no longer afford to pay their mortgages. If farmers could not pay mortgages—loans from the bank used to buy houses, farms, or other properties—then their farms went into foreclosure. The bank that loaned the money would take the property.

In the North, fifty percent of the residents of Harlem did not have jobs because of the worsening economy. The few available jobs usually went to white workers first and then to black workers, if they were lucky. The black workers were paid lower wages than the white workers for the same job. To save money, several generations of family members lived in the same run-down Harlem tenement. These crowded living conditions created an unhealthy environment and spread diseases such as tuberculosis and pneumonia.

When Democrat Franklin D. Roosevelt, from the state of New York, was sworn in as president of the United States in 1933, he was faced with the great challenge of a failing economy. He was determined to put

A sharecropper family, evicted from the farm they worked in Missouri, wait at a roadside camp with their belongings, in 1939.

Understanding To Kill a Mockingbird

Excerpts from Claudia Durst Johnson's student guide *Understanding To Kill a Mockingbird* offer a look at the real life of Mrs. Peacolia Barge when she was a young black girl living in a small town outside of Birmingham, Alabama, during the Depression. In her guide, Johnson compares Barge's true small-town experience with those of the fictional white protagonists, Scout and Jem, in the book and movie *To Kill a Mockingbird*.

Mrs. Barge describes her family's experiences during the Great Depression:

> *They were all shotgun houses, mostly two-room places. No electricity, of course. Even after TVA came to the Birmingham area, we had no electricity until my father, who could be very stubborn and hot-tempered, fought and fought until he managed to get electricity run to our house. The thing we hated most about not having electricity was that we couldn't use a radio. It wasn't until about 1940 that we got a radio.*

> *Except for the few white people who lived in the Quarters, as a child I didn't know many white people or have a sense of being discriminated against. My friends were right there in the Quarters. There were very, very few children there, so I remember primarily being with the adults. It wasn't until after I started school that I became aware that we couldn't go to certain parks, couldn't swim in certain places.*

> *During the thirties my mother had to begin taking in washing and ironing for white people, so I began to see the white people she worked for. Then later I came to realize other differences. For example, there were no hospitals for black people. The one or two hospitals that would take black people put them in the base[ment of the hospital an]d of course the black doctor, who had been taking care of you [would] not be allowed to practice—to attend you in the white [hospital.]*

> *We were always poor, but the Depression was definitely worse. People who had had jobs lost them or, like my father, were laid off for periods of time. And if you worked, the pay was often something like 3 or 4 dollars a week. What my mother always said that people used the old plantation skiffs [strategies] to survive: growing gardens, canning, making absolutely everything and buying almost nothing.*

> *Well, of course, we weren't allowed to register to vote. Even though I was a schoolteacher for twenty years, I didn't register to vote until the late sixties.*

A group of African American advisers, referred to as Franklin D. Roosevelt's "black cabinet," during the New Deal

America back to work, however. Upon entering office, Roosevelt implemented a sweeping series of social programs that he called the New Deal (1933–1938) to bring relief to the ailing economy. He called for a banking holiday, which closed the banks for a week and stemmed the panic of withdrawals that had caused many banks to collapse or go out of business.

The new president also passed legislation to help farmers keep their farms, homeowners keep their homes, and factories stay open and pay their workers. Safeguards were put in place to protect savings, instill confidence in investments, and provide financial relief to families who were struggling. This was done through newly formed federal agencies such as the Federal Deposit Insurance Corporation (FDIC) to insure bank depositors; the Securities and Exchange Commission (SEC) to regulate the stock market; and the Federal Emergency Relief Administration to provide funds to states in the form of grants for poor people. The Social Security Act of 1935 provided unemployment insurance, old-age insurance, and financial help to states to provide for blind and homeless children. The Fair Labor Standards Act of 1938 set a minimum wage rate of forty cents per hour and a forty-hour work week for factory workers.

African Americans who were part of the Roosevelt administration became advisers to the president during the New Deal and were referred to as the "black brain trust" or the "black cabinet." Mary McLeod Bethune, an activist and educator, was the head of the Negro Affairs section of the National Youth Administration, which provided job training to young men and women who were not in school. Robert Weaver, a Negro Affairs adviser in the Department of the Interior, advocated for black workers on federal construction projects through a plan that guaranteed jobs to a percentage of skilled and unskilled black workers.

First Lady Eleanor Roosevelt supported programs for children, unemployed women, and African Americans. Mrs. Roosevelt became her husband's eyes and ears (FDR was confined to a wheelchair after a bout with polio) as she traveled the country inspecting projects funded by New Deal legislation. When she returned to Washington, she would inform the president of the discrimination against blacks that she observed in the South and would urge him to do something about it. Her appeals caused FDR to issue executive orders that prohibited discrimination in New Deal projects.

Other programs under the New Deal that provided jobs to the unemployed included the Tennessee Valley Authority (TVA), which put people to work constructing dams and power grids to bring electric power to rural areas. There were also reforestation projects to increase crop production

LEFT: Hale Woodruff was an African American artist who specialized in landscapes, murals, and woodcuts during the Depression. As an arts educator, he introduced his students to the African American aesthetic but also encouraged them to draw from their own cultural experience.

RIGHT: Mary McLeod Bethune was an American educator, a civil rights leader, and a member of President Roosevelt's black cabinet.

Jim Crow at Fort Dix

An excerpt from an article titled "A Negro in the CCC," which appeared in *The Crisis* magazine, by Luther C. Wandall, a New Yorker, provides a firsthand account of his experience.

We reached Camp Dix about 7:30 that evening. As we rolled up in front of headquarters an officer came out to the bus and told us: "You will double-time as you leave this bus, remove your hat when you hit the door, and when you are asked questions, answer 'Yes, sir,' and 'No, sir.'"

And here it was that Mr. James Crow [Jim Crow] first definitely put in his appearance. When my record was taken at Pier I, a "C" [for Colored] was placed on it. When the busloads were made up at Whitehall street an officer reported as follows: "35, 8 colored." But until now there had been no distinction made.

But before we left the bus the officer shouted emphatically: "Colored boys fall out in the rear." The colored from several buses were herded together, and stood in line until after the white boys had been registered and taken to their tents. This seemed to be the established order of procedure at Camp Dix.

This separation of the colored from the whites was completely and rigidly maintained at this camp. One Puerto Rican, who was darker than I, and who preferred to be with the colored, was regarded as pitifully uninformed by the [white] officers.

in the southeastern United States. The Works Progress Administration (WPA) directed work programs that employed people to build and work on projects, including government buildings, parks, and other public facilities.

The Works Progress Administration hired artists, writers, and theatrical professionals as part of its Federal Art Project, Federal Writers' Project, and Federal Theatre Project. Many African American writers, artists, and actors who were prolific during the Harlem Renaissance worked in these arts projects and produced work that was showcased throughout the United States. Visual artists Jacob Lawrence, Hale Woodruff, and Aaron Douglas; sculptor Augusta Savage; photographers Morgan and Marvin Smith; and authors Richard Wright and Zora Neale Hurston worked for the WPA.

The Civilian Conservation Corps (CCC) established in 1933 was an important early program of the New Deal. The Corps employed young men from ages seventeen to twenty-eight in conservation jobs that created park systems, maintained existing parks, and constructed roads across America. The CCC was a major employer for African American men during the Depression. Of the 3 million enrolled in the CCC, 250,000 were black and lived in approximately 150 all-black camps under the direction of white military officers. Although discrimination was prohibited in federal programs, segregation was not.

The New Deal programs provided African Americans with the opportunity to work in factories, construction, and other jobs sponsored by the federal government. President Roosevelt's role as an implementor of social programs that helped African Americans in their quest for equality was a major factor in blacks switching their support from the Republican Party (the party of Abraham Lincoln) to the Democratic Party (formerly the predominant party of the South and its plantation owners).

The Great Depression finally subsided as the United States entered World War II and its factories were transformed into industries that manufactured weapons, ships, and aircraft. Unemployment decreased and Americans experienced the possibility for prosperity, although they were faced with fighting in the Second World War.

WORLD WAR II

TWO AND A half million African Americans enlisted in the U.S. military during World War II, and five hundred thousand were deployed to Europe. This global conflict between the Allies (United States, Great Britain, France, China, and Russia) and the Axis powers (Germany, Italy, and Japan) was the deadliest and costliest war ever waged. The war was the most technologically advanced because of the design and improvement in aircraft (B-17, B-24, B-26, and B-29 bomber planes), bombs ("buzz bombs" that blitzed London), battleships (aircraft carriers), and atomic weapons (used in the

Training for War, by African American painter William H. Johnson, shows a troop of African American soldiers preparing for battle during World War II. Johnson's painting documents the segregation in the U.S. Armed Forces at the time.

Women were given jobs in the defense industry during World War II for positions that men generally held. Women, black and white, worked in factories like the Douglas Aircraft Factory, making airplanes, while the men were away fighting the war.

bombing of Hiroshima and Nagasaki, Japan). The debate over whether the use of nuclear bombs was necessary to end the war rages on today. The Hiroshima and Nagasaki bombings of August 6, 1945, and August 9, 1945, resulted in the deaths or eventual deaths of around two hundred thousand people. The Cold War Era (when the United States and the Soviet Union were in conflict but did not engage directly in military action) followed World War II, and more and more nations armed themselves with nuclear weapons.

During World War II, the United States military was still segregated and most of the black military men were assigned to noncombat duty, with the exception of the all-black 92nd "Buffalo Soldiers" Infantry Division, which saw combat in western Italy, and the 761st "Black Panther" Tank Battalion, which led a drive from France to Germany. Activists A. Philip Randolph, founder of the Brotherhood of Sleeping Car Porters, and Walter White, executive secretary of the NAACP, were determined to end discrimination in the armed services and employ African Americans in the defense industries. Civil rights activists and members of the black community around the country were waging the "Double Victory" campaign to end racism at home and fascism (a dictatorship in which individuals have no rights other than to serve the governing party) abroad.

Randolph and White met with President Franklin Roosevelt to request that he abolish segregation in the armed services and start hiring blacks in jobs in the defense industry. Roosevelt was reluctant to agree to Randolph and White's demands for fear he would anger southern politicians, and the War Department was adamant that the armed services remain segregated. With prodding from his wife, Eleanor, who believed in the equality of all citizens, and pressure from the African American leaders, Roosevelt found himself in a very difficult situation. Randolph upped the ante when he called for thousands of black men to march on Washington for jobs in the defense industries and integration of the armed services. The march was set for July 1, 1941, and momentum grew around the country. Randolph informed the president that one hundred thousand black men were going to march on Washington.

Wanting to avoid a major incident, Roosevelt asked Randolph to call off the march, but Randolph refused. After much debate and deliberation, President Roosevelt relented and issued Executive Order 8802, which banned discrimination in the defense industry for companies holding government contracts for war production. Randolph called off the march on Washington. The order also banned discrimination in the training for jobs in the defense industry and established the Fair Employment Practices Commission, which monitored the industry for discriminatory practices. As a result of Executive Order 8802, many blacks—both men and women—moved out west to work in the aircraft and shipbuilding industries, as well as to other parts of the country to work at plants that made ships and ammunitions and housed supply facilities. Researchers of African American history have called this the Second Black Migration.

President George W. Bush presents the Congressional Gold Medal to Dr. Roscoe Brown and other Tuskegee Airmen, during ceremonies honoring the Tuskegee Airmen on Thursday, March 29, 2007, at the U.S. Capitol. Dr. Brown commanded the 100th Fighter Squadron of the 332nd Fighter Group during World War II.

THE TUSKEGEE AIRMEN

IN 1941, CONGRESS legislated that all-black combat units should be formed in the military, as an experiment. Among these units was the 99th Pursuit Squadron established by the U.S. Army Air Corps (the precursor to the Air Force), which became part of the Tuskegee Airmen. Rigid testing and much tougher requirements, such as previous flight experience and higher education, were instituted to discourage African Americans from applying to the all-black air corp. But many qualified black candidates did apply and were accepted, to the surprise of those in the War Department. The higher-ups in that department really had believed that blacks were inferior to whites and would not qualify as pilots.

Despite the tremendous obstacles, 994 African Americans from all over the United States became Tuskegee Airmen during World War II. The all-black combat unit trained at the Tuskegee Army Airfield in Alabama and would eventually become the 332nd Fighter Group. The 332nd was commanded by West Point graduate Captain Benjamin O. Davis, Jr., whose father Benjamin O. Davis, Sr., was America's first black general.

The Tuskegee Airmen were an all-black air corps trained at Tuskegee Army Airfield in Alabama. The 332nd Fighter Group of the Army Air Corps received numerous awards for their heroic efforts in World War II.

Although Floyd Carter became a Tuskegee Airman in 1946, a year after World War II ended, he was still a trailblazer. Lieutenant Floyd J. Carter, (Ret.), volunteered in 1943 after seeing a subway sign in New York City that read: "You Too Can Fly." When he asked for an application at the recruiting station, the white female recruiter said, "They don't take Negroes in the Army Air Forces." Carter responded, "Lady, I didn't ask you to recruit me, I asked you for an application." A sergeant had overheard the conversation and told the woman to give Floyd an application, so he took three for his friends to sign up, too.

"I had to take a test, there were three hundred guys and there were only two Negroes taking the test, me and a friend of mine. After the test was over the Colonel came to read the names of the men who passed. And I was one of the ones who passed."

From New York, Carter went to Mississippi, but before he left New York, the white colonel at the recruiting station told him, "'They are going to do everything they can to destroy you. If you can take it, you win, if you give up, they win.' All the aviation cadets went to Mississippi for testing to see if we could fly."

Forty black recruits were sent to Tuskegee for six months to train as pilots. Thirteen out of the forty received their wings, including Carter. "I qualified for navigation, bombardier and pilot," explained Carter. "I went to bombardier and navigation school in Texas and graduated as a navigator and bombardier. I was part of the first class of student officers who went through pilot training at Tuskegee."

Carter received his wings in 1946 and was among the last to graduate from the Tuskegee Army Air Field in Tuskegee, Alabama, too late for World War II, which ended in 1945. But Carter, certified as a pilot, bombardier, and navigator, would go on to train white flyers and participate in the Korean War and the Vietnam War in an integrated Air Force.

During World War II, the Tuskegee Airmen were members of the 99th Fighter Squadron and the 332nd Fighter Group and flew missions over North Africa, the Mediterranean, and Sicily. The Black Airmen "completed 15,000 sorties in approximately 1,500 missions, destroyed over 260 enemy aircraft, sank one enemy destroyer and demolished numerous enemy installations." And unlike World War I, when the United States of America did not acknowledge the role of black men in the military, the

Tuskegee Airmen were recognized for their contribution to the war effort. The group was "awarded numerous high honors including Distinguished Flying Crosses, Legions of Merit, Silver Stars, Purple Hearts, the Croix de Guerre, and the Red Star of Yugoslavia. A Distinguished Unit Citation was awarded the 332nd Fighter Group 'for outstanding service and extraordinary heroism' in 1945."

In 2007, although late in coming, the Tuskegee Airmen received the United States Congress's highest civilian award, the Congressional Gold Medal, in recognition of their heroism in World War II. The bill to award the medals passed unanimously and was sponsored by Congressman Charles Rangel (D-NY) in the House of Representatives and Senator Carl Levin (D-Mich.) in the Senate. The law was signed by President George W. Bush in April 2006.

Many of the Tuskegee Airmen went on to successful careers. Among them were Percy Sutton, media entrepreneur, who became New York City's Manhattan borough president; Dr. Roscoe C. Brown, the former president of Bronx Community College, City University of New York; Wendell Freeland, an attorney and civil rights activist from Pittsburgh, Pennsylvania; and brothers Robert Higginbotham, a retired orthopedic surgeon, and Mitchell Higginbotham, a retired probation officer from California.

Among those heralded for their achievements during World War II were two other African Americans: Dorie Miller and Dr. Charles Drew.

Dorie Miller was awarded the Navy Cross for his heroics performed in the line of duty at Pearl Harbor on December 7, 1941.

Members of the Women's Army Corps (WAC), expediting soldiers' mail at a camp post office

Miller, a navy mess attendant stationed on board the U.S.S. *West Virginia*, was awarded the Navy Cross, the highest award given to an African American during World War II, for his heroism when his ship was attacked by the Japanese at Pearl Harbor in Hawaii on December 7, 1941. He commandeered a machine gun on the deck of the *West Virginia* and shot down four enemy planes. Miller's heroic act was not initially recognized by the navy until civil rights groups and the black press campaigned for the navy to recognize him.

Dr. Charles Drew attended Amherst College in Massachusetts and McGill University Medical School in Canada. Drew became a researcher in blood chemistry and developed blood banking. Through his process, blood can be stored for a longer period of time by separating the plasma from whole blood and refrigerating the elements separately. The research was conducted at Columbia University's Presbyterian Hospital in New York

City, in 1938, when Drew received a two-year Rockefeller Fellowship. He also discovered that blood plasma could be transfused to a patient with any blood type without causing medical problems. His discoveries on blood banking and blood transfusions were instrumental in saving thousands of lives on the battlefield during World War II.

By 1944, the U.S. Navy began admitting African American women in the Women Accepted for Volunteer Emergency Service (WAVES), an emergency services program made up of nurses and other medical personnel. In 1945, Phyllis Daley became the first African American woman to be commissioned as a nurse in the U.S. Navy.

The U.S. Army allowed African American nurses to join in 1941, but only in limited numbers. By 1944, the quota was lifted and five hundred black nurses joined the ranks of army nurses to serve in World War II.

Black women enlisted in all branches of the military, including WAVES, the Women's Army Corps (WAC), and the SPARS, an acronym for the Coast Guard motto "Semper Paratus, Always Ready." African Americans Harriet Ida Pickens and Frances Wills became the first female black WAVES officers in 1944, helped by the efforts of Mary McLeod Bethune, a member of Roosevelt's black cabinet.

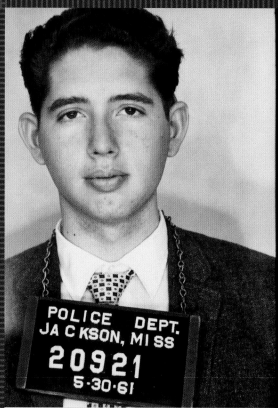

POLICE DEPT.
JACKSON, MISS
20921
5-30-61

POLICE DEPT.
JACKSON, MISS
21242
7-24-61

POLICE DEPT.
JACKSON, MISS
2097A

POLICE DEPT.
JACKSON, MISS
21046
6-21-61

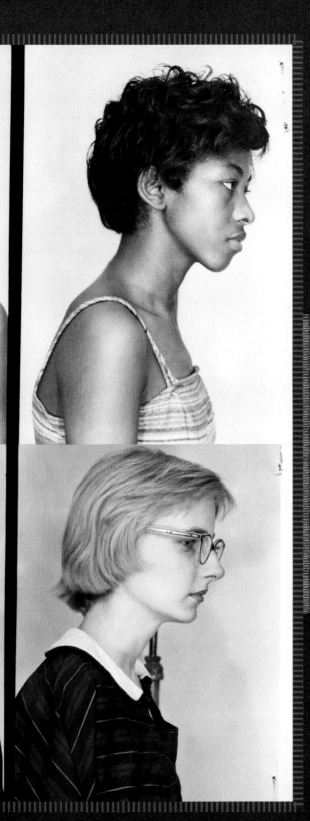

PART VI

THE CIVIL RIGHTS MOVEMENT TO THE BLACK POWER MOVEMENT

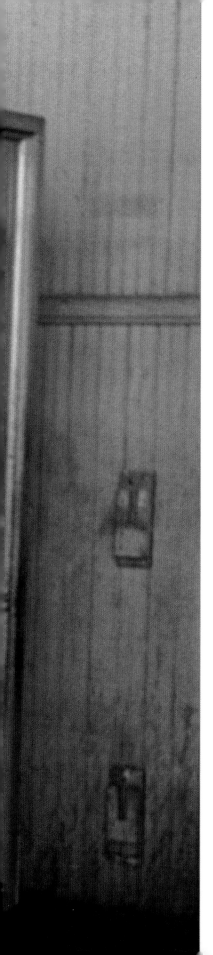

DESPITE THEIR ADVANCEMENTS made during World War II, the African American men and women returning from war-torn Europe and the Pacific, as well as those black men and women in the States who had worked in factories and other jobs, were still faced with overwhelming racism. They suffered a campaign of violence, mutilation, and murder waged by white supremacists. Dogged by a flood of false information that demeaned their intellect, morality, and integrity, African Americans had much to overcome as they continued their demand for equal rights.

Black colleges and universities were filled with students studying to become teachers, nurses, doctors, and lawyers. African American athletes had already broken color barriers during the 1930s and 1940s. Jesse Owens, a black sprinter, brought home four gold medals from the 1936 Summer Olympics held in Nazi Germany. Boxer Joe Louis became the second African American world heavyweight champion, holding the title from 1937 to 1949 (Jack Johnson was the first African American champion, from 1908 to 1915). Jackie Robinson became the first African American to play Major League Baseball when he debuted with the Brooklyn Dodgers in 1947.

The National Association for the Advancement of Colored People (NAACP) and the National Urban League (NUL) continued to fight for equality, as they had since the opening years of the twentieth century. These organizations were joined by the Congress of Racial Equality (CORE), founded in 1942. Together the NAACP, NUL, and CORE would wage the battle for equal rights in an effort to ensure that African Americans attained full citizenship.

By the late 1940s and mid-1950s, major legislation had begun to end discrimination. In 1948, President Harry S. Truman desegregated the United States Armed Forces by issuing Executive Order 9981. The Legal Defense and Education Fund of the NAACP, headed up by attorney Thurgood Marshall, who would later become the first African American U.S. Supreme Court justice, in 1967, began working on overturning the "separate but equal" clause relating to separate schools for black and white students. He was assisted by a young Constance Baker Motley, who became the first African American woman to serve as a federal judge. In their legal campaign to end race-based schooling, Marshall and Motley would fight to end the racism codified in the 1896 *Plessy v. Ferguson* ruling, which had legalized segregation in all public facilities.

LEFT: Jack Johnson became the first African American world heavyweight boxing champion after a bruising fifteen-round battle with white champion James Jeffries. Johnson's win in "the fight of the century" in Reno, Nevada, on July 4, 1910, sparked race riots across the United States.

RIGHT: Sports teams were also segregated. The Negro Leagues had an all-black New York Yankees baseball team, photographed here in 1934.

BROWN V. BOARD OF EDUCATION OF TOPEKA

THE HARD WORK of Marshall, Motley, and their colleagues resulted in the Supreme Court's landmark 1954 decision in the *Brown v. Board of Education of Topeka* case, which began the gradual unraveling of the *Plessy v. Ferguson* ruling. The historic case grouped together five cases in which African Americans sued school districts in five different states for providing separate and inferior schools (and therefore an inferior education) for black students. One of the cases involved a Virginia school district, where sixteen-year-old Barbara Rose Johns led a group of students in protest because their black school was inferior to the local white school. The *Brown v. Board of Education* Supreme Court ruling made it illegal to have separate public schools for whites and blacks and marked the beginning of the modern civil rights movement. Although it would be some time before states in the South and other parts of the United States actually enforced the law to desegregate the schools, the Brown decision was the beginning of the breaking down of racial barriers of segregation.

George E. C. Hayes, Thurgood Marshall, and James Nabrit celebrate the Supreme Court Decision in *Brown v. Board of Education*, 1954, which declared segregation illegal in public schools.

In 1957, the first civil rights legislation since 1875 was passed. The Civil Rights Act of 1957 created the Civil Rights Division within the Department of Justice and the Civil Rights Commission established by President Dwight Eisenhower, which protected the voting rights of all American citizens, guaranteed under the Constitution's Fifteenth Amendment.

These advancements drew the ire of white supremacists and breathed new life into the white terrorist group the Ku Klux Klan, which organized rallies, cross burnings, and lynchings, launching a reign of terror against blacks in the South and the Midwest. In the Pacific Northwest, where there were not many blacks, the Klan focused its hatred on Catholics and other ethnic groups.

THE MURDER OF EMMETT TILL

EMMETT TILL, A fourteen-year-old black teenager from Chicago, Illinois, was kidnapped while visiting his family in Money, Mississippi, in the summer of 1955. He was mutilated and killed for allegedly whistling at a white woman. The Till murder caused outrage and protests across the country.

Two white men were tried for the murder, but the all-white, all-male jury found them innocent of the crime. Till's body was returned to Chicago for the funeral and his mother insisted on an open casket to remind the world what had happened to her son. It is estimated that tens of thousands of mourners were at the viewing. Emmett Till's battered body was photographed and the pictures were published in African American publications (*Jet* magazine on September 15, 1955, and *The Chicago Defender* on September 17, 1955), galvanizing blacks and their white supporters nationwide to fight vigorously against racial violence and inequality. The acquittal of the two men also caused an uproar in the European media.

With the murder of young Emmett Till symbolizing the violence and injustices experienced by African Americans, organizations were established to protest and change these inequities in American society. The Southern Christian Leadership Conference (SCLC) was founded in 1957 by Reverend Martin Luther King, Jr., Dr. Ralph Abernathy, and other organizers to coordinate protest activities in the South. Before that, King and Abernathy had established the Montgomery Improvement Association (MIA) in December 1955, which successfully desegregated the Montgomery, Alabama, bus system through a massive, nonviolent 381-day bus boycott. King, a new resident of Montgomery and the minister at the Dexter Avenue Baptist Church, headed up the MIA, while E. D. Nixon, a Pullman porter (a man who worked on the railroad helping passengers with their needs) and the president of the local NAACP chapter, organized the boycott.

Emmett Till and his mother, Mamie Bradley, in 1955. Emmett was murdered by the Ku Klux Klan while visiting relatives in the South during his summer vacation.

THE MONTGOMERY BUS BOYCOTT

THE MONTGOMERY BUS boycott was a protest by the black community in response to the arrest of Rosa Parks, a black passenger and the secretary of the local NAACP chapter, who was on her way home from her job as a seamstress at a department store when she refused to give up her seat on the bus to a white man. Through her choice to not give up her seat on the bus, Parks was enacting Dr. King's belief in nonviolent resistance, when a person or group refuses to obey a specific law that they consider wrong. This

Rosa Parks riding a Montgomery, Alabama, bus in December 1956, after the Supreme Court outlawed segregation on buses

form of peaceful protest had been used successfully in India's campaign for independence from Great Britain by Mohandas Gandhi, also known as Mahatma Gandhi.

The Montgomery bus boycott was the first organized demonstration of the modern-day civil rights era in which an entire community of African Americans participated in a protest that lasted a little over a year and effectively ended bus segregation in the Alabama city. Because of the widespread media coverage and the huge financial blow dealt the city with the drop in black riders, the white community was pressured to negotiate with the protesters.

When the U.S. Supreme Court upheld, in November 1956, a lower court's ruling that segregated buses were unconstitutional, the Montgomery city fathers had to integrate the bus system. From the success of this first boycott, key organizers coordinated civil disobedience actions through sit-ins, boycotts, and marches throughout the South and in other parts of the country. Prominent members of the SCLC during the early years included Fred Shuttlesworth, Charles K. Steele, Andrew Young, Joseph Lowery, and Hosea Williams.

The federal rulings that upheld integration on buses and in schools were a first step to full citizenship for African Americans. Although the "separate but equal" statute regarding schools for blacks and whites had been ruled unconstitutional by the Supreme Court in 1954, many districts, especially in the South, steadfastly refused to allow blacks to attend their white schools, while others complied with the ruling to desegregate and enroll black students. Still, in other parts of the country, some districts dragged their feet in implementing plans and made attempts to get around the ruling. In some instances, mostly in southern states, white protesters intimidated and threatened physical harm to blacks who tried to integrate white schools.

LITTLE ROCK NINE INTEGRATES CENTRAL HIGH SCHOOL

THE LITTLE ROCK Nine is an example of a group of brave African American students who integrated their school. In this case it was Central High School in Little Rock, Arkansas, on September 4, 1957. When they arrived at Central High School as the first black students, Minnijean Brown, Elizabeth Eckford, Ernest Green, Thelma Mothershed, Melba Pattillo, Gloria Ray, Terrance Roberts, Jefferson Thomas, and Carlotta Walls were met with racist taunts and death threats from the angry white protesters.

Governor Orval Faubus deployed the Arkansas National Guard to block the Little Rock Nine from entering the school. It took three weeks, an order by President Dwight Eisenhower, and the United States 101st Air Borne Division to protect the students as they finally gained entrance to the high school. Once inside, the black students were confronted by angry white students calling them names and threatening them with physical harm.

Minnijean Brown was expelled from Central High for fighting back when she dumped a bowl of chili on the head of one of her white abusers. Ernest Green was the first black student to graduate from Central High School in June 1958. Jefferson Thomas and Carlotta Walls graduated in 1960, and the remaining five students either moved from Little Rock or transferred to other schools. Others would follow these brave students in their pursuit of equal education. In her memoir, *In My Place*, journalist Charlayne Hunter-Gault wrote about her experiences as the first African

American to integrate in 1961 and then graduate from the University of Georgia. In 1962, James Meredith was the first black student to enroll in the University of Mississippi, also known as "Ole Miss."

As a footnote to the violent history of the 1950s South, African American documentary filmmaker Keith Beauchamp, haunted by the image he saw in an old copy of a 1955 *Jet* magazine when he was ten or eleven years old of Emmett Till's open casket, decided to make a documentary about Till's murder. In *The Untold Story of Emmett Louis Till* (2005), Beauchamp revisited the community of Money, Mississippi, where Till was killed, and interviewed witnesses, including blacks who were still fearful of reprisals for speaking out fifty years later.

The two white men accused of Till's murder had been acquitted and a third alleged participant, who was not charged, was interviewed in the film and denied his involvement. In a 1956 *Look* magazine article, one of the accused men had admitted to murdering young Till. However, the men could not be retried because of the "double jeopardy" rule: Once found innocent of a crime, one cannot be tried again for the same crime. The two men have since died, but in 2004, the United States Department of Justice reopened the Emmett Till case, based on new information provided by

Members of the Little Rock Nine, the students who integrated Little Rock's Central High School in 1957, on their way to class, under the protection of the United States Army

Members of the Washington Freedom Riders Committee en route to Washington, D.C., from New York City, hold signs from bus windows to protest segregation, on May 30, 1961

interviews eventually included in Beauchamp's film. In 2005, Till's body was exhumed and an autopsy was performed. The case was closed in 2007 for lack of evidence to indict any remaining suspects.

The 1960s were a very turbulent time in America. Voter registration drives in southern communities took place to register black voters who were afraid to register because of violence and intimidation tactics at the polls. There were boycotts of transportation systems that sent black riders to separate waiting areas and to the back of the bus or train. Protest marches and sit-ins occurred at white-owned businesses that refused to serve blacks. As discontentment grew among African Americans, race riots erupted in New York City (1964), Watts (in Los Angeles, 1965), Detroit (1967), and Newark (1967).

FREEDOM RIDERS AND FREEDOM SUMMER

THE CONGRESS OF Racial Equality (CORE) organized "Freedom Rides" with black and white volunteers traveling through the South and the Midwest on buses to test out the December 5, 1960, U.S. Supreme Court decision that banned segregated bus and train terminals (a 1946 Supreme Court ruling had already banned segregation in interstate bus travel). Many of the Freedom Riders were jailed and beaten, and buses were firebombed during these trips, but the riders were successful in bringing national attention to states that were not enforcing the new law.

In his book *Breach of Peace: Portraits of the 1961 Mississippi Freedom Riders,* Eric Etheridge pays tribute to the Freedom Riders in a collection of personal essays of eighty people, along with mug shots from their arrests in 1961. In an article about the book entitled "The Freedom Riders, Then and Now" by Marian Smith Holmes in the February 2009 *Smithsonian* magazine, two of the Freedom Riders describe how they felt:

> As soon as he heard the call for riders, Robert Singleton remembers, he "was fired up and ready to go." He and his wife, Helen, had both been active in their local NAACP and they took twelve volunteers with them from California. "The spirit that permeated the air at that time was not unlike the feeling Barack Obama has rekindled among the youth of today," says Singleton, now 73 and an economics professor at Loyola Marymount University in Los Angeles.
>
> Peter Ackerberg, a lawyer who now lives in Minneapolis, said that while he'd always talked a "big radical game," he had never acted on his convictions. "What am I going to tell my children when they ask me about this time?" he recalled thinking. Boarding a bus in Montgomery, Alabama, "I was pretty scared," he told Etheridge. "The black guys and girls were singing . . . They were so spirited and so unafraid. They were really prepared to risk their lives." Today, Ackerberg recalls acquiescing and saying "sir" to a jail official who was "pounding a blackjack [a club or baton]." Soon after, "I could hear the blackjack strike [rider C. T. Vivian's] head and him shrieking; I don't think he ever said 'sir.'"

ABOVE: African American voters went to the polls in the South in the 1960s, some voting for the first time in their lives.

BOTTOM: African American students from North Carolina's A&T State University, who were refused service at a lunch counter, stage a sit-down protest at the F.W. Woolworth store in Greensboro, North Carolina, on February 2, 1960.

By the mid-1960s, groups of students on campuses across the United States became involved in the civil rights movement. The Student Non-violent Coordinating Committee (SNCC) was founded in 1960 at Shaw University in Raleigh, North Carolina. Black student activists James Forman, John Lewis (later U.S. representative, D-GA), and Robert Parris Moses were the early leaders. In 1966, Stokely Carmichael (who later changed his name to Kwame Ture), an activist from Howard University who also coined the term "Black Power," took over as head of SNCC.

Along with CORE, SNCC's main focus was to assist with voter registration drives in Mississippi, Alabama, and Georgia and with sit-ins at department stores in Charlotte, North Carolina. SNCC created Freedom Schools, as part of its Mississippi Freedom Summer Project in 1964, whose main goal was voter registration and organizing the Mississippi Freedom Democratic Party (MFDP). SNCC recruited black and white college students to teach and encourage African American students not only in academics, but also in developing leadership skills to become politically active in the struggle for civil rights.

The violent attacks against African Americans and white supporters of the civil rights movement politicized all age groups. Two events left indelible marks on the American psyche. In June 1964, in Philadelphia, Mississippi, Michael Schwerner and Andrew Goodman, who were white, and James Chaney, an African American, were killed while working to register

black voters and investigating the burning of a local church. The three young men were arrested by the police supposedly for speeding. They were detained at the police station and handed over to the local Ku Klux Klan, who murdered the men.

Michael Schwerner, James Chaney, and Andrew Goodman (left to right), each in their twenties, were civil rights workers murdered by the Ku Klux Klan in June 1964, during Freedom Summer in Mississippi.

The national media attention on the deaths of the three civil rights workers focused the American public on the violence experienced by those working in the movement like never before. However, forty years would pass before eighty-year-old Edgar Ray Killen would be charged with orchestrating the killing of Schwerner, Goodman, and Chaney. He was convicted in 2005 on three counts of manslaughter and sentenced to sixty years in prison.

In September 1963, a bomb was placed under the steps of the 16th Street Baptist Church in Birmingham, Alabama, killing four young girls, ages eleven through fourteen. Although one member of the Ku Klux Klan, Robert Chambliss, was finally convicted of the crime in 1977, it was not until 2000 that his three accomplices, also members of the Ku Klux Klan, would be made public by the FBI.

Many fought to achieve participation for African Americans in the electoral process in Mississippi. Blacks who were denied the right to vote and whites sympathetic to their cause formed a new political party. The Mississippi Freedom Democratic Party (MFDP) wanted its representatives to attend the Democratic National Convention in Atlantic City, New Jersey, in August 1964, as official delegates. Barred from the state's all-white Democratic Party, the MFDP sent its own delegates to the Atlantic

City convention to protest their exclusion and request that the MFDP, as the only legitimate party representing the state, replace the all-white Mississippi delegation.

In a televised Credentials Committee meeting, Fannie Lou Hamer, an MFDP delegate, gave impassioned testimony about her harrowing experiences trying to register to vote in Mississippi. Lyndon Johnson, the Democratic presidential nominee, was incensed by the controversy and, to end the debacle, offered a compromise that would give the MFDP two "at-large" seats (that allowed the MFDP delegates to observe but not vote). The MFDP declined, and its delegation was not recognized or seated at the convention.

The official Mississippi Delegation, except for three members, walked out of the convention because of the compromise that asked delegates to support a full slate of Democratic candidates in the upcoming elections. MFDP delegates then borrowed convention passes and sat in the seats vacated by the Mississippi delegates, until the seats were removed and the MFDP delegates were thrown out. The MFDP delegates returned the next day and sang freedom songs in protest.

Many celebrities participated in the civil rights movement by hosting fund-raisers, donating large sums of money for staffing or living expenses, or by recording record albums to raise money. Working for the cause were singer and actor Harry Belafonte; comedian Dick Gregory; actor Sidney Poitier; singer Sam Cooke; actress Lena Horne; singer and dancer Sammy Davis, Jr.; singer Nina Simone; gospel singer Mahalia Jackson; author James Baldwin; and Ruby Dee and Ossie Davis, a husband-and-wife duo whose activism rivaled their acting fame.

Dee and Davis began their activism very early in their careers and supported causes that campaigned for workers rights, human rights, and civil rights. In the 1960s, their focus was on the struggle for equality for African Americans. The couple acted as mistress and master of ceremonies at the August 1963 March on Washington for Jobs and Freedom. The march was planned by A. Philip Randolph, Bayard Rustin, Whitney Young, John Lewis, and Martin Luther King, Jr., to lobby for President John F. Kennedy's civil rights legislation. Ruby Dee and Ossie Davis also marched and protested with Martin Luther King at the Selma-to-Montgomery March for voting rights in March 1965.

Fannie Lou Hamer was a delegate representing the Mississippi Freedom Democratic Party at the Democratic National Convention in Atlantic City, New Jersey, in 1964. Hamer and her delegation were not allowed to be seated, and she made an impassioned statement to the Credentials Committee about voting fraud in Mississippi.

In their book, *With Ossie and Ruby: In This Life Together*, Davis talked about a pivotal moment for him when he was in Washington, D.C., attending Howard University in 1939. Marian Anderson, the African American opera singer, was banned from performing at Constitution Hall by the Daughters of the American Revolution (DAR). With the help of First Lady Eleanor Roosevelt, Anderson instead performed her concert on the steps of the Lincoln Memorial on April 9, 1939. Ossie Davis remembered Anderson's performance as "an act of defiance" that "married in my mind forever the performing arts as a weapon in the struggle for freedom. It made a connection that, for me and for thousands of other artists, has never been severed. It was a proclamation and commitment."

Protest music or music of social justice was very important to the civil rights movement. Not only was it a means of spreading the message of freedom and equality, it was also a way to raise money to continue the fight. Folk singers, white and black, contributed their time and talent to the cause. Pete Seeger is credited with popularizing what became the anthem of the struggle, "We Shall Overcome," and adding the verse, "We'll walk hand in hand." Seeger also suggested to SNCC leadership that they form the SNCC Freedom Singers, of which Dr. Bernice Johnson Reagon, founder of the singing group Sweet Honey in the Rock, was an original member. The

Opera singer Marian Anderson is congratulated by Secretary of the Interior Harold Ickes, who introduced Anderson at her outdoor concert at the Lincoln Memorial, after the Daughters of the American Revolution refused to let her sing at Constitution Hall in 1939 because she was African American.

Freedom Singers performed at concerts around the country with the proceeds going to SNCC.

In an interview with Amy Goodman of *Democracy Now!*, during Pete Seeger's ninetieth birthday celebration at Madison Square Garden in New York City in May 2009, Dr. Reagon talked about meeting Pete Seeger and the formation of the SNCC Freedom Singers:

> *I didn't know him as Pete Seeger. I met him as a human being because of the Albany, Georgia, civil rights movement in the 1960s . . . he actually thought the singing in Southwest Georgia was so powerful that they should organize a singing group . . . and said to Jim Forman of SNCC, "If you organized a group, you would have a group that could travel all over the country singing songs about the movement, and they might also bring financial support to the movement."*

Other folk musicians who participated in the civil rights movement were Joan Baez; Odetta; Bob Dylan; and Peter, Paul and Mary.

CIVIL RIGHTS, WEST COAST STYLE

BY THE MID-1960S, SNCC had emerged as a more politically radical group attracting younger activists, along with the Black Panther Party. Both groups were strikingly different alternatives to the more conservative and nonviolent SCLC and the NAACP in their approach to achieving full civil rights. The Black Panther Party, which advocated Black Power, was established by Huey Newton and Bobby Seale in Oakland, California, in 1966, and attracted a large following of young blacks with branches eventually in many cities across the country, including San Francisco, New York City, Baltimore, and Chicago.

The Black Panther Party, considered a radical militant group that promoted black self-defense and black self-sufficiency by offering free health clinics, programs to feed kids, drug rehabilitation programs, and racial pride, was targeted by the FBI's COINTELPRO, the federal counter-intelligence program. The program used covert operations to watch and track the activities of domestic groups, including civil rights activists,

Black Panthers national chairman Bobby Seale (left) and defense minister Huey Newton (right) in Oakland, California

antiwar protesters, student activists, religious organizations, and black militants who protested against various political and social issues. COIN-TELPRO infiltrated the Black Panthers, and many of the party's organizers were either killed or jailed during their confrontations with police.

The civil rights movement on the West Coast had the same goals as the movement in other parts of the country: gain full equality for black citizens in jobs, education, and housing. The NAACP and the SCLC were very active in organizing boycotts, marches, and rallies in support of efforts to help African Americans gain their voting rights, integrate businesses and public facilities, desegregate transportation systems and schools, and protest discrimination against African Americans in the South and on the West Coast, in general. Martin Luther King; Ralph Abernathy; Roy Wilkins, executive secretary of the NAACP; and Thurgood Marshall attended the 1956 NAACP Convention in San Francisco at the Civic Center. And Malcolm X, an important minister in the Nation of Islam, visited the West Coast in 1963. But tensions were brewing in California, as they were in many states, and black citizens were becoming impatient with the slow movement toward equality.

On August 11, 1965, the black community of Watts in South Central Los Angeles exploded in violence, triggered by a confrontation between the family of a black motorist and a white cop during the arrest of the motorist, who was suspected of drunken driving. The residents were fed up with the police brutality, lack of jobs, poor housing conditions, and discrimination, and this incident with the police was the last straw. For six days, rioters burned and looted white-owned businesses, leveling blocks and blocks of stores in the Watts community. Thirty-four people died, more than one thousand were injured, and six hundred buildings were destroyed. Governor Pat Brown formed a commission to study the causes of the riots, and the December 1965 report titled "Violence in the City: An End or a Beginning?" concluded that African Americans in Watts were frustrated because of the lack of jobs, poor living conditions, and inferior schools. However, no programs were implemented by the state to remedy the findings nor did the state establish a rebuilding plan for the community.

Angela Davis, a political activist and university professor, worked closely with the Black Panthers for the release of the Soledad Brothers (George Jackson, Fleeta Drumgo, and John Cluchette), who were charged with murdering a prison guard at the maximum-security San Quentin State Prison in California in January 1970. Jonathan Jackson, the brother of George Jackson, entered the Marin County Courthouse in California in August 1970 with an automatic weapon. He freed three San Quentin prisoners who were at the courthouse and took a judge as a hostage. Jackson's plan was to hold the judge hostage until the Soledad Brothers were released. The bungled plan resulted in Jonathan Jackson's death, along with the deaths of the judge and two prisoners, during an attempt to escape from the courthouse. Angela Davis, who was the chair of the Soledad Brothers Defense Committee, was linked to the shotgun used in the killing of the judge.

The FBI placed Davis on the Ten Most Wanted List and launched a massive nationwide hunt during the summer of 1970, flooding black communities from the East Coast to the West Coast with wanted posters of Angela Davis with her trademark large Afro hairstyle. To many African American women it felt as though every black woman with an Afro was under suspicion as many were stopped and questioned, causing much anxiety in the black communities in America. The hunt lasted more than

Angela Davis, a political activist, speaking at a rally against the death penalty, outside the state capitol building in Raleigh, North Carolina, on July 4, 1974

two months and ended in New York City with Davis's capture. Angela Davis, who became somewhat of a folk hero during her time on the run from the FBI, was tried on conspiracy, kidnapping, and murder charges and was acquitted of all charges. Davis is still an activist and teaches and lectures on women's rights, racial equality, and social issues associated with incarceration.

MLK AND MALCOLM X

AS THE MOOD of the country grew more volatile, a series of political leaders were assassinated by zealots who attempted to stop their work in the civil rights movement. Medgar Evers, a field secretary for the NAACP, was one of the first major civil rights leaders to be assassinated. He was killed in June 1963 in the driveway of his home in Jackson, Mississippi. In August of that same year, a group of civil rights organizations—SCLC, NAACP, CORE, NUL (National Urban League), and the BSCP (Brotherhood of Sleeping Car Porters)—sponsored what came to be called the March on Washington for Jobs and Freedom, which also supported the civil rights legislation introduced to Congress by President John F. Kennedy (1961–1963). With an audience of several hundred thousand black and white supporters on the Mall in Washington, D.C., Reverend Martin Luther King, Jr., delivered his iconic "I Have a Dream" speech from the steps of the Lincoln Memorial in August 1963.

King, the son of a Baptist preacher and civil rights activist, came to his nonviolent approach to achieve equality through prayer and struggle. His first boycott, the 1955 Montgomery bus boycott, was a test of his ability to stay focused on the goal of desegregating the bus system and not to be distracted by the hate-filled challenges he experienced. These included being arrested, the bombing of his home with his wife and small child inside, and receiving death threats on the phone.

Tonya Bolden describes in her book *MLK: Journey of a King* how King dealt with his dilemma of getting angry versus being nonviolent when confronted with extreme acts of racism. At one point during the bus boycott, when King's home was bombed and after calming his supporters, Bolden describes his reaction:

> *[King was] on the verge of corroding hate . . . he dug deep for the strength to love. He knew that it was neither the kind of love that he felt for Yoki [his young daughter], his parents, or his friends, nor the kind of love he had for Coretta [his wife], but rather agape [pronounced ah-gah-pay], a Greek word for a higher, harder love: a love that has nothing to do with liking a person, a love worthy of people who do you no good and even do you wrong.*

That love was what kept him from hating.

On November 22, President John F. Kennedy was assassinated in Dallas, Texas, and Vice President Lyndon B. Johnson became president of the United States. On July 2, 1964, Johnson signed the Civil Rights Act of 1964 into law. The 1964 act prohibited segregation in schools and in public accommodations and banned racial discrimination in employment. The law also cut off aid to federally funded programs that discriminated, continued the tenure of the Commission on Civil Rights established in 1957, and created the Equal Employment Opportunity Commission. The Voting Rights Act of 1965, signed into law by President Johnson on August 6, strengthened the voting rights of African Americans by making it illegal to require literacy tests and other obstacles that prevented blacks from registering to vote.

Martin Luther King, Jr., was assassinated on April 4, 1968, in Memphis, Tennessee, where he had gone to lead a march in support of striking sanitation workers. Riots in more than one hundred cities, including Washington, D.C.; Baltimore; Denver; and Chicago followed the news of King's murder. As hundreds of thousands mourned King's death, the United States Congress passed the Civil Rights Act of 1968, also referred to as the Fair Housing Act, banning discrimination in the sale, rental, or financing of housing. President Lyndon Johnson signed the act into law on April 11, a week after King's assassination.

Malcolm X was often perceived as the polar opposite of Martin Luther King, who believed in a nonviolent resistance approach to attaining equal rights for blacks. Malcolm, a member of the controversial Nation of Islam, was viewed as a radical who preached hate and the separation of the black and white races. His mantra was "by any means necessary," which for many meant that Malcolm would resort to violence to achieve his goals. In 1965 Malcolm made a pilgrimage to Mecca (the holiest city of the Islamic religion, located in Saudi Arabia), where he began his transformation from a

Rev. Dr. Martin Luther King, Jr., speaks to the crowd gathered around the Reflecting Pool on the Mall in Washington, D.C., during the March on Washington, August 1963.

ABOVE: Malcolm X, a religious civil rights leader

BELOW: President Lyndon B. Johnson signed the Civil Rights Act of 1968 on April 11, 1968. This bill was a follow-up to the Civil Rights Act of 1964.

black separatist into a human rights activist fighting for all oppressed people around the world. After his return to the United States, Malcolm X, who then became known as El-Hajj Malik El-Shabazz, established the Organization of Afro-American Unity in June 1965 to connect African Americans and Africans on a global level.

Malcolm grew up in a large family—there were eight children—in Lansing, Michigan. King's childhood was in Atlanta, Georgia, where he was raised with his two siblings. Malcolm's father was a lay Baptist preacher and a follower of Marcus Garvey, whose movement encouraged blacks to emigrate to Africa and build a life away from the racism of America. King's father was the pastor of the Ebenezer Baptist Church in Atlanta and a civil rights leader who was active in the NAACP.

Both Martin Luther King, Jr., and Malcolm X were exposed to racism in their early years, which had a tremendous influence on them later in life. Although Malcolm's path to becoming a human rights activist and leader was very circuitous—serving time in prison for robbery and joining the Nation of Islam—he did make a significant contribution to the civil rights movement in the United States by aggressively and eloquently challenging African Americans to love themselves, practice self-determination, and expand their self-knowledge, before he was assassinated on February 21, 1965.

The news media emphasized the differences between the two leaders. Martin Luther King was portrayed as a passive, more conciliatory activist. Malcolm X was depicted as a firebrand who initially advocated black separatism and who later transformed into a human rights activist who reached out to King and other civil rights leaders through proposing a broad coalition of organizations working in concert for equality for blacks.

There was an occasion when the two were captured in a photograph for a brief moment at a press conference, when the leaders came to the Capitol to view the debate on the civil rights legislation being considered by Congress, on March 26, 1964, in Washington, D.C. The series of photos of Malcolm and King, smiling and shaking hands, are the only photographs of the two leaders together. They may have had different tactics, but they were pursuing the same goal of equality for African Americans, and toward the end of their lives a respect for each other emerged. After he returned from his pilgrimage to Mecca, Malcolm's changed attitude regarding King was indicated in a telegram that he sent King, asking if he needed help after being jailed for trying to integrate a whites-only motel in St. Augustine on June 11, 1964:

Rev. Martin Luther King and Malcolm X greet each other at the U.S. Capitol in Washington, D.C., on March 26, 1964, during the debate on the Civil Rights Bill of 1964.

June 30, 1964
Dr. Martin Luther King
St. Augustine, FL

We have been witnessing with great concern the vicious attacks of the white races against our poor defenseless people there in St. Augustine. If the Federal Government will not send troops to your aid, just say the word and we will immediately dispatch some of our brothers there to organize self defense units among our people and the Ku Klux Klan will then receive a taste of its own medicine. The day of turning the other cheek to those brute beasts is over.

The Organization of Afro-American Unity
Malcolm X, Chairman
Theresa Hotel
Harlem, NY

King also reached out after Malcolm X was assassinated. He sent Betty Shabazz, Malcolm's widow, a telegram that expressed his feelings about Malcolm:

> *While we did not always see eye to eye on methods to solve the race problem, I always had a deep affection for Malcolm and felt that he had a great ability to put his finger on the existence and the root of the problem. He was an eloquent spokesman for his point of view and no one can honestly doubt that Malcolm had a great concern for the problems we face as a race.*

The Big Six, men who were regarded as the leaders of the civil rights movement in the 1960s, included Martin Luther King, Jr.; A. Philip Randolph; Roy Wilkins; James Farmer; John Lewis; and Whitney Young.

Roy Wilkins, as the head of the NAACP from 1955 to 1977, believed in social change through legislation. Wilkins founded, along with A. Philip Randolph and Arnold Aronson, a leader of the National Jewish Community Relations Advisory Council, the Leadership Conference on Civil Rights (LCCR), an important civil rights coalition that coordinated the national legislative campaign of every major civil rights law since 1957. *Brown v. Board of Education* of 1954, the Civil Rights Act of 1964, and the Voting Rights Act of 1965 were the significant legislative victories that added to Wilkins's stature as the "Senior Statesman" of the civil rights movement.

James Farmer, cofounder of CORE and its first chairman, organized the Freedom Rides. In 1968, Farmer, a Republican, was defeated by Shirley Chisholm—a Democrat who would become the first woman and African American to seek the presidential nomination—for Brooklyn, New York's 12th Congressional seat. Farmer was later appointed by President Richard Nixon (1969–1974) as assistant secretary for Health, Education, and Welfare.

John Lewis, as a student at Fisk University, was a founding member of SNCC and participated in sit-ins at lunch counters and was a volunteer on the Freedom Rides. Lewis was elected to the United States Congress in 1986 as the representative from Georgia's fifth district. The congressman, a powerful politician, is the senior chief deputy whip—or minority leader of the U.S. House of Representatives—for the Democratic Party in the House and a member of the Ways & Means Committee.

Whitney Young, as president of the National Urban League in 1961,

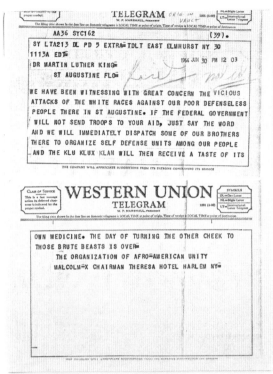

was a negotiator who helped gain equal opportunity for blacks in government services, including the military, and in businesses.

These men's efforts toward equal rights for African Americans were legendary, and many of these activists went on to become instruments of change, along with other important figures of the civil rights movement:

Andrew Young was a young minister when he joined the SCLC in 1960. He became its executive director in 1964. Young worked side by side with MLK in Birmingham, St. Augustine, and Selma as they campaigned for civil rights and voting rights. He was with him in Memphis in April 1968, when King was assassinated. Young continued his work in the movement and went on to become the mayor of Atlanta, Georgia; the U.S. congressman representing Georgia's fifth district; and the U.S. ambassador to the United Nations.

Julian Bond, a founding member and communications director of SNCC, was elected to three terms to the Georgia House of Representatives, beginning in 1965, and served in the Georgia Senate from 1974 to 1987.

Jesse Jackson, a young civil rights activist, was among the supporters with Martin Luther King, Jr., when King was assassinated in Memphis. He has continued King's mission of equal opportunity through his organization, Operation PUSH (People United to Save Humanity), now called the

LEFT: Rev. Martin Luther King, Jr., Ralph Abernathy, and Rev. Andrew Young (left to right) lead a group of African American church members to the Dallas County Courthouse to register to vote, March 1965.

RIGHT: A Western Union telegram dated June 30, 1966, that Malcolm X sent to Martin Luther King, offering to send reinforcements to combat the Ku Klux Klan in St. Augustine, Florida

RIGHT: U.S. medal winners Tommie Smith (center) and John Carlos (right) protest with raised fists during the playing of "The Star-Spangled Banner" at the Olympic Games in Mexico City, October 1968. Australian Peter Norman (left) supported their protest and wore a badge identical to Smith and Carlos, identifying the Olympic Project for Human Rights.

LEFT: Stokely Carmichael (Kwame Ture), the leader of the Student Nonviolent Coordinating Committee, speaking to a group of demonstrators outside of the U.S. Capitol, protesting the action by the House of Representatives denying Congressman Adam Clayton Powell his seat in Congress, 1967

Rainbow/PUSH Coalition. The organization's mission is to increase minority hiring in Fortune 500 companies and investments in the inner cities.

The civil rights movement in the United States changed after the assassination of King, which set the stage for the emergence of the Black Power Movement of the 1960s and 1970s. Younger black activists like Stokely Carmichael, H. Rap Brown, Huey Newton, Bobby Seale, and Fred Hampton were at the vanguard of a more militant and aggressive movement of black pride, black self-sufficiency, and black self-determination.

Black Power was about racial identity and love of oneself ("Black is Beautiful") as well as creating political power for blacks. Young African American men and women grew their hair into "naturals," or Afros, as a show of pride. Others changed their names to those of African or Muslim origin or replaced their last names with the letter "X" to denote that they did not know their real last names because their ancestors had been kidnapped from their African homes and given Christian names by the slaveholders in the New World. The Black Power salute, fist thrust into the air, was a show of solidarity among supporters. Intricate handshakes and clothing, such as the loose-fitting African-style shirt called a dashiki, became part of the style that some Black Power activists, their supporters, and young people adopted.

Proponents of the movement believed that educating African Americans about their culture and history would bring about a more informed and cohesive race—a stronger race with its own organizational structure and its own political and economic institutions. This social independence would enable African Americans to operate from a position of solidarity and strength.

THE BLACK ARTS MOVEMENT

THE BLACK ARTS Movement, a cultural movement that has been referred to as the Second Black Renaissance, was based in New York, with arts groups springing up in Chicago, Detroit, New Orleans, Houston, Miami, San Francisco, and Los Angeles from the mid-1960s to the mid-1970s. In a 1968 essay titled "The Black Arts Movement," author and scholar Larry Neal wrote that the movement was the "aesthetic and spiritual sister of the Black Power concept."

African American authors, poets, artists, playwrights, actors, dancers, and musicians reflected pride in their race and heritage through their works, which became known as the "black aesthetic." The content and motivation of the works of the Black Arts Movement was to promote the message of black pride and black identity that was prevalent among African Americans at the time.

Poet Imamu Amiri Baraka (formerly LeRoi Jones) is considered the primary force of the Black Arts Movement. Authors Ishmael Reed, Alice Walker, Steve Cannon, Rosa Guy, Maya Angelou, Calvin Hernton, Askia Touré, Tom Dent, John O. Killens, and others formed the literary core of the movement, along with poets Sonia Sanchez, Nikki Giovanni, and Haki Madhubuti (formerly Don L. Lee).

The Last Poets, a group of poets and musicians, and musician Gil Scott-Heron represented the revolutionary spoken-word arts genre in which their fiery poems about the disenfranchisement of black people were set to

Ntozake Shange, author and playwright, wrote and produced the groundbreaking choreopoem and Obie Award–winning play *For Colored Girls Who Have Considered Suicide When the Rainbow Is Enuf*.

The Jackson 5 were a staple of the Motown sound in the 1970s.

music. These early rappers, along with other creative figures in the Black Arts Movement, empowered many young African Americans to embrace their blackness and express themselves through the literary, visual, and performing arts.

Playwrights Ed Bullins, Ron Milner, and Ntozake Shange, and theatrical producers Barbara Ann Teer, Woodie King, and others were instrumental in the black theater wing of the movement.

Artist Tom Feelings and his wife, writer Muriel Feelings, published two books for children on African culture during this period, *Jambo Means Hello: A Swahili Alphabet Book* (1974) and *Moja Means One: A Swahili Counting Book* (1971), introducing young people to African life. These books also enabled young African American readers to see images of people who looked like them and to learn about their African heritage. Prior to the Black Arts Movement, there were very few, if any, books that celebrated African culture and history in a positive way for young readers. In their books, the couple combine beautiful illustrations with compelling stories for young people of all races.

Cultural institutions such as the Negro Ensemble Company (1967), the Studio Museum in Harlem (1968), and the Dance Theatre of Harlem (1969) were founded during the period as African Americans were searching for artistic freedom and acceptance. The New Federal Theatre (1970), the New Lafayette Theatre (1970), and Barbara Ann Teer's National Black Theatre (1970) offered performance space for plays, poetry readings, and concerts. Other black arts institutions were founded across the United States in the San Francisco Bay Area, including Oakland, as well as in Chicago and Detroit.

Music has always been an important part of the African American struggle. From the work songs sung by slaves to the songs of freedom performed at protest rallies to rap lyrics about social issues chanted by hip-hop artists, black music has included spirituals, blues, jazz, rock and roll, rhythm and blues, and hip-hop. Artists such as Mahalia Jackson, Ma Rainey, Billie Holiday, John Coltrane, Thelonious Monk, Miles Davis, the Temptations, Mary J. Blige, Beyoncé, Mariah Carey, Alicia Keys, Prince, and Jay-Z brought their extraordinary talents to a broad audience, providing a window into the experiences of African Americans. Whether singing about keeping the faith, not having a job, or about a failed romance, black music has always told a story to which many listeners related.

The Dance Theatre of Harlem performs *Concerto Barocco*, choreographed by George Balanchine, 1974.

Motown Record Corporation, an African American music company founded by Berry Gordy, Jr., in 1959, was at the forefront of the black music explosion in the 1960s. Gordy started Motown in Detroit, Michigan. He created a stable of singers, songwriters, and musicians, which included Stevie Wonder, Gladys Knight and the Pips, Marvin Gaye, Martha & the Vandellas, the Supremes, the Four Tops, the Temptations, Smokey Robinson & the Miracles, the Jackson 5, and the Shirelles. Later in the 1960s, Motown's influence as a successful engine of hit-making songs from black artists that appealed to both black and white audiences began to decline because the music did not keep up with the changing times and shied away from dealing with social issues in their lyrics. In 1972, Gordy moved the company from Detroit to Los Angeles, California, to make movies, leaving many artists in the Motown stable back in Detroit. Gordy sold Motown to Music Corporation of America (MCA) in 1988, and the company moved to New York City. Polygram acquired Motown in 1994 but was itself purchased by Seagram's in 1998, incorporating Motown into the Universal Music Group.

With Gordy in L.A., producer Norman Whitfield introduced a harder edge to the Motown sound. Beginning with hits like Marvin Gaye's "I Heard It Through the Grapevine" and Edwin Starr's "War," the company effectively moved away from its softer side. Gaye's "What's Going On" was another political anthem. This time his lyrics were about police brutality and riots during these troubled times. Gaye's lyrics illustrate the pain and suffering of the 1970s in the black community and the campaign for equality for blacks.

"What's Going On"

Mother, mother, there's too many of
   you crying
Brother, brother, brother, there's far
   too many of you dying
You know we've got to find a way
To bring some lovin' here today, hey

Father, father, we don't need to
   escalate
You see, war is not the answer, for
   only love can conquer hate
You know we've got to find a way
To bring some lovin' here today, oh

Picket lines—sister—and picket
   signs—sister
Don't punish me—sister—with
   brutality—sister
Talk to me—sister—so you can
   see—sister

Oh, what's goin' on—what's goin' on,
   what's goin' on—what's goin' on
Yeah, what's goin' on—what's goin' on,
   oh, what's goin' on—what's goin' on
Ah ah—ay-ay-ay-ay-ay—right on—
   right on—ay-ay-ay-ay-ay

(M. Gaye/A. Cleveland/R. Benson)
1971

AFRICAN AMERICANS ADVANCE

THIS PAGE: Congresswoman Shirley Chisholm flashes a victory sign at her campaign headquarters in Brooklyn, New York, November 1972. Chisholm was the first African American woman elected to Congress, in 1969. She retired in 1982.

PREVIOUS PAGE: *Stone of Hope*, part of the Martin Luther King, Jr., National Memorial on the Mall in Washington, D.C.

AFRICAN AMERICANS MADE great strides during the civil rights movement in the 1950s and 1960s, virtually rolling back the Jim Crow laws that had severely limited the rights of blacks. The successful outcome of the 1954 *Brown v. Board of Education* case made separate education for blacks and whites illegal. With the enactment of the Civil Rights Act of 1964, the Voting Rights Act of 1965, and the Civil Rights (Fair Housing) Act of 1968, blacks were guaranteed the right to be served at public accommodations and the right to equal employment, the right to vote, and the right to live where they wanted to.

The journey for African Americans has been a long and difficult one. From the slave ships of the Middle Passage to the abolition movement to the civil rights movement—the struggle has been constant. As the doors to equal opportunity opened in education, the voting booth, and housing, the next generation of African Americans became beneficiaries of the dream: to become participants in American society. Beginning in the 1970s, African Americans made significant inroads in politics and government, business, technology and science, sports, entertainment, and the arts. According to the U.S. Census Bureau, from 1970 to 2002 the number of black elected officials increased from 1,469 to 9,430.

AFRICAN AMERICAN ELECTED AND APPOINTED OFFICIALS

SHIRLEY CHISHOLM, A Democrat from Brooklyn, New York, became the first African American woman elected to the U.S. Congress, in 1968. In 1972, Chisholm became the first African American to seek the nomination for president of the United States. To date, a total of 132 African Americans have served in the U.S. Congress: 6 in the Senate and 126 in the House. The Congressional Black Caucus, an organization of elected black Congress members, was formed in 1971. By 1975, there were approximately 3,500 black elected officials in forty-five states. In 1991, Clarence Thomas became the second African American to be appointed to the U.S. Supreme Court, succeeding Justice Thurgood Marshall, the first black justice.

Since the Civil War only four African Americans have served as state governors. P. B. S. Pinchback, the acting lieutenant governor of Louisiana, became interim governor for thirty-five days after Governor Henry Clay Warmoth was brought up on impeachment charges in 1872. More than one hundred years would pass before another African American governor would be elected: L. Douglas Wilder, who was elected in Virginia in 1989. Deval Patrick was elected governor of Massachusetts in 2006, and David Paterson, the lieutenant governor of New York State, was appointed governor in 2008, after Eliot Spitzer resigned from office amid scandal.

Carl Stokes of Cleveland, Ohio, and Richard Hatcher of Gary, Indiana, were the first African Americans elected mayors of major U.S. cities, in 1967. They were followed by many more. Among them are Tom Bradley, Los Angeles; Coleman Young, Detroit; Ernest "Dutch" Morial, New Orleans; Harold Washington, Chicago; David Dinkins, New York City; Marion Barry, Washington, D.C.; Sharon Pratt-Kelly (the first African American woman elected to the office of mayor of a major American city), Washington, D.C.; Willie Brown, San Francisco; Sheila Dixon, Baltimore; Stephanie Rawlings-Blake, Baltimore; Marcus Knight, Lancaster, Texas; and Carson Ross, Blue Springs, Mississippi. Karen Freeman-Wilson was elected the first female African American mayor of Gary Indiana in November of 2011. She joins Cory Booker of Newark, New Jersey; Michael Nutter of Philadelphia, Pennsylvania; and Dave Bing of Detroit, Michigan, among the group of young black mayors leading major U.S. cities in the twenty-first century.

POWELL AND RICE

On the federal level, several African Americans were appointed to positions in the executive branch of the government. Ret. U.S. general Colin Powell, appointed by President George H. W. Bush, was the first African American chairman of the Joint Chiefs of Staff. In his role, Powell, a four-star general, became the highest-ranking military officer in the armed forces. His duties as chairman included advising the president, the National Security Council, the Department of Homeland Security, and the secretary of defense in matters of national security, and protecting the United States from military threats. The Harlem-born Powell served as chairman of the Joint Chiefs of Staff from 1989 to 1993, and in 2001, under President George W. Bush, he was appointed secretary of state, again becoming the first

African American to hold that position. Although Powell's military career was stellar, his career in government presented real challenges for him. As the spokesman for the Bush administration at a United Nations Security Council session, Powell was charged with the task of making a case for international support to invade Iraq because the Iraqis allegedly possessed weapons of mass destruction (WMD). His appearance at the U.N. was a low point in his career, because it was later determined that the information given to Powell by the Department of Defense and senior administration officials on Iraq's WMDs was based on inaccurate intelligence. Colin Powell resigned as secretary of state in 2004 and was replaced by Condoleezza Rice, the second African American to be appointed to the position and the first African American woman.

In an interview with the *Washington Times* on March 28, 2008, Condoleezza Rice, secretary of state and the highest-ranking African American in President George W. Bush's administration, spoke about the status of African Americans. "Black Americans were a founding population," Rice said. "Africans and Europeans came here and founded this country

LEFT: General Colin Powell served as the first African American chairman of the Joint Chiefs of Staff under President George H. W. Bush, and then went on to become, under President George W. Bush, the first African American secretary of state.

RIGHT: Condoleezza Rice was the first African American woman to become secretary of state and the second African American to hold the position, after Colin Powell.

together—Europeans by choice and Africans in chains. That's not a very pretty reality of our founding." She continued, "Descendants of slaves did not get much of a head start, and I think you continue to see some of the effects of that . . .That particular [national] birth defect makes it hard for us [Americans] to confront racism, hard for us to talk about it, and hard for us to realize that it has continuing relevance for who we are today."

Secretary Rice's comments emphasize how difficult it is for some to overcome racism, even in the twenty-first century, nearly 150 years since the end of the Civil War and more than 55 years after *Brown vs. Board of Education*. Recent incidents that illustrate the persistence of racial injustice include, in December 2006, six black high school students in Jena, Louisiana, being arrested and charged with attempted murder for beating up a white student after three nooses were found hanging from a tree in the schoolyard. The nooses, a reminder to African Americans of the lynchings of blacks by the Ku Klux Klan, appeared after a black student sat under a tree where only white students gathered.

Other incidents that have been attributed to race and that involved the police were the murders of Amadou Diallo in February 1999 and Sean Bell in November 2006. Amadou Diallo, a 23-year-old West African immigrant, was killed in the vestibule of his apartment building in February 1999 by four New York City police officers, who mistook the wallet in Diallo's hand for a gun. Five New York City police officers shot Bell and his companions after they left a bachelor party in celebration of Bell's marriage planned for the next day. In each case, all the officers involved were acquitted of murder.

AFRICAN AMERICAN CEOS

AS THE NATION entered the twenty-first century, in the business world, black chief executive officers became heads of Fortune 500 companies (the five hundred largest companies in the United States) in the fields of finance, media, retail, health insurance, technology, and energy. Prior to 2000, other African Americans who led the way in business include Robert L. Johnson, who founded Black Entertainment Television (BET), the first

Ursula M. Burns is the chairman and chief executive officer of Xerox Corporation.

Some African Americans Who Have Headed Major Corporations in the Twenty-First Century:

URSULA M. BURNS
Xerox Corporation

KENNETH CHENAULT
American Express Company

AYLWIN LEWIS
Sears Holding Corporation

E. STANLEY O'NEAL
Merrill Lynch

RODNEY O'NEAL
Delphi

CLARENCE OTIS
Darden Restaurants Inc.

RICHARD PARSONS
Time Warner

FRANKLIN RAINES
Fannie Mae

RONALD WILLIAMS
Aetna Inc.

black-controlled company to be listed on the New York Stock Exchange, and Reginald F. Lewis, considered a pioneer in leverage buyouts.

A graduate of Harvard Law School, Lewis and several colleagues established an African American law firm on Wall Street that specialized in corporate law, investments in minority-owned businesses, and served as counsel to corporations such as General Foods and Equitable Life. In 1983, Lewis formed TLC Group, L.P., and completed a $22.5 million leveraged buyout of the McCall Pattern Company, which he retooled into a leaner and more profitable corporation. He sold McCall in 1987 for $65 million, a ninety-to-one return on his investment. Following his financial success with the McCall buyout, Lewis purchased the international division of Beatrice Foods (sixty-four companies in thirty-one countries) in 1987 for $985 million with support from Drexel Burnham Lambert and investor Michael Milken. This was the largest offshore leveraged buyout by an American company. Lewis changed the name of his company to TLC Beatrice International, Inc., and reduced its debt, thereby increasing its net worth and making the company—with $1.5 billion in revenue—one of the Fortune 500. Reginald Lewis died in 1993 at the age of fifty.

AFRICAN AMERICANS ON THE CUTTING EDGE OF SCIENCE AND TECHNOLOGY

BLACK INVENTORS PUSHED the envelope of technology with their inventions in this century. Dr. Mark Dean, who has worked at IBM since the 1980s, created the ISA system bus, an interface that allows multiple devices, including a modem and printer, to be connected to a personal computer, or PC. He also holds three patents of IBM's original nine patents for the PC.

Lonnie G. Johnson, an inventor and former NASA engineer, invented the Super Soaker water gun in 1988 and sold it to a major toy company. The high-power squirt gun is considered one of the top twenty best-selling toys in the world. Johnson, whose idol was black inventor George Washington Carver, graduated in 1973 with an engineering degree and a master's in nuclear engineering in 1975 from Tuskegee Institute (now Tuskegee University), where Carver did his research as an agricultural scientist and inventor in the early 1900s. Johnson joined the Air Force and worked in the Strategic Air Command, where he helped develop the stealth bomber. As a systems engineer with the NASA (National Aeronautics and Space Administration) Jet Propulsion Laboratory, Johnson was part of the team working on the Galileo mission to Jupiter and the Cassini mission to Saturn. Johnson left the military and founded his own company, Johnson Research and Development, and holds eighty patents, and twenty pending, for inventions such as the ceramic battery, and for rollers that set the hair into curls without electric current. Johnson's latest project is the Johnson Thermoelectric Energy Converter (JTEC), which converts solar energy into electric energy at an extremely efficient rate. This invention could revolutionize the power grid by creating a clean, renewable source of energy by using solar energy instead of coal.

Another African American who contributed to space exploration at NASA was Charles F. Bolden, Jr. He was nominated by President Barack Obama and confirmed by the U.S. Senate as the administrator of NASA on July 17, 2009, the first African American to head that agency on a permanent basis. In NASA's Budget Summary for Fiscal Year 2012, Bolden describes the agency's future as "transitioning from an engineering focus on building the ISS [International Space Station] to an emphasis on research and technology development." The new NASA is inspiring students through science and technology competitions to pursue careers in earth science, aeronautics, and engineering. A retired major general of the U.S. Marine Corps, Bolden joined the NASA Astronaut Office in 1980 and traveled on four space shuttle missions between 1986 and 1994. He was the commander of two shuttle missions—the *Atlantis* and *Discovery*—and he piloted the *Columbia* in 1986 and the *Discovery* in 1990, from which his team deployed the Hubble Space Telescope. It was the first joint American-Russian shuttle mission to include a cosmonaut as a crew member.

Neil deGrasse Tyson is an astrophysicist and the Frederick P. Rose Director of the Hayden Planetarium in the Department of Astrophysics at the American Museum of Natural History in New York City. A graduate of Harvard and Columbia universities, Tyson has researched star formation, exploding stars, dwarf galaxies, and the structure of the Milky Way. The author of ten books on subjects such as the cosmos, black holes, and the controversy over the planetary status of Pluto, Tyson has written for dozens of professional publications, appeared on numerous television programs, and has been interviewed on the radio many times. He is the go-to expert on everything extraterrestrial and describes very complex theories about the universe in comprehensible terms. He currently hosts *StarTalk*, a radio program that brings science to a wider audience using celebrity guests.

Neil deGrasse Tyson is the recipient of the NASA Distinguished Public Service Medal, the highest award given by NASA to a nongovernment citizen, and he even had an asteroid named for him, 13123 Tyson, by the International Astronomical Union.

Charles F. Bolden, Jr., is the Administrator of the National Aeronautics and Space Administration (NASA). A former NASA astronaut and retired major general from the U.S. Marine Corps, Bolden was appointed to the position by President Barack Obama in 2009.

Muhammad Ali, formerly Cassius Clay, with supporters at the Armed Forces Examining and Entrance Station in Houston, Texas, 1967, after being stripped of his heavy-weight championship title for draft evasion because of religious reasons as well as opposition to the Vietnam War

BLACK ATHLETES
EXCEL IN THEIR FIELDS

SINCE THE MID-TWENTIETH century, African American athletes have broken records and won awards, bringing them and the African American community and its accomplishments to worldwide attention. They have been well represented in a number of athletic associations and leagues, from track and field (Evelyn Ashford, Michael Johnson, Jackie Joyner-Kersee, and Carl Lewis), to gymnastics (Dominique Dawes), basketball (Kobe Bryant, LeBron James, Cynthia Cooper, Earvin "Magic" Johnson, Michael Jordan, Lisa Leslie, and Teresa Weatherspoon), football (Jim Brown, Jerry Rice, and Michael Vick), and baseball (Barry Bonds and Derek Jeter). (Although mired in controversy over a steroids abuse case, Barry Bonds was not convicted or stripped of his awards, and he remains an all-time record holder and the recipient of many awards in Major League Baseball history.) At the

Manhattan borough president Hulan Jack and Mrs. Annie Gibson greet tennis champion Althea Gibson (center) at the airport in New York City. Althea became the first African American to win a major tennis tournament when she won the French Open in 1956.

2006 Winter Olympics, speed skater Shani Davis won a gold medal, making him the first African American to achieve that honor in an individual sport at the Olympic Winter Games. At times, the media spotlight also illuminated the issue of racism in America.

Muhammad Ali, three-time heavyweight champion of the world (1964, 1974, and 1978), was a trailblazer. As a conscientious objector and a member of the Nation of Islam, he refused to serve in the Vietnam War in 1966. (A conscientious objector is a person whose religious beliefs prevent him or her from fighting in wars.) Ali was stripped of his title and convicted of a felony for refusing to obey the draft. A U.S. Supreme Court decision in 1971 overturned Muhammad Ali's conviction. He regained his title in a match with champ Joe Frazier in 1974. Ali retired from the ring in 1981. In 1984, he was diagnosed with Parkinson's disease, a neurological disorder that affects motor function. Despite his disability, Muhammad Ali continues to pursue and fund humanitarian causes around the world. Ali's daughter, Laila Ali, made her boxing debut in 1999 and went on to win twenty-three more bouts. Laila was named the super middleweight champion by the International Boxing Association in 2002 and the super middleweight champion by the International Women's Boxing Federation in 2005.

Althea Gibson made her mark in tennis when she became the first African American to win the French Open (1956), Wimbledon (1957), and the

U.S. Open (1958). Arthur Ashe continued Gibson's legacy when he became the first African American to win the U.S. Open Men's Singles in 1968. Beginning in the late 1990s, the Williams sisters, Venus and Serena, burned up the courts winning Wimbledon, the Australian Open, the French Open, the U.S. Open, and other major tennis events with their one-hundred-plus-mile-per-hour serves.

The Olympics has been an important international arena where blacks have represented the United States of America. Wilma Rudolph became the first American woman to win three gold medals as a member of the U.S. Track Team, in the 1960 Summer Olympics held in Rome, Italy. At the 1968 Olympic Games in Mexico City, as track-and-field gold medalist Tommie Smith and bronze medalist John Carlos received their awards, they became the first athletes to protest racism in America on a world stage, when they raised their fists above their heads in a Black Power salute.

Track-and-field athlete Carl Lewis won four gold medals (100 meters, 200 meters, long jump, and the 400-meter relay) at the 1984 Olympics in Los Angeles. He won them in the same events that Jesse Owens did during the 1936 Olympics in Berlin. Lewis's wins from competing in the 1984, 1988, 1992, and 1996 Olympics earned him a total of one silver and nine gold medals.

One of the last racial barriers in sports for African Americans to break through was golf, not because blacks did not play the game, but because their race caused them to be banned from the country clubs, golf courses, and associations important to professional competition. Lee Elder (the first African American to play the Masters Tournament, in 1975), Charlie Sifford (the first African American to become a PGA Tour member, in 1960), and Ted Rhodes (who, with two other golfers, sued PGA for discrimination in 1948) were pioneers in the sport and paved the way for others.

Tiger Woods, the golf phenom who, at twenty-one years old, broke several records when he won the 1997 Masters Tournament in Augusta, Georgia, is a recipient of that legacy. He broke the tournament's 1965 record held by Jack Nicklaus by one stroke, becoming the youngest winner and the first African American winner. Tiger has gone on to win an unprecedented number of golf tournaments, setting a very high standard for his competitors. In 2005, he won six championships and was named the PGA Tour Player of the Year for the seventh time in nine years. Woods went on to win the Australian Masters in November 2009, but suffered setbacks in his personal life that resulted in a two-year career losing streak that included twenty-six tournaments without a win. In a comeback bid, Woods won the 2011 Chevron World Challenge, although not a PGA Tour event, in December of that year.

BLACK ENTERTAINMENT AND MEDIA

ENTERTAINMENT HAS BEEN an area where African Americans have thrived since the civil rights era, especially in the field of music. But black Americans have found it more difficult to make an impact in film and television. Before the 1970s, some exceptions were Academy Award–winner Hattie

The cast of *The Cosby Show* in the 1984–1985 season. The network television show was groundbreaking in its depiction of an affluent African American family.

McDaniel, who won for Best Supporting Actress in the 1939 film *Gone With the Wind*, and singer Nat King Cole (father to singer Natalie Cole), who was the first African American to host a network television show. *The Nat "King" Cole Show*, a variety program, aired on NBC-TV in 1956.

Although film and television programs featuring black actors increased during the Black Power Movement of the 1970s, some of the roles were still stereotypical. The actors played exaggerated caricatures of themselves or others, like the bug-eyed comedian Jimmie Walker, who played J.J. on *Good Times*, or comedian Flip Wilson, who appeared in drag as the character Geraldine on his comedy and variety program, *The Flip Wilson Show*. With *The Cosby Show* (1984–1992), a new awareness was born of who black people were and how they lived. The Huxtables, an upper-middle-class black family living in an urban setting with a father who was a doctor and a mother who was an attorney, broke new ground in how black families were perceived by white America.

Other programs followed *The Cosby Show* with more realistic characterizations of black life. *My Wife and Kids*, starring Damon Wayans, of the Wayans comedy dynasty, and Tisha Campbell-Martin, from the comedy *Martin* starring comedian Martin Lawrence, was a family sitcom in the *Cosby* style that premiered in 2001 and ended its run in 2005. And today, Malcolm-Jamal Warner, *Cosby* alum, and Tracee Ellis Ross, Diana Ross's daughter and the star of *Girlfriends*, are the leads in a family sitcom that deals with the everyday challenges facing all families—this just happens to be an African American family.

The extraordinarily successful talk show host and philanthropist Oprah Winfrey has created a media empire that includes *The Oprah Winfrey Show*, which aired for twenty-five years on network television; *O, The Oprah Magazine*; Harpo Productions, a company that makes TV movies and feature films; the Oprah Winfrey Network (OWN), a cable television network; and Oprah Radio, a channel on Sirius Satellite Radio. Oprah has extended her reach worldwide with her Angel Network, which helps people around the globe to live better lives, and through the Oprah Winfrey Leadership Academy for Girls in South Africa. The multiple Emmy Award–winning media executive and humanitarian has helped hundreds of thousands of people in the United States, too, including the victims of the catastrophic 2005 Hurricane Katrina, by helping rebuild neighborhoods in New Orleans and the Gulf States. Oprah also campaigned for a bill (signed into law in 1993 by President Bill Clinton) to establish a database of convicted child abusers.

Filmmaker Spike Lee has documented African American stories in his feature films *She's Gotta Have It*, *Jungle Fever*, *Do the Right Thing*, *School Daze*, and *Malcolm X*. Lee has also focused on major events in the African American community with the release of several films, including *Get on the Bus* in 1996, to mark the one-year anniversary of the Million Man March, which took place in Washington, D.C. The film follows a group of men on their trip from California to Washington to attend the march for unity, atonement, and brotherhood, organized by Minister Louis Farrakhan of the Nation of Islam, and portrays the discoveries they make about themselves and each other along the way. In 1997, Lee collaborated with HBO in the production of a feature-length documentary titled *4 Little Girls* about the 1963 church bombing in Birmingham. The film was nominated in 1997 for an Academy Award in the Best Documentary Feature category. In 2006, Lee also produced a four-part HBO documentary for the cable network, *When the Levees Broke: A Requiem in Four Acts*, about the devastation in New Orleans from Hurricane Katrina.

Spike Lee is an actor, director, producer, and screenwriter who examines race relations and other issues in his work.

In the 1970s, the emergence of hip-hop counteracted the activities of the local Bronx gangs like the Savage Nomads, the Savage Skulls, the Seven Immortals, the Black Spades, the Ghetto Brothers, and the Mongols. The decaying neighborhoods of the New York City borough were a hotbed of drugs and crime, and gangs arose as a means of protecting their South Bronx communities and controlling the illegal activities of heroin addicts. The gangs became defenders of their own turf and performed their own brand of justice. President Lyndon Johnson's Great Society agenda to fight poverty and crime and to create better communities through urban renewal and beautification programs was not working in the South Bronx or in other urban centers across the United States.

In 1974, former Black Spade gang leader Afrika Bambaata formed the Universal Zulu Nation (a group of graffiti artists, breakdancers, rappers, and DJs), which replaced their gang lifestyle with the cultural phenomenon know as hip-hop. Bambaata, who is widely credited for naming the movement, inspired gang members to exchange their weapons for rap lyrics, spawning competitive rap and dance performances that became cultural showdowns, and street art that turned subways, abandoned buildings, and walls into canvases. The person who was instrumental in pioneering the hip-hop sound was DJ Kool Herc, also known as Clive Campbell, who hosted dance parties with his sister in the recreation room of their apartment building at 1520 Sedgwick Avenue in the Bronx. Herc's trademark move featured him on two turntables, spinning (playing) two copies of the same record. He would isolate the break (the place in a song where the music shifts into a different register) on one record and, when it reached the end, start the second record at the beginning of the break, extending that section of the song even longer. Break-dancers would showcase their acrobatic moves, each one trying to outdo the other as MCs took to the mike with their own special brand of rhyme. As the parties grew in popularity, they were moved outside to local parks, where DJs hooked up their turntables to outdoor power supplies.

Rappers emerged as ghetto poets delivering their poems or improvised lyrics in rhyme and to the beat. Rapping refers to the words or rhymes accompanying the music played by the DJ. A rap is the creative delivery of topics, ranging from social issues to politics, in a definite rhyming pattern overlaying the beats. The word *rap* reemerged during the Black Power Movement in the 1960s. This form of expression also evolved from the African oral tradition, Jamaican-style "toasting" (talking over music), and the language of the jazz musicians popularized in Harlem Renaissance poems, particularly those by Langston Hughes. Gangsta rap, which deals with violence in the inner city and includes lyrics about drug dealing, drive-by shootings, and making money illegally, has been criticized by the mainstream for its sometimes obscene and misogynistic lyrics.

Other important contributors to music include Grandmaster Flash, who introduced "back spinning" (playing the record backward) and "phasing" (the aligning of two tracks, so when one track ends the other track continues without a break in the music), while Grand Wizard Theodore

Grandmaster Flash spins the vinyl during a game between the Cleveland Cavaliers and the New York Knicks at Madison Square Garden, November 6, 2009.

Donna Summer, known as the Queen of Disco in the 1970s

popularized the method known as "scratching" (moving the record back and forth on the turntable to create a scratching sound with the needle).

By the end of the 1970s, the music industry was primed for this new era. Record sales of disco—dance music that started in New York City in the 1960s with rhythmic, long-playing songs that had a repetitive beat— had been declining. Manu Dibango's "Soul Makossa" (1972) and Donna Summer's "Love to Love You Baby" (1975) had dominated the 1970s discotheque scene at clubs like Studio 54 and the black-owned Leviticus in Manhattan. Hip-hop replaced the disco craze. The Sugarhill Gang is credited with the first hip-hop single, "Rapper's Delight," in 1979. Early hip-hop artists include Kurtis Blow, Chuck D, Mos Def, Doug E. Fresh, LL Cool J, and the female group Salt-N-Pepa. The hip-hop industry has expanded and crossed over to a larger, more commercial audience with impresarios Russell Simmons; P. Diddy; Jay-Z; and record executives Damon Dash, L. A. Reid, and Jermaine Dupri. African American artists, including Rihanna, Nicki Minaj, Lil Wayne, Mary J. Blige, Drake, the Black Eyed Peas with will.i.am, Beyoncé, Chris Brown, and Kanye West, continue to top the charts with their innovative music.

PART **VIII**

AFRICAN AMERICANS TODAY

THIS PAGE: President Barack Obama with his wife, Michelle, daughters, Sasha and Malia, and mother-in-law, Marian Robinson, at the 2010 National Christmas Tree Lighting Ceremony on December 9 at the Ellipse, south of the White House, Washington, D.C.

PREVIOUS PAGE: President Barack Obama speaks to a group of supporters at the Downtown Marriott in Kansas City, Missouri, in 2008 during his presidential campaign.

AMERICANS STILL HAVE a ways to go toward understanding one another, but a giant step was taken in 2008. Although the United States remains an imperfect union, a major shift occurred on November 4 when an overwhelming number of voters—young, old, black, white, Hispanic, Asian, both male and female—cast their ballots to elect Illinois senator Barack Obama as the first African American president of the United States of America.

PRESIDENT BARACK OBAMA

SOME OBSERVERS REGARDED the election of Obama as evidence that most American voters are now more influenced by a candidate's political platform than by his or her racial identity. More than 62 percent of registered voters cast their ballots in the election, the majority being Democrats. At polls around the country, there were two-, three-, and even eight-hour waits.

This historic election was preceded by a feverish campaign in which Democratic contender Barack Obama, who opted out of the public financing for his campaign and was therefore not limited in his fund-raising efforts, raised an astounding 600 million dollars. He also created an impressive ground campaign of hundreds of thousands of volunteers who knocked on doors, telephoned potential voters, and, if needed, drove voters to and from the polls on Election Day.

In contrast, his rival, Republican candidate John McCain, was limited to 85 million dollars in public financing and funding from the Republican National Committee, bringing his total to about 250 million dollars. Having a smaller campaign fund put McCain at a huge disadvantage in advertising, in staffing, and in building an extensive ground operation to get out the voters in key states.

Barack Obama also changed traditional campaigning by using the Internet to solicit funds in amounts as small as five dollars, which added up to considerable sums. He also made it easy for volunteers to use the

Internet as a tool to call undecided voters in battleground states, host fundraising events, and connect with other volunteers in the same community to coordinate get-out-the-vote activities. The Obama campaign was also extremely tech-savvy. The campaign used social networking sites such as Facebook, Myspace, YouTube, and BlackPlanet as well as blogs to communicate the candidate's message of "Change You Can Believe In" and his mantra of "Yes We Can" to voters. The campaign also used other forms of media, including a thirty-minute infomercial broadcast on major networks a few days before the election and innovative strategies using satellite television and cell phones. His campaign even text-messaged his supporters with Obama's pick for vice president, Delaware senator Joseph Biden, before the news was announced to the national media.

Obama faced many challenges in his campaign. First, he was up against former First Lady Hillary Clinton, a white woman and a fellow Democrat, whose husband, Bill Clinton, had been president from 1993 to 2001. The long and bitter primary campaign between the two was tinged with racism, sexism, and accusations from both sides ranging from elitism, dishonesty, and lack of integrity. Barack Obama won the primary and became the Democratic Party's nominee, then went on to win the general election.

In the end, the American people were decisive in their selection of Barack Obama for their president and were given the opportunity to reflect on the history of African Americans in general and Barack Obama's unique history in particular. The son of a white mother from Kansas and an African father from Kenya, he was raised by his white grandparents in Hawaii. Obama said during the keynote address at the 2004 Democratic National Convention, the year he sought his first term in the United States Senate, "I stand here knowing that my story is part of the larger American story . . . and that, in no other country on earth, is my story even possible."

In Philadelphia, on March 18, 2008, not long before the presidential Pennsylvania primary slated for April 22, 2008, Obama addressed the issue of race in America more directly in response to the firestorm created by incendiary remarks made by his then pastor Reverend Jeremiah Wright. In a sermon he gave on race in America, Reverend Wright made remarks that were interpreted by Hillary Clinton and others as preaching a hatred of America, raising questions about whether Barack Obama shared his pastor's beliefs.

In his speech, Obama took the opportunity to educate people about the history of African Americans in the United States and to distance himself from Reverend Wright's angry words. He began with the words of the Constitution: "We, the people, in order to form a more perfect union," and went on to say:

> *The document they produced was eventually signed but ultimately unfinished. It was stained by this nation's original sin of slavery...*
>
> *This was one of the tasks we set forth at the beginning of this campaign—to continue the long march of those who came before us, a march for a more just, more equal, more free, more caring and more prosperous America.*
>
> *I chose to run for the presidency at this moment in history because I believe deeply that we cannot solve the challenges of our time unless we solve them together—unless we perfect our union by understanding that we may have different stories, but we hold common hopes; that we may not look the same and we may not have come from the same place, but we all want to move in the same direction—towards a better future for our children and our grandchildren...*

President Barack Obama's time in the Oval Office has been extremely challenging for the Democratic president, whose political agenda has been repeatedly blocked by a Republican Congress determined to make him a one-term president. Nevertheless, President Obama's administration—faced with a slow economy, staggering unemployment, and a decimated housing market—has been able to implement many new policies on the national front, including health care reform, student loan reform, an economic stimulus bill, loans to automakers to stimulate jobs, and the restructuring of financial regulations. On the international front, President Obama has withdrawn American troops from Iraq, reduced the number of American troops in Afghanistan, ordered the assassination of Osama Bin Laden, and supported, with American allies, the overthrow of Muammar Gaddafi, the Libyan dictator.

The flag of the United States, "whose broad stripes and bright stars" represent all Americans

CONCLUSION

The election of Barack Obama was a watershed moment in American history that many African Americans did not expect to see in their lifetimes. Almost four hundred years after the first Africans were brought to Jamestown, Virginia, to build a new country, a majority of registered voters in this country was able to see beyond race, to the future.

THE JOURNEY FOR African Americans has been painful and complex, and the ability to overcome these daunting obstacles is something to celebrate. A race of people numbering in the millions were kidnapped from their homeland, held in bondage, forced to live and work in a foreign environment, and forbidden to learn to read and write—it is a magnificent feat to survive all those challenges. With the election of Barack Obama, more people than ever have developed an interest in discovering black America and its history and culture. This broadening interest in African Americans opens up many possibilities for all of us to discover more about one another and about our histories and cultures. Perhaps in getting to know all of our stories, a greater understanding and knowledge will help us find that we are more alike than we are different.

Discovering Your Own History

AFRICAN AMERICANS HAVE long been interested in finding out who they are and where they came from. Unlike some Americans who can trace their lineage with the help of historical records and documents, it has been more difficult for African Americans, who were taken from their families during the slave trade. Now several companies are offering DNA testing to trace the genealogical ancestry of African Americans. For people who have more information about their kinships, the use of research on the Internet, photographs, birth certificates, and census records can lead to fascinating discoveries. Wilbur Jones is an example of this type of discovery.

WILBUR JONES SEARCHES FOR HIS ROOTS

Spurred on by the groundbreaking ABC-TV 1977 miniseries *Roots*, which was based on the best-selling book by Alex Haley published in 1976, millions of African Americans began searching for their connection to their own African ancestors.

Wilbur Jones, a seventy-five-year-old human resources consultant, was also curious. In an interview Jones stated, "I was very interested in black history as a young man, and I was always trying to define black as it related to me, more than what I was getting from the textbooks. I wanted to find out about blacks in the United States; I wanted to find out about blacks in Africa."

Jones's family began holding reunions in 1983, and they continue to this day, on a biannual basis. The reunions are held in Hartford, Connecticut, and include his mother's side of the family, the Jacksons, and his father's side of the family, the Joneses. Both families, which are present in recorded history after the Civil War, lived in the neighboring counties of Schley and Sumter in southwestern Georgia. A large contingent of both families migrated to Connecticut in the 1920s.

The reunions bring together family from near and far, and the stories flow. Passed down from generation to generation, bits and pieces of history have emerged. And one of those stories, told over and over again, was about Nancy Carter, Jones's great-great-grandmother on his mother's side, and the family's connection to Jimmy Carter of Plains, Georgia, the thirty-ninth president of the United States. As the family legend goes, Nancy Carter had been born in Virginia, and was "sold south" as a slave and ended up in Georgia.

She was a slave on Wiley Carter's plantation in Plains, Georgia. Wiley Carter was President Jimmy Carter's great-great-grandfather. Jones's great-great-grandmother, Nancy Carter, was one of the slaves listed in the probate of Wiley Carter's will. According to the probate, Nancy Carter and her children were "sold" to the designated heirs of Wiley Carter—his wife and his children. Nancy had a daughter named Celie.

Wilbur Jones's quest for more information about his family began on the Internet. He accessed sites specializing in genealogy and found census records that listed family members. "With the Carter family, for example, I knew my mother was Mabel Jackson, her mother was Ida Blanch, her mother was Celie Carter, and her mother was Nancy Carter," explained Jones about tracing his maternal descent line.

Mr. Jones also researched President Carter's family background and found census records that listed the number of slaves on Carter's great-great-grandfather's plantation, but not their names. "I found the records for Wiley Carter in 1850 and in 1860. On those slavery listings, I found a mulatto woman, who would have been Nancy Carter, my great-great-grandmother. That would have been Celie's mother." Other family members were helping Jones's research, and his cousin Eugene found an article in a newspaper in a library in Americus, Georgia. "The article stated that Wiley Carter had brought my great-great-grandmother, Nancy Carter, from Virginia. And that she remained a faithful retainer of the Carter family after the Civil War," explained Jones. "That was the article that I was looking for that shows the connection between President Jimmy Carter of Plains, Georgia, and my family."

Wilbur Jones wrote a letter to President Carter telling him about his discoveries. Jimmy Carter wrote back and invited Jones to Plains to compare their research. "I drove up the road to his ranch-style house. The President was out on the porch to greet me; he was very casually dressed, no socks, just moccasins. I was very nervous, but he was very kind and welcoming," said Jones. "We met for over an hour discussing our families. President Carter proceeded to bring out the documentation that he had talked about in his letter. It was Wiley Carter's will. He showed me a list of slaves, and on the list was Nancy Carter, my great-great-grandmother, and her daughter Celie Carter. There were three or four people listed with Nancy who I recognized as her children."

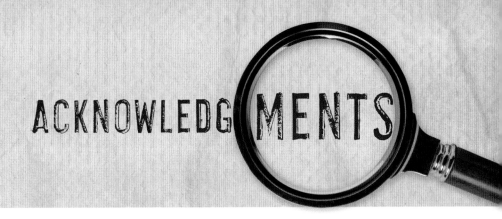

ACKNOWLEDGMENTS

I WOULD LIKE to convey my deepest gratitude and thanks to the wonderful people at Abrams Books who worked long and hard to make *Discovering* a reality: Howard Reeves, my editor, for understanding and appreciating where I wanted to go. Your patience and guidance have been invaluable. To the rest of the team at Abrams—Jenna Pocius (who was tireless in her dedication to this project), Brett Wright, Scott Auerbach, Maria Middleton, Alissa Faden, and Jennifer Graham—thanks so much for your diligence and attention to the details of my book.

For assisting me with my early research of the Jamestown Settlement, my thanks to historian Nancy Egloff at the Jamestown–Yorktown Foundation in Jamestown, Virginia. Special appreciation and love to my traveling companion to Jamestown, my sister, Gale Colden, who passed away in 2009. Also thanks to Shira Kalman-Hicks for helping with the research in the early stages of the book.

Special thanks to Tonya Bolden for our uplifting chats and support during the process of completing my book. To Donald Bogle, my dear, dear friend who acknowledges me in all of his books, so one good turn deserves another, thank you, Donald. To Angela Cox, my longtime friend and colleague, thank you for being a great listener and a great friend. And to Marie Brown, I really appreciate all of your love and support during each and every one of my projects. And to my family, especially my husband, Stuart, and my children, Siad and Gibwa, thank you for helping me achieve my dream. I love you guys.

NOTES

PAGE #

I. EXPLORATION OF THE NEW WORLD AND SETTLEMENTS IN COLONIAL AMERICA

3   *Prince Henry of Portugal... establishing Portuguese colonies.* Charles Johnson, Patricia Smith, and the WGBH Series Research Team, *Africans in America: America's Journey through Slavery* (New York: Houghton Mifflin Harcourt, 1998), 5.

3–4   *The first such European structure... between Africans and Europeans.* Ibid, 6.

4   *"Some served in royal courts... tenant farmers."* "Slavery in Africa," Digital History, accessed January 6, 2012, http://www.digitalhistory.uh.edu/database/article_display. cfm?HHID=64.

The Black Explorers

4   *Pedro Alonzo (Alonso) Niño... to the New World.* African American World Timeline, accessed January 6, 2012, http://www.pbs.org/wnet/aaworld/timeline/early_01.html, and "Did Your Family Sail with Columbus?," originally published in *Vista* (July 7, 1991), reproduced on the Florida Museum of Natural History Web site, accessed January 6, 2012, http://www.flmnh.ufl.edu/caribarch/columbus.htm.

4–5   *Juan Las Canarias... on the* Santa María. Madeleine Burnside, "Marooned: Africans in the Americas 1500–1750," accessed January 6, 2012, http://www.kislakfoundation.org/millennium-exhibit/burnside1.htm.

5   *Esteban Gómez... what is now New York City.* Ira Berlin and Leslie M. Harris, eds., *Slavery in New York* (New York: The New Press, published in conjunction with the New-York Historical Society, 2005, exhibition catalog), 33.

5   *On Juan Garrido.* Amy Howard, "Juan Garrido: African Conquistador," St. Augustine tourism Web site, accessed January 6, 2012, http://www.augustine.com/history/black_history/juan_garrido/index.php.

5–7   *On Estevanico, an enslaved black Moor.* "African Explorers of Spanish America," *NPS Ethnography*, accessed December 23, 2011, http://www.nps.gov/history/ethnography/aah/aaheritage/SpanishAmb.htm, and "Events in the West from 1500 to 1650," *PBS: The West*, accessed December 23, 2011, http://www.pbs.org/weta/thewest/events/1500_1650.htm.

5–7   *On Estevanico, his early life and journey to America.* Kitty Morse, "Esteban of Azemmour and His New World Adventures," *Saudi Aramco World* 53, no. 2 (March/April 2002), 2–9, accessed December 23, 2011, http://www.saudiaramcoworld.com/issue/200202/esteban.of.azemmour.and.his.new.world.adventures.htm, and Donald E. Chipman, "Estevanico," Texas State Historical Association, *The Handbook of Texas Online*, accessed January 6, 2012, www.tshaonline.org/handbook/online/articles/EE/fes8.html. *The Handbook of Texas Online* is a joint project of the University of Texas Libraries (http://www.lib.utexas.edu) and the Texas State Historical Association (http://www.tshaonline.org).

6   *"Estevanico's abilities... rather than slave."* Alvar Núñez Cabeza de Vaca, translated by Cyclone Covey, *The Journey and Ordeal of Cabeza de Vaca: His Account of the Disastrous First European Exploration of the American Southwest* (Mineola, NY: Dover Publications, 2003), 92.

6   *"[Estevanico] was wearing... a blessing."* Morse, "Esteban of Azemmour and His New World Adventures."

7   *When Estevanico arrived... trying to escape.* Ibid, 2–9.

Additional sources on Estevanico and his journey are from the "joint report" of Cabeza de Vaca, Andrés Dorantes de Carranza, and Alonso de Castillo Maldonado; Cabeza de Vaca, *The Journey and Ordeal*; and Madeleine Turrell Rodack, trans. and ed., *Adolph F. Bandelier's The Discovery of New Mexico by the Franciscan Monk Friar Marcos de Niza in 1539* (Tucson: University of Arizona Press, 1981). Original documentary sources have been used to construct a narrative of Estevanico's adventures in John Upton Terrell, *Estevanico the Black* (Los Angeles: Westernlore Press, 1968), which served as the basis for this account. Terrell includes an extensive bibliography of the original sources and selected secondary sources that discuss the role of Estevanico.

Jamestown, the First Surviving British Colony

8   *On the capture of the earliest documented Africans.* John Thornton, "Notes and Documents: The African Experience of the '20. and Odd Negroes' Arriving in Virginia in 1619," *William and Mary Quarterly* 55, no. 3 (July 1998): 422–434, and Martha W. McCartney et al., *A Study of the Africans and African Americans on Jamestown Island and at Green Spring, 1619–1803* (Williamsburg, VA: National Park Service/The Colonial Williamsburg Foundation, 2003).

8   *On the number of Africans brought to Jamestown in 1619.* Kingsbury, *Records*, 3:243, and Lyon Gardiner Tyler, ed., *Narratives of Early Virginia* (New York: Scribner, 1907), 337.

10   *"About the latter end... easiest rate they could."* Sluiter, Engel, "New Light on the '20. and Odd Negroes' Arriving in Virginia, August 1619, *William and Mary Quarterly* 54, no. 2 (April 1997): 395–398, and Susan M. Kingsbury, *Records of the Virginia Company of London, 1606–1626* (Washington, DC: Government Printing Office, 1906–35), 3:243.

11   *On Angelo's journey to the Jamestown Colony.* McCartney, et al., *A Study of the Africans and African Americans on Jamestown Island and at Green Spring, 1619–1803.* Further information from *Adventurers of Purse and Person, VIRGINIA 1607–1624/5*, 3rd ed., revised and edited by Virginia M. Meyer and John Frederick Dorman, F.A.S.G. (Richmond: Order of First Families of Virginia, 1987).

12   *On the Africans' shared culture and identity helping them adapt to the Jamestown environment.* Thornton, "Notes and Documents: The African Experience of the '20. and Odd Negroes' Arriving in Virginia, August 1619," 431–433, and "Africans in the Chesapeake," *NPS Ethnography*, accessed December 23, 2011, http://www.nps.gov/history/ethnography/aah/aaheritage/ChesapeakeA.htm.

Free Black Planters

13   On the free blacks of Virginia living in Northampton County

as property owners and planters in the mid 1660s. Ibid., 83. This population was able to free themselves from their indentures or from servitude as "slaves" by satisfying their terms as indentured servants or purchasing their freedom. Many free blacks married, prospered, and had families.

13   On the Africans listed in Northampton county records. Breen and Innes, *Myne Owne Ground*, 69.

A Family Named Johnson

13-4   On Anthony and Mary Johnson. "Antonio, the Negar" appears in the 1625 census as a servant in the Bennett household. "Mary a Negro woman," from T.H. Breen and Stephen Innes, *"Myne Owne Ground": Race and Freedom on Virginia's Eastern Shore, 1640–1676* (New York: Oxford University Press, 1980), 8–10. Court records from Northampton County, 1651–1654, ibid., 16–19, and Carol Berkin, *First Generations: Women in Colonial America* (New York: Hill and Wang/Farrar, Straus and Giroux, 1996), 103–109.

14   *"make a sizable claim"* "The Practise of Slavery," *Virtual Jamestown*, accessed December 23, 2011, http://www.virtualjamestown.org/practise.html.

14   *John Jr. married . . . in Somerset County, Maryland.* Ryan Charles Cox, "The Johnson Family: The Migratory Study of an African-American Family on the Eastern Shore," Edward H. Nabb Research Center for Delmarva History & Culture, accessed January 26, 2012, http://nabbhistory.salisbury.edu/settlers/profiles/johnson5.html.

Dutch New Amsterdam

15   *"Company slaves"* Berlin and Harris, eds., *Slavery in New York*, 31.

15   *Based on some . . . Angola, the Congo, and Portugal.* Ibid., 31–32.

15   *"The Company's slaves acted . . . white workers."* Ibid., 37.

15   On the use of Company Negroes in conflicts with Native Americans. Ibid., 42.

16   On the "half-freedom" granted the Company Negroes of the Dutch West India Company in 1640s by Director William Kieft. Ibid., 42–45.

Chattel Slavery

18   *"negro named John Punch . . . here or elsewhere."* Breen and Innes, *Myne Owne Ground*, 28.

18   *"mortgaged, inherited . . . from the land."* David Brion Davis, *Slavery in Colonial Chesapeake* (Williamsburg, VA: The Colonial Williamsburg Foundation, 1986), 5.

18   On indentured servitude. Ibid., 7.

18   *"There were several reasons . . . jobs and wages."* Ibid., 7.

19   *"Indentured servants . . . white servants."* Ibid., 7.

II. SLAVERY

23   On the importation of African slaves to the Americas from 1700 to the early 1800s. Colin A. Palmer, ed., *Encyclopedia of African-American Culture and History*, Vol. 5, 2nd ed. (New York: Macmillan Reference, 2005), 2062–2063.

23   *"By the 1560s . . . Africans also increased."* Davis, *Slavery in Colonial Chesapeake*, 2.

23   *"The need for slave labor . . . agriculture required."* Ibid., 2.

24   *"8,000 to 45,000 annually . . . 18,000 slaves a year."* Johnson, et al., *Africans in America*, 47.

24   On the Atlantic slave trade and triangular trade routes. "Black Presence: Britain and the Trade," National Archives and Records Administration, accessed January 8, 2012, http://www.nationalarchives.gov.uk/pathways/blackhistory/africa_caribbean/britain_trade.htm.

Slave Society in Colonial America

26   *"Sequences of Legal Maneuvers . . . in Virginia"* William Waller Hening, *Hening's Statutes, Being a Collection of All the Laws of Virginia from the First Session of the Legislature, in the Year 1619* (Richmond: W.W. Gray, 1819).

28   *"all Negroes, Mulattoes, and Indians"* James Oliver Horton and Lois E. Horton, *Slavery and the Making of America* (New York: Oxford University Press, 2005), 32.

Slave Verse and Narratives: In Their Own Words

28-9   On Phillis Wheatley. "Phillis Wheatley," The Massachusetts Historical Society, accessed January 8, 2012, http://www.masshist.org/endofslavery/?queryID=57.

29-30   *"One day . . . a large sack."* Olaudah Equiano, *The Interesting Narrative of the Life of Olaudah Equiano, or Gustavas Vassa, the African*, 9th ed. (London: printed by the author, 1794), 17.

31   *"I had objected . . . three hundred dollars."* Harriet Jacobs, *Incidents in a Life of A Slave Girl* (Mineola, NY: Dover Publications, 2001), 163.

Educating the Enslaved

33-4   On the Reverend Alexander Garden starting a school for slave children in South Carolina in 1743. Kimberly Sambol-Tosco, "The Slave Experience: Education, Arts, & Culture," *Slavery and the Making of America*, accessed January 8, 2012, http://www.pbs.org/wnet/slavery/experience/education/history2.html.

33   *"Learning a skill . . . Garden's School."* Walter B. Edgar, *South Carolina: A History* (Columbia, SC: University of South Carolina, 1998), 176.

34   *"to Catechize and Instruct . . . Jesus Christ."* Thelma Wills Foote, *Black and White Manhattan: The History of Racial Formation in Colonial New York* (New York: Oxford University Press, 2004), 128–129.

35   On Primus Hall and the Abiel Smith School. "Abiel Smith School," National Park Service, accessed December 23, 2011, http://www.nps.gov/boaf/historyculture/abiel-smith-school.htm.

Early Black Churches

36 On the Silver Bluff Church. Walter H. Brooks, "The Priority of the Silver Bluff Church and its Promoters," *Journal of Negro History* 7, no. 2 (April 1922), 172–196, and Karen Ruffle, "Walter H. Brooks," *Documenting the American South*, accessed January 8, 2012, http://docsouth.unc.edu/church/brooks/summary.html.

36 *"regular pastor . . . David George [ca. 1742–1810]."* Robert J. Priest and Alvaro L. Nieves, ed., *This Side of Heaven: Race, Ethnicity, and Christian Faith* (New York: Oxford University Press, 2007), 118.

Blacks in the Revolutionary War

38 *"10 pound reward . . . on penalty of law."* "Crispus Attucks (1723–1770), framingham.com, accessed January 8, 2012, http://www.framingham.com/history/profiles/crispus.

39 *"That your Petitioners apprehend . . . agreement whatever."* "The Struggle for Freedom," The Massachusetts Historical Society, accessed January 8, 2012, http://www.masshist.org/endofslavery/?queryID=55.

40 *Peter Salem of Framingham . . . at Concord.* Gail Buckley, *American Patriots: The Story of Blacks in the Military from the Revolution to Desert Storm* (New York: Random House, 2001), 8.

40 "The Battle of Lexington." James G. Basker, ed. *Amazing Grace: An Anthology of Poems About Slavery, 1660–1810* (New Haven: Yale University Press, 2002), 231, and Buckley, *American Patriots*, 8–9.

41 On the black Minutemen who fought alongside Peter Salem during the American Revolution in Boston. Buckley, *American Patriots*, 11–12, and "African Americans in the Revolutionary Period," *The American Revolution*, accessed December 23, 2011, http://www.nps.gov/revwar/about_the_revolution/african_americans.html.

42 On the number of enslaved African Americans before the American Revolution and the number who served. "African Americans in the Revolutionary Period," *The American Revolution*.

Black Patriots Who Fought for Independence

42-3 On Prince Hall. "Bill of Sale for drumheads, Prince Hall to Boston Regiment," *Africans in America*, accessed January 8, 2012, http://www.pbs.org/wgbh/aia/part2/2h44.html and "African Americans and the End of Slavery in Massachusetts," *The Massachusetts Historical Society*, http://www.masshist.org/endofslavery/?queryID=53.

43 *fortifications at Castle Island in Boston Harbor* William C. Nell, *The Colored Patriots of the American Revolution with Sketches of Several Distinguished Colored Persons, to Which Is Added a Brief Survey of the Condition and Prospects of Colored Americans*, introduction by Harriet Beecher Stowe (Reprint, New York: Arno Press, 1968), 29.

43-4 On Prince Whipple and his journey to America. Ibid., 16.

44 On Caesar Tarrant, a slave from Hampton, Virginia. Buckley, *American Patriots*, 28.

44 On land in Ohio granted to Caesar Tarrant's daughter. Ibid., 28.

45 On Joseph Ranger. Burke Davis, *Black Heroes of the American Revolution* (Boston: Sandpiper/Harcourt, 1976), 20.

45 *"[H]e had fired eight times . . . our breastwork [barriers]."* *Virginia Gazette*, December 13, 1775, an extract from a letter from Colonel Woodford to Edmond Pendleton, Esquire, president of the Convention about the Battle of Great Bridge, on the bravery of William Flora in defeating the British.

45 On James Forten. Buckley, *American Patriots*, 29. More information can be found at "James Forten Historical Marker," ExplorePAHistory.com, accessed January 8, 2012, http://explorepahistory.com/hmarker.php?markerId=1-A-28C, in Davis, *Black Heroes of the American Revolution*, 23–26, and at Scott A. Miltenberger, "Forten, James," *Encyclopedia of African American History, 1619–1895: From the Colonial Period to the Age of Frederick Douglass*, edited by Paul Finkelman, *Oxford African American Studies Center*, accessed January 8, 2012, http://www.oxfordaasc.com/article/opr/t0004/e0213.

46 *"as a tribute to their courage and devotion in the cause of American Liberty."* Nell, *The Colored Patriots*, 24–25.

46 *"every able-bodied negro, mulatto . . . into this service."* and *"the service of his master . . . of slavery."* Nell, *The Colored Patriots*, 50–51.

46-7 On the First Rhode Island's Battle at Pine's Bridge. Lincoln Diamant, "When a Black Unit Battled the British," *The New York Times*, May 12, 1996.

47 On the disbanding of the First Rhode Island Regiment. Note: The First Rhode Island Regiment was disbanded at Saratoga, New York, in 1783. Gretchen A. Adams, "'Deeds of Desperate Valor': The First Rhode Island Regiment," *The American Revolution: National Discussions of Our Revolutionary Origins*, accessed January 26, 2012, http://revolution.h-net.msu.edu/essays/adams2.html.

47 On Parting Ways. "Parting Ways," Plymouth County Web site, accessed January 8, 2012, http://www.seeplymouth.com/partingways.htm, and Parting Ways Museum of Afro-American EthnoHistory, accessed January 8, 2012, http://www.partingways.org.

Fighting for the Loyalist Cause

48-9 On Lord Dunmore's Ethiopian regiment. Lt. Colonel Michael Lee Lanning, U.S. Army (Ret.), *African Americans in the Revolutionary War,* New York: Citadel Press, 2000, 50–59.

49 On Colonel Tye and the Black Brigade. "Colonel Tye," *Africans in America*, accessed January 8, 2012, http://www.pbs.org/wgbh/aia/part2/2p52.html, and Jonathan D. Sutherland, *African Americans at War: An Encyclopedia* (Santa Barbara, CA: ABC-CLIO, 2004), 420–421.

Patriot Spies

50 On James Armistead Lafayette. Davis, *Black Heroes of the American Revolution*, 53–60.

52 On Saul Matthews. Ibid., 57–58.

52–3 On Samuel Fraunces. Charles L. Blockson, "Black Samuel Fraunces: Patriot, White House Steward and Restaurateur Par Excellence," accessed December 23, 2011, http://library.temple.edu/collections/blockson/fraunces.jsp.

54 *"an estimated 75,000 . . . left the 13 states."* Bob Blythe, "The Odyssey of the Black Loyalists," *The Unfinished Revolution,* accessed January 8, 2012, http://www.nps.gov/revwar/unfinished_revolution/black_loyalists.html.

54 "One corps of black drummers . . . the Sierra Leone colony." Buckley, *American Patriots,* 35.

54 On *The Book of Negroes.* "Book Three of the Book of Negroes," *Black Loyalists: Our History, Our People,* accessed December 23, 2011, www.blackloyalist.com/canadiandigitalcollection/documents/official/black_loyalist_directory_book_three.htm.

Blacks in the War of 1812

55 *"One-sixth of the U.S. Navy . . . September 11, 1814."* Buckley, *American Patriots,* 46.

57 *"black second lieutenants . . . Santo Domingo army."* Ibid., 48–49.

Slave Rebellions, Revolts, and Insurrections

57 On Maiden Lane incident. Lorraine B. Diehl, "Skeletons in the Closet: Uncovering the Rich History of the Slaves of New York," *New York,* October 5, 1992, 78–86.

61 *"If John Brown did not end . . . arms was at hand."* "Frederick Douglass at Harpers Ferry," National Park Service, accessed January 8, 2012, http://www.nps.gov/hafe/historyculture/frederick-douglass-at-harpers-ferry.htm.

III. THE ROAD TO THE CIVIL WAR

The American Colonization Society and *The Liberator*

67 *"Let no man . . . with our* blood?" *Walker's Appeal, in Four Articles, Together with a Preamble, to the Coloured Citizens of the World, But in Particular, and Very Expressly, to Those of the United States of America,* 3rd ed., with an introduction by James Turner (Baltimore: Black Classic Press, 1993).

The Underground Railroad

71 On Shadrach Minkins. "The Ordeal of Shadrach Minkins," The Massachusetts Historical Society, accessed December 23, 2011, http://www.masshist.org/longroad/01slavery/minkins.htm.

71–2 On Anthony Burns. "The 'Trial' of Anthony Burns," The Massachusetts Historical Society, accessed December 23, 2011, http://www.masshist.org/longroad/01slavery/burns.htm, and "Fugitive Slave Anthony Burns Arrested," *Mass Moments,* accessed December 23, 2011, http://www.massmoments.org/moment.cfm?mid=153.

72 *"Protesters suspended a coffin . . . painted on its side"* "The Trial of Anthony Burns," The Massachusetts Historical

Society, accessed January 26, 2012, http://www.masshist.org/longroad/01slavery/burns.htm, and "Fugitive Slave Anthony Burns Arrested May 24, 1854," *Mass Moments,* accessed January 26, 2012, www.massmoments.org/moment.cfm?mid=153.

Black Abolitionists

73 *"The practice . . . their homes."* Frederick Douglass, *The Life and Times of Frederick Douglass, From 1817 to 1882, Written By Himself,* introduction by the Right Hon. John Bright, M.P., edited by John Lobb, F.R.G.S. (London: Christian Age Office, 1882), 2–3.

74 *"sailor named Stuart . . . life with me."* Ibid., 172.

74 On Douglass's marriage and work as a caulker. Ibid., 173.

76 On the African Free School Number 2. Berlin and Harris, eds., *Slavery in New York,* 183.

76–7 On Rev. Henry Highland Garnet. Milton C. Sernett, "Common Cause: The Antislavery Alliance of Gerrit Smith and Beriah Green," *New York History Net,* accessed December 23, 2011, www.nyhistory.com/gerritsmith/bgreen.htm, and "Highland Henry Garnet," *Africa Within,* accessed December 23, 2011, http://www.africawithin.com/bios/henry_garnet.htm.

77 On William Still. James Oliver Horton, "William Still: From Slave to Conductor," Slavery in America, accessed January 26, 2012, http://www.slaveryinamerica.org/narratives/bio_william_still.htm.

78 *"In these Records . . . cost of life."* William Still, *Still's Underground Rail Road Records,* revised ed. (Philadelphia: self-published, 1886), xix.

80 *"for the head of the woman. . . slaves from their masters."* Sarah Hopkins Bradford, *Scenes in the Life of Harriet Tubman* (Auburn, NY: W.J. Moses, stereotyped by Dennis Bro's & Co., 1869), 21.

80 *"The date of . . . 80 miles from here."* Ibid., 49–50.

80 *"torpedoes placed . . . the rebel troops."* Ibid., 39–42.

80 *"valuable information . . . battery positions."* Ibid., 41–42, and "Black Dispatches," CIA, accessed December 23, 2011, https://www.cia.gov/library/publications/additional-publications/civil-war/p20.htm.

New York City: A Destination for Fugitive Slaves

82 *"famous antislavery advocates . . . Frederick Douglass"* and *"included Booker T. Washington . . . running in 1868."* "Our History," Plymouth Church, accessed December 23, 2011, http://www.plymouthchurch.org/our_history.php.

83 On William Alexander Brown. James V. Hatch and Ted Shine, *Black Theatre USA: Plays by African Americans, the Early Period, 1847–1938, Revised and Expanded Edition* (New York: The Free Press/Simon & Schuster, 1996), 1.

83 On the Colored Sailors' Home. Leslie M. Harris, *In the Shadow of Slavery: African Americans in New York City, 1626–1863* (Chicago: The University of Chicago Press, 2003), 238, and Tonya Bolden, *Maritcha: A Nineteenth-Century American Girl* (New York: Harry N. Abrams, 2005), 10.

83–4 On black businesses in colonial New York. Howard Dodson, Christopher Moore, and Roberta Yancy, *The Black New Yorkers: The Schomburg Illustrated Chronology* (New York: John Wiley & Sons, Inc., 2000), 79.

84 On David Ruggles. "David Ruggles Home," *MAAP* (*Mapping the African American Past*), accessed December 23, 2011, http://maap.columbia.edu/place/7.html, and Harris, *In the Shadow of Slavery*, 212–213.

Early Black Newspapers

85–7 On the black press. "African American Newspapers," *Accessible Archives*, accessed December 23, 2011, http://www.accessible.com/accessible/about/aboutAA.jsp.

90 On Reconstruction newspapers. "About Us," *The New Orleans Tribune*, accessed January 8, 2012, http:// theneworleanstribune/aboutus.htm.

Black Inventors

89 On Sarah E. Goode. Mary Bellis, "Colors of Innovation: Early History of African American Inventors," About.com, accessed January 26, 2012, http://inventors.about.com/od/blackinventors/a/Early_History.htm.

The Civil War: Battle for Freedom

92 *"Approximately 180,000 . . . joined the fight."* "History of African Americans in the Civil War," *Civil War Sailors & Soldiers System*, accessed December 23, 2011, http://www.civilwar.nps.gov/cwss/history/aa_history.htm.

93 *"General James Blunt . . . my command.'"* Ibid.

93 On the 1st Louisiana Native Guard. Jerome S. Handler and Michael L. Tuite Jr., "Retouching History: The Modern Falsification of a Civil War Photograph," on the author's Web site, accessed December 23, 2011, http://people.virginia.edu/~jh3v/retouchinghistory/essay.html, and "Louisiana Native Guard in the Civil War," National Park Service, accessed January 14, 2012, http://www.nps.gov/guis/historyculture/louisiana-native-guard-in-the-civil-war.htm.

93 On the Louisiana Native Guards. "Port Hudson," National Park Service, accessed January 8, 2012, http://www.nps.gov/history/nr/travel/louisiana/por.htm.

94 *"After being shot . . . troops to follow."* "Medal of Honor Recipient," National Archives and Records Administration, accessed December 23, 2011, http://www.archives.gov/education/lessons/blacks-civil-war/medal-of-honor.html.

Draft Riots of 1863 in New York City

98 *"This is the place . . . dance and game"* Charles Dickens, *American Notes for General Circulation in Two Volumes* (London: Chapman and Hall 1842), 212.

98 *"All that . . . is here."* Ibid., 216.

Black Dispatches

99 *"One of the first . . . Union re-supply."* "Black Dispatches: Black American Contributions to Union Intelligence During the Civil War," CIA, accessed December 23, 2011, https://www.cia.gov/library/center-for-the-study-of-

intelligence/csi-publications/books-and-monographs/black-dispatches/index.html.

100 *"An accomplished role player"* and *"different identities . . . or laborer"* and *"local conditions . . . troop dispositions."* Ibid.

100 On Mary Touvestre. "Black Dispatches," CIA, accessed December 23, 2011, https://www.cia.gov/library/publications/additional-publications/civil-war/p20.htm.

101 On Robert Smalls. Robert Smalls, accessed December 23, 2011, http://www.robertsmalls.org.

IV. RECONSTRUCTION AND JIM CROW

The Freedmen's Bureau

106–7 On the Freedmen's Bureau. "The Freedmen's Bureau, 1865–1872," National Archives and Records Administration, accessed January 8, 2012, http://www.archives.gov/research/african-americans/freedmens-bureau.

106–7 On the Freedmen's Bureau bank. Reginald Washington, "The Freedman's Savings and Trust Company and African American Genealogical Research," *Federal Records and African American History* 29, no. 2 (Summer 1997), National Archives and Records Administration, accessed January 8, 2012, http://www.archives.gov/publications/prologue/1997/summer/freedmans-savings-and-trust.html.

Freed Men and Women Advance in Education and Politics

110 On P. B. S. Pinchback, Oscar J. Dunn, and Cesar C. Antoine. Buckley, *American Patriots*, 119.

Westward Expansion: The Buffalo Soldiers

114–5 On the new army. Buckley, *American Patriots*, 111.

114–5 On the Buffalo Soldiers. "Experiencing War: Buffalo Soldiers: The 92nd in Italy," Library of Congress, accessed December 23, 2011, http://www.loc.gov/vets/stories/ex-war-buffalosoldiers.html, and Buffalo Soldiers: Greater Washington DC Chapter, accessed December 23, 2011, http://www.buffalosoldiers-washington.com.

Blacks Migrate West to Kansas and Beyond

116 *"between 1850 . . . the Far West."* "The Far West," *In Motion: The African-American Migration Experience*, The Schomburg Center for Research in Black Culture, accessed January 8, 2012, http://www.inmotionaame.org/migrations/topic.cfm?migration=6&topic=3.

116 *"The number . . . in 1900."* and *"as sharecroppers . . . skilled craftsmen."* "Late Nineteenth-Century Texas," Texas State Historical Association, accessed January 8, 2012, http://www.tshaonline.org/handbook/online/articles/LL/npl1.html.

116 On the Homestead Act of 1862. "Teaching with Documents: The Homestead Act of 1862," National Archives and Records Administration, accessed January 31, 2012, http://www.archives.gov/education/lessons/homestead-act/.

116 On Benjamin "Pap" Singleton. Bobby L. Lovett, "Benjamin 'Pap' Singleton," *The Tennessee Encyclopedia of History and Culture*, accessed January 8, 2012, http://tennessee encyclopedia.net/entry.php?rec=1208.

117 On Nicodemus, Kansas. "The Story of Nicodemus," National Park Service, accessed December 23, 2011, http://www.nps.gov/features/nicodemus/intro.htm.

117-8 On Nat Love. Nat Love, *The Life and Adventures of Nat Love* (originally published in 1907 by Wayside Press, Los Angeles, reprinted with and introduction by Brackette F. Williams, University of Nebraska Press: 1995).

118 On Bill Pickett. "Famous Cowboys," BlackCowboys.com, accessed January 26, 2012, http://www.blackcowboys.com/billpickett.htm.

118 On "Stagecoach Mary" Fields. Richard W. Slatta, The Mythical West: *An Encyclopedia of Legend, Lore, and Popular Culture* (Santa Barbara, CA: ABC-CLIO, 2001), 141.

118-9 On Mary Ellen Pleasant. Mary Ellen Pleasant, accessed January 8, 2012, http://www.mepleasant.com, Lerone Bennett Jr., "A Historical Detective Story, Part I: The Mystery of Mary Ellen Pleasant," *Ebony* 48, no. 8 (June 1993), 56–64, excerpted from *Ebony* 34, no. 6 (April 1979), 90–96, and Bennett, "A Historical Detective Story, Part II: The Mystery of Mary Ellen Pleasant," *Ebony* 48, no. 11 (September 1993), 52–62.

Booker T. Washington and W. E. B. Du Bois

120-2 On Booker T. Washington. "Booker T. Washington," *The Rise and Fall of Jim Crow*, accessed January 8, 2012, http://www.pbs.org/wnet/jimcrow/stories_people_booker.html.

121 *"Our greatest danger . . . at the top."* "The Atlanta Compromise Speech (1895)," *The Rise and Fall of Jim Crow*, accessed January 8, 2012, http://www.pbs.org/wnet/jimcrow/stories_events_speech.html.

122 *"I never thought . . . about him."* Ralph McGill, "W. E. B. Du Bois," *The Atlantic Monthly* 216, no. 5 (November 1965), 78–81, accessed January 8, 2012, http://www.theatlantic.com/past/docs/unbound/flashbks/black/mcgillbh.htm.

123 *"Men of America . . . exceptional men."* W. E. B. Du Bois, "The Talented Tenth," *The Negro Problem: A Series of Articles by Representative Negroes To-day* (New York: James Pott & Company, 1903), 31–75, excerpted at the Gilder Lehrman Center for the Study of Slavery, Resistance & Abolition at The MacMillan Center, accessed January 8, 2012, http://www.yale.edu/glc/archive/1148.htm.

123-4 *"bartered away . . . to win back."* McGill, "W. E. B. Du Bois."

124 *"As we . . . mutual progress."* "The Atlanta Compromise Speech (1895)."

124 *"I also have . . . decision in 1896"* McGill, "W. E. B. Du Bois."

The Great Migration North

127 *"[A] mob of . . . the colored section."* Walter F. White, "The Eruption of Tulsa," *The Nation* 112 (June 29, 1921), 909–910, accessed January 8, 2012, http://historymatters.gmu.edu/d/5119.

128 On the number of African Americans who died and were injured in the Tulsa Riot. Dr. Robert L. Brooks and Dr. Alan H. Witten, "The Investigation of Potential Mass Grave Locations for the Tulsa Riots," *Tulsa Race Riot: A Report by the Oklahoma Commission to Study the Tulsa Race Riot of 1921* (Tulsa: Oklahoma Historical Society, February 28, 2001), 123–132, accessed December 23, 2011, http://www.okhistory.org/trrc/freport.pdf.

128 *"The backbone . . . American community."* Scott Ellsworth, "The Tulsa Race Riot," *Tulsa Race Riot*, 40.

128 *"black-owned . . . photography studio."* Ibid., 40–41 *beautiful, modern homes* Ibid., 43.

129 *"First, the Negro . . . superior race."* White, "The Eruption of Tulsa."

129 *"early July 1921 . . . black rebuilding."* Ellsworth, "The Tulsa Race Riot," 88.

V. TWO WORLD WARS AND THE BLACK CULTURAL AWAKENING

World War I: Black Soldiers Fight on Two Fronts

133 On the number of African American soldiers in World War I. "Photographs of the 369th Infantry and African Americans During World War I," National Archives and Records Administration, accessed January 8, 2012, http://www.archives.gov/education/lessons/369th-infantry.

133 *"Although a citizen . . . black officers."* "A French Directive," *The Crisis* 18 (May 1919), 16–18.

134 On serving as Y secretaries in France. Addie W. Hunton and Kathryn M. Johnson, *Two Colored Women with the American Expeditionary Forces* (Brooklyn: Brooklyn Eagle Press, 1920), accessed January 8, 2012, http://digitalgallery.nypl.org/nypldigital/id?1149597.

134 On the Harlem Hellfighters. "369th Infantry Regiment Memorial," City of New York Parks & Recreation, accessed January 8, 2012, http://www.nycgovparks.org/sub_your_park/historical_signs/hs_historical_sign.php?id=19562.

134 On James Reese Europe. "James Reese Europe, 1881–1919," Library of Congress, accessed January 8, 2012, http://lcweb2.loc.gov/diglib/ihas/loc.natlib.ihas.200038842/default.html.

Black Cultural Awakening

135 On the IRT and subway service to the boroughs of New York City. "New York City Transit—History and Chronology," MTA, accessed December 23, 2011, http://www.mta.info/nyct/facts/ffhist.htm.

137 On the famous residents of Strivers' Row. "Striver's Row," New York Architecture, accessed January 26, 2012, http://nyc-architecture.com/HAR/HAR013.htm.

137 *"better, cleaner . . . ever lived in before."* James Weldon Johnson, *Black Manhattan* (New York: Knopf, 1930, reprinted with introduction by Sondra Kathryn Wilson, New York: Da Capo Press, 1991), 148.

139 On the Negro Factories Corporation. Booker T. Washington, *The Negro in Business* (Atlanta: Hertel, Jenkins & Co., 1907), 197–205.

140-1 On Madam C. J. Walker. A'Lelia Bundles, *On Her Own Ground: The Life and Times of Madam C. J. Walker* (New York: Scribner, 2002), 286.

140-1 On the "Dark Tower" and the "Joy Goddess" of the Harlem Renaissance. "A'Lelia Walker: 'Joy Goddess' of the Harlem Renaissance," accessed January 8, 2012, http://www.madamcjwalker.com/bios/alelia-walker, and Bundles, *On Her Own Ground*, 281–283.

144 On Florence Mills. Cary D. Wintz and Paul Finkelman, ed., *Encyclopedia of the Harlem Renaissance*, vol. 1, *A–J* (New York: Routledge, 2004), 143.

144 On Harlem theaters. Bernard L. Peterson Jr., *The African American Theatre Directory, 1816–1960: A Comprehensive Guide to Early Black Theatre Organizations, Companies, Theatres, and Performing Groups*, foreword by Errol Hill (Westport, CT: Greenwood Press, 1997), 114.

145-6 On Harlem nightlife. Steven Watson, *The Harlem Renaissance: Hub of African-American Culture, 1920–1930* (New York: Pantheon Books, 1995), 124–144, accessed January 8, 2012, http://xroads.virginia.edu/~UG97/blues/watson.html.

The Great Depression and the New Deal

150 On FDR's New Deal programs. "The New Deal," Roosevelt Institute, accessed January 8, 2012, http://www.rooseveltinstitute.org/policy-and-ideasroosevelt-historyfdr/new-deal.

149 *"They were all . . . until the late sixties."* Claudia Durst Johnson, "Interview: Growing Up Black in the 1930s in McCulley's Quarters, Alabama," *Understanding To Kill a Mockingbird* (Westport, CT: Greenwood Press, 1994), 172–174.

150-1 On FDR's "black cabinet." "The 'Black Cabinet,'" In Motion: The African-American Migration Experience, accessed January 31, 2012, http://www.inmotionaame.org/gallery/detail.cfm?migration=9&topic=8&id=487435&type=image.

152 On the number of blacks enrolled in the CCC. "African Americans in the Civilian Conservation Corps," New Deal Network, accessed January 8, 2012, http://newdeal.feri.org/aaccc/index.htm.

152 *"We reached Camp Dix . . . by the officers."* Luther C. Wandall, "A Negro in the CCC," *The Crisis* 42 (August 1935), 244, 253–254.

World War II

155 On Executive Order 8802. "FDR, A. Philip Randolph and the Desegregation of the Defense Industries," The White House Historical Association, accessed December 23, 2011, http://www.whitehousehistory.org/whha_classroom/classroom_9-12-pressure-defense.html.

The Tuskegee Airmen

156 On FDR, Randolph, and the white desegregation of armed rorces. "FDR, A. Philip Randolph and the Desegregation of the Defense Industries," The White House Historical Association.

156 On the Tuskegee Airmen. Stephen Sherman, "The Tuskegee Airmen," accessed January 8, 2012, http://acepilots.com/usaaf_tusk.html.

158 *"They don't . . . at Tuskegee."* Interview of Tuskegee Airman Floyd Carter by author, January 27, 2007.

158 *"completed 15,000 sorties . . . enemy installations."* "The Tuskegee Airmen," *Legends of Tuskegee*, accessed December 23, 2011, http://www.nps.gov/history/museum/exhibits/tuskegee/aircombat.htm.

159 *"awarded numerous . . . in 1945."* Ibid.

159-60 On Dorie Miller. "Remember Pearl Harbor," National Park Service, accessed January 30, 2012, http://www.nps.gov/pwso/honor/miller.htm, and "Cook Third Class Doris Miller's Navy Cross Citation," Naval History and Heritage Command, accessed January 8, 2012, http://www.history.navy.mil/faqs/faq57-4a.htm.

160 On Dr. Charles Drew. "Dr. Charles Drew (1904–1950)," American Red Cross, accessed January 8, 2012, http://www.redcross.org/museum/history/charlesdrew.asp.

161 On African American women in the military. Kathryn Sheldon, "Brief History of Black Women in the Military," Women in Military Service for America Memorial Foundation, http://www.womensmemorial.org/Education/BBH1998.html.

VI. THE CIVIL RIGHTS MOVEMENT TO THE BLACK POWER MOVEMENT

The Murder of Emmett Till

168 *The acquittal of . . . the European media.* (L'Humanite). Margaret M. Russell, "Justice Delayed: Reopening the Emmett Till Case," *Santa Clara Magazine* (Spring 2006), accessed January 8, 2012, www.scu.edu/scm/spring2006/justice.cfm.

The Montgomery Bus Boycott

168-9 On Rosa Parks and the Montgomery bus boycott. "Rosa Parks," *International Civil Rights: Walk of Fame*, accessed December 23, 2011, http://www.nps.gov/features/malu/feat0002/wof/Rosa_Parks.htm.

Little Rock Nine Integrates Central High School

170 On the integration of Central High School by the Little Rock Nine. "Little Rock Central High School Historical Site," National Park Service, accessed January 8, 2012, http://www.nps.gov/nr/travel/civilrights/ak1.htm, and Carlotta Walls LaNier with Lisa Frazier Page, *A Mighty Long Way: My Journey to Justice at Little Rock Central High School* (New York: One World/Ballantine Books, 2009).

Freedom Riders and Freedom Summer

173 *"As soon as he heard . . . he ever said "sir.""* Eric Etheridge, *Breach of Peace: Portraits of the 1961 Mississippi Freedom Riders*, preface by Roger Wilkins, introduction by Diane McWhorter (New York: Atlas & Co., 2008).

174 On the Mississippi Freedom Summer Project. Lisa Cozzens, "Mississippi & Freedom Summer," accessed January 8, 2012, http://www.watson.org/~lisa/blackhistory/civilrights-55-65/missippi.html.

175 On MFDP at the Democratic National Convention in Atlantic City. "Mississippi Freedom Democratic Party (MFDP)," Civil Rights Documentation Project, accessed January 8, 2012, http://usm.edu/crdp/html/cd/mfdp.htm.

177 *"an act of defiance . . . proclamation and commitment."* Ossie Davis and Ruby Dee, *With Ossie and Ruby: In This Life Together* (New York: William Morrow, 1998), 86.

178 *"I didn't know . . . the movement."* Amy Goodman, "Legendary Folk Singer & Activist Pete Seeger Turns 90, Thousands Turn Out for All-Star Tribute Featuring Bruce Springsteen, Joan Baez, Bernice Johnson Reagon and Dozens More," *Democracy Now!*, May 4, 2009, accessed January 8, 2012, http://www.democracynow.org/2009/5/4/legendary_folk_singer_activist_pete_seeger.

Civil Rights, West Coast Style

179–80 On the Watts Riot, August 11, 1965. "Watts Riots," *A Huey P. Newton Story*, accessed January 31, 2012, http://www.pbs.org/hueypnewton/times/times_watts.html.

MLK and Malcolm X

182 *"[King was] on the verge . . . do you wrong."* Tonya Bolden, *MLK: Journey of a King* (New York: Harry N. Abrams, 2007), 28–29.

185–6 *"June 30, 1964 . . . Harlem, NY."* "Telegram to Martin Luther King," malcolm-x.org, accessed January 8, 2012, http://www.malcolm-x.org/docs/tel_mart.htm, and "Telegram from Malcolm X," Martin Luther King, Jr., and the Global Freedom Struggle, accessed January 8, 2012, http://mlk-kpp01.stanford.edu/index.php/encyclopedia/documentsentry/telegram_from_malcolm_x.

186 *"While we did not . . . as a race."* "Telegram from Martin Luther King, Jr., to Betty al-Shabazz," Martin Luther King, Jr., and the Global Freedom Struggle, accessed January 8, 2012, http://mlk-kpp01.stanford.edu/index.php/encyclopedia/documentsentry/telegram_from_martin_luther_king_jr_to_betty_al_shabazz.

The Black Arts Movement

191 "What's Going On," lyrics by M. Gay, A. Cleveland and R. Benson, 1971.

VII. AFRICAN AMERICANS ADVANCE

African American Elected and Appointed Officials

197–8 *"Black Americans . . . who we are today."* "Rice Hits U.S. 'Birth Defect,'" *The Washington Times*, March 28, 2008, accessed January 8, 2012, http://www.washingtontimes.com/news/2008/mar/28/rice-hits-us-birth-defect.

Black Entertainment and Media

207–8 On the emergence of hip-hop. "The Evolution of Rap Music in the United States," Yale.edu, accessed February 13, 2012, http://www.yale.edu/ynhti/curriculum/units/1993/4/93.04.04.x.html#b, and "Hip Hop," UIC.edu, accessed February 13, 2012, http://www.uic.edu/orgs/kbc/hiphop/overview.htm.

VIII. AFRICAN AMERICANS TODAY

President Barack Obama

215 *"The document . . . and our grandchildren."* "A More Perfect Union," Barack Obama's speech on race in America on March 18, 2008, in Philadelphia during presidential campaign.

AFTERWORD

218–20 Interview with Wilbur Jones by author, September 6, 2007.

SELECT BIBLIOGRAPHY

An asterisk (*) indicates resources suitable for young readers.

BOOKS

Adventurers of Purse and Person, VIRGINIA, 1607–1624/5, 3rd ed. Revised and edited by Virginia M. Meyer and John Frederick Dorman, F.A.S.G. Richmond: Order of First Families of Virginia, 1987.

Bandelier, Adolph F. *The Discovery of New Mexico by the Franciscan Monk Friar Marcos de Niza in 1539*, Translation by Madeleine Turrell Rodack. Tucson: University of Arizona Press, 1981.

Berkin, Carol. *First Generations: Women in Colonial America*. New York: Hill and Wang/Farrar, Straus and Giroux, 1996.

*Bradford, Sarah Hopkins. *Scenes in the Life of Harriet Tubman*. Auburn, NY: W.J. Moses, by Dennis Bro's & Co., 1869.

*Berlin, Ira, and Leslie M. Harris, editors. *Slavery in New York*. New York: The New Press, published in conjunction with The New-York Historical Society, 2005. Exhibition catalog.

*Bolden, Tonya. *Maritcha: A Nineteenth-Century American Girl*. New York: Harry N. Abrams, 2005.

*Breen, T.H., and Stephen Innes *"Myne Owne Ground": Race and Freedom on Virginia's Eastern Shore, 1640–1676*. New York: Oxford University Press, 1980.

Buckley, Gail. *American Patriots: The Story of Blacks in the Military from the Revolution to Desert Storm*. New York: Random House, 2001.

Bundles, A'Lelia. *On Her Own Ground: The Life and Times of Madam C.J. Walker*. New York: Scribner, 2002.

*Davis, Burke. *Black Heroes of the American Revolution*. Boston: Sandpiper/Harcourt, 1976.

*Davis, David Brion. *Slavery in Colonial Chesapeake*. Williamsburg, VA: The Colonial Williamsburg Foundation, 1986.

Davis, Thulani. *My Confederate Kinfolk: A Twenty-First Century Freedwoman Confronts Her Roots*. New York: Basic Books, 2006.

Dickens, Charles. *American Notes for General Circulation in Two Volumes*. London: Chapman and Hall, 1842. Reprinted, New York: Cambridge University Press, 2009.

*Dodson, Howard, Christopher Moore, and Roberta Yancy. *The Black New Yorkers: The Schomburg Illustrated Chronology*. New York: John Wiley & Sons, Inc., 2000.

*Douglass, Frederick. *The Life and Times of Frederick Douglass: From 1817–1882, Written by Himself*. Introduction by the Right Hon. John Bright, M.P., edited by John Lobb, F.R.G.S. London: Christian Age Office, 1882.

Edgar, Walter B. *South Carolina: A History*. Columbia, SC: University of South Carolina, 1998.

Estlin, John Bishop. *A Brief Notice of American Slavery, and the Abolition Movement*. Bristol: H.C. Evans, 1846.

*Etheridge, Eric. *Breach of Peace: Portraits of the 1961 Mississippi Freedom Riders*. Preface by Roger Wilkins, introduction by Diane McWhorter. New York: Atlas & Co., 2008.

*Equiano, Olaudah. *The Interesting Narrative of the Life of Olaudah Equiano, or Gustavas Vassa, the African*, 9th ed. London: printed by the author, 1794.

Foote, Thelma Wills. *Black and White Manhattan: The History of Racial Formation in Colonial New York*. New York: Oxford University Press, 2004.

Harris, Leslie M. *In the Shadow of Slavery: African Americans in New York City, 1626–1863*. Chicago: The University of Chicago Press, 2003.

Hatch, James V., and Ted Shine. *Black Theatre USA: Plays by African Americans, the Early Period, 1847–1938, Revised and Expanded Edition*. New York: The Free Press/Simon & Schuster, 1996.

Hening, William Waller. *Hening's Statutes, Being a Collection of All the Laws of Virginia from the First Session of the Legislature, in the Year 1619*. Richmond: W.W. Gray, 1819.

Horton, James Oliver, and Lois E. Horton. *Slavery and the Making of America*. New York: Oxford University Press, 2005.

*Jacobs, Harriet. *Incidents in the Life of a Slave Girl*. Mineola, NY: Dover Publications, 2001.

*Johnson, Charles, Patricia Smith, and the WGBH Series Research Team. *Africans in America: America's Journey through Slavery*. New York: Houghton Mifflin Harcourt, 1998.

*Johnson, Claudia Durst. "Interview: Growing Up Black in the 1930s in McCulley's Quarters, Alabama," in *Understanding* To Kill a Mockingbird: *A Student Casebook to Issues, Sources, and Historic Documents*. Westport, CT: The Greenwood Press, 1994.

Johnson, James Weldon. *Black Manhattan*. New York: Knopf, 1930. Reprinted with introduction by Sondra Kathryn Wilson. New York: Da Capo Press, 1991.

Jones-Wilson, Faustine C., Charles A. Asbury, Margot Okazawa-Rey, et al., editors. *Encyclopedia of African-American Education*. Westport, CT: The Greenwood Press, 1996.

*LaNier, Carlotta Walls, with Lisa Frazier Page. *A Mighty Long Way: My Journey to Justice at Little Rock Central High School*. New York: One World/Ballantine Books, 2009.

McCartney, Martha W., et al. *A Study of the Africans and African Americans on Jamestown Island and at Green Spring, 1619–1803*. Williamsburg, VA: National Park Service/The Colonial Williamsburg Foundation, 2003.

*Nell, William C. *The Colored Patriots of the American Revolution with Sketches of Several Distinguished Colored Persons, to Which Is Added a Brief Survey of the Condition and Prospects of Colored Americans*. Introduction by Harriet Beecher Stowe. Boston: Robert F. Wallcut, 1855. Reprint, New York: Arno Press, 1968.

Palmer, Colin A., editor. *Encyclopedia of African-American Culture and History: The Black Experience in the Americas*, Vol. 5, 2nd ed. New York: Macmillan Reference, 2005.

Priest, Robert J., and Alvaro L. Nieves, editors. *This Side of Heaven: Race, Ethnicity, and Christian Faith*. New York: Oxford University Press, 2007.

Slatta, Richard W. *The Mythical West: An Encyclopedia of Legend, Lore, and Popular Culture*. Santa Barbara, CA: ABC-CLIO, 2001.

Still, William. *Still's Underground Rail Road Records*, revised ed. *Philadelphia: Self-published, 1886.

Terrell, John Upton. *Estevanico the Black*. Los Angeles: Westernlore Press, 1968.

Walker, David. "Article IV. Our Wretchedness in Consequence of the Colonizing Plan," in *Walker's Appeal, in Four Articles, Together with a Preamble, to the Coloured Citizens of the World, But in Particular, and Very Expressly, to Those of the United States of America*, 3rd ed. Boston: David Walker, 1830. Reprinted with an introduction by James Turner. Baltimore: Black Classic Press, 1993.

Washington, Booker T. *The Negro in Business*. Atlanta: Hertel, Jenkins & Co., 1907.

Wintz, Cary D., and Paul Finkelman, editors. *Encyclopedia of the Harlem Renaissance*, vol. 1, *A–J*. New York: Routledge, 2004.

MAGAZINES AND PERIODICALS

"A French Directive." *The Crisis* 18 (May 1919): 16–18.

Blockson, Charles L. "Black Samuel Fraunces: Patriot, White House Steward and Restaurateur Par Excellence." Accessed December 23, 2011. http://library.temple.edu/collections/blockson/fraunces.jsp.

Diehl, Lorraine B, "Skeletons in the Closet: Uncovering the Rich History of the Slaves of New York." *New York*, October 5, 1992, 78–86.

Horle, Records of the Courts of Sussex County, DE, 107. Jane Johnson, Marriage Record, 1682, Somerset County Courthouse, Princess Anne, Maryland (microfilm, CR 50, 078, Edward H. Nabb Research Center for Delmarva History and Culture, Salisbury University, Salisbury, Maryland), folio 210. Found in Liber IKL, 1649-1720. See Appendix F on page 75 for a copy of the original record.

Morse, Kitty. "Esteban of Azemmour and His New World Adventures." *Saudi Aramco World* 53, no. 2 (March/April 2002): 2–9.

Sluiter, Engel. "New Light on the '20. and Odd Negroes' Arriving in Virginia, August 1619." *The William and Mary Quarterly* 54, no. 2 (April 1997): 395–98.

Thornton, John. "Notes and Documents: The African Experience of the '20. and Odd Negroes' Arriving in Virginia in 1619." *William and Mary Quarterly* 55, no. 3 (July 1998): 422–34.

Wandall, Luther C. "A Negro in the CCC." *The Crisis* 42 (August 1935): 244, 253–54.

WEB SITES

*"Abiel Smith School." National Park Service. Accessed December 23, 2011. http://www.nps.gov/boaf/historyculture/abiel-smith-school.htm.

"African American Newspapers." *Accessible Archives*. Accessed December 23, 2011. http://www.accessible.com/accessible/about/aboutAA.jsp.

*"African Americans in the Revolutionary Period." *The American Revolution*. Accessed December 23, 2011. http://www.nps.gov/revwar/about_the_revolution/african_americans.html.

*The African Burial Ground. Accessed December 23, 2011. http://www.africanburialground.gov.

"African Explorers of Spanish America." *NPS Ethnography*. Accessed December 23, 2011. http://www.nps.gov/history/ethnography/aah/aaheritage/SpanishAmb.htm.

"Africans in the Chesapeake." *NPS Ethnography*. Accessed December 23, 2011. http://www.nps.gov/history/ethnography/aah/aaheritage/ChesapeakeA.htm.

"Black Dispatches." Central Intelligence Agency. Accessed December 23, 2011. https://www.cia.gov/library/publications/additional-publications/civil-war/p20.htm.

"Black Dispatches: Black American Contributions to Union Intelligence During the Civil War." Central Intelligence Agency. Accessed December 23, 2011. https://www.cia.gov/library/center-for-the-study-of-intelligence/csi-publications/books-and-monographs/black-dispatches/index.html.

*"Book Three of the Book of Negroes." *Black Loyalists: Our History, Our People*. Accessed December 23, 2011. http://www.blackloyalist.com/canadiandigitalcollection/documents/official/black_loyalist_directory_book_three.htm.

Buffalo Soldiers; Greater Washington DC Chapter. Accessed December 23, 2011. http://www.buffalosoldiers-washington.com.

*"David Ruggles Home." *MAAP* (*Mapping the African American Past*). Accessed December 23, 2011. http://maap.columbia.edu/place/7.html.

"Dorantes de Carranza, Andrés." Texas State Historical Association. Accessed December 23, 2011. http://www.tshaonline.org/handbook/online/articles/DD/fdo20.html.

"Events from 1500 to 1650." *PBS: The West*. Accessed December 23, 2011. http://www.pbs.org/weta/thewest/events/1500_1650.htm.

*"Experiencing War: Buffalo Soldiers: The 92nd in Italy." Library of Congress. Accessed December 23, 2011. http://www.loc.gov/vets/stories/ex-war-buffalosoldiers.html.

*"Famous Cowboys." *Black Cowboys*. Accessed January 14, 2012. http://www.blackcowboys.com/billpickett.htm.

*"FDR, A. Philip Randolph and the Desegregation of the Defense Industries." The White House Historical Association. Accessed December 23, 2011. http://www.whitehousehistory.org/whha_classroom/classroom_9-12-pressure-defense.html.

"Frederick Douglass at Harpers Ferry." National Park Service, U.S. Department of the Interior. Accessed January 14, 2012. http://www.nps.gov/hafe/historyculture/frederick-douglass-at-harpers-ferry.htm.

*"Fugitive Slave Anthony Burns Arrested." *Mass Moments*. Accessed December 23, 2011. http://www.massmoments.org/moment.cfm?mid=153.

Handler, Jerome S., and Michael L. Tuite Jr. "Retouching History: The Modern Falsification of a Civil War Photograph." On the author's website. Accessed December 23, 2011. http://people.virginia.edu/~jh3v/retouchinghistory/essay.html.

"Highland Henry Garnet." *Africa Within*. Accessed December 23, 2011. http://www.africawithin.com/bios/henry_garnet.htm.

*"History of African Americans in the Civil War." *Civil War Sailors & Soldiers System*. Accessed December 23, 2011. http://www.civil war.nps.gov/cwss/history/aa_history.htm.

"Jacobs School." *Harriet Jacobs Documents*. Accessed December 23, 2011. http://www.yale.edu/glc/harriet/13.htm.

*"Louisiana Native Guard in the Civil War." National Park Service, U.S. Department of the Interior. Accessed January 14, 2012. http://www.nps.gov/guis/historyculture/louisiana-native-guard-in-the-civil-war.htm.

"Medal of Honor Recipient." National Archives and Records Administration. Accessed December 23, 2011. http://www.archives.gov/education/lessons/blacks-civil-war/medal-of-honor.html.

*"New York City Transit—History and Chronology." MTA. Accessed December 23, 2011. http://www.mta.info/nyct/facts/ffhist.htm.

*"The Ordeal of Shadrach Minkins." The Massachusetts Historical Society. Accessed December 23, 2011. http://www.masshist.org/longroad/01slavery/minkins.htm.

"Our History." Plymouth Church. Accessed December 23, 2011. http://www.plymouthchurch.org/our_history.php.

"The Practise of Slavery." *Virtual Jamestown*. Accessed December 23, 2011. http://www.virtualjamestown.org/practise.html.

"A Report by the Oklahoma Commission to Study the Tulsa Race Riot of 1921." Oklahoma Historical Society. Accessed December 23, 2011. http://www.okhistory.org/trrc/freport.htm.

*Robert Smalls. Accessed December 23, 2011. http://www.robert smalls.org.

*"Rosa Parks." *International Civil Rights: Walk of Fame*. Accessed December 23, 2011. http://www.nps.gov/features/malu/feat0002/wof/Rosa_Parks.htm.

Sernett, Milton C. "Common Cause: The Antislavery Alliance of Gerrit Smith and Beriah Green." *New York History Net*. Accessed December 23, 2011. http://www.nyhistory.com/gerritsmith/bgreen.htm.

*"The Story of Nicodemus." National Park Service. Accessed December 23, 2011. http://www.nps.gov/features/nicodemus/intro.htm.

Texas State Historical Association. Accessed December 23, 2011. http://www.tshatshaonline.org.

*"The 'Trial' of Anthony Burns." The Massachusetts Historical Society. Accessed December 23, 2011. http://www.masshist.org/longroad/01slavery/burns.htm.

*"The Tuskegee Airmen." *Legends of Tuskegee*. Accessed December 23, 2011. http://www.nps.gov/history/museum/exhibits/tuskegee/aircombat.htm.

University of Texas Libraries. Accessed December 23, 2011. http://www.lib.utexas.edu.

*Washington Crossing Historical Park. Accessed December 23, 2011. http://www.ushistory.org/washingtoncrossing.

*Weidman, Budge. "Preserving the Legacy of the United States Colored Troops." National Archives and Records Administration. Accessed December 23, 2011. http://www.archives.gov/education/lessons/blacks-civil-war/article.html.

ART CREDITS

Foundations. **Page 88**: The Granger Collection, NYC. **Page 89**: The Granger Collection, NYC. **Page 90**: The Granger Collection, NYC. **Page 91**: Library of Congress. **Page 92**: Library of Congress. **Page 93**: Courtesy of The U.S. National Archives. **Page 94**: Moorland-Springarn Research Center, Howard University. **Page 95**: Courtesy of The U.S. National Archives. **Page 96**: Library of Congress. **Page 97**: HarpWeek, LLC. **Page 100**: Library of Congress; Picture Collection, The Branch Libraries, The New York Public Library, Astor, Lenox and Tilden Foundations. **Page 102–103**: Library of Congress. **Page 104–105**: Library of Congress. **Page 106**: HarpWeek, LLC. **Page 111**: Library of Congress. **Page 112**: Library of Congress. **Page 113**: Picture Collection, The New York Public Library, Astor, Lenox and Tilden Foundations. **Page 114**: The Granger Collection, NYC. **Page 116**: Library of Congress. **Page 117**: The Granger Collection, NYC. **Page 118**: The Granger Collection, NYC. **Page 119**: Art Resource/Art Resource, NY. **Page 121**: Library of Congress. **Page 122**: The Granger Collection, NYC. **Page 123**: Special Collections and University Archives, University of Massachusetts Amherst Libraries. **Page 125**: The Museum of Modern Art / Licensed by SCALA / Art Resource, NY. **Page 127**: Library of Congress. **Page 129**: Oklahoma Historical Society. **Page 130–131**: General Research & Reference Division, Schomburg Center for Research in Black Culture, The New York Public Library, Astor, Lenox and Tilden Foundations. **Page 132**: Library of Congress. **Page 135**: National Portrait Gallery, Smithsonian Institute / At Resource, NY. **Page 136**: Photographs and Prints Division, Schomburg Center for Research in Black Culture, The New York Public Library, Astor, Lenox and Tilden Foundations. **Page 137**: Photographs and Prints Division, Schomburg Center for Research in Black Culture, The New York Public Library, Astor, Lenox and Tilden Foundations. **Page 138**: Manuscripts, Archives and Rare Books Division, Schomburg Center for Research in Black Culture, The New York Public Library, Astor, Lenox and Tilden Foundations. **Page 139**: Milstein Division of United States History, Local History & Genealogy, The New York Public Library, Astor, Lenox and Tilden Foundations. **Page 140**: Photographs and Prints Division, Schomburg Center for Research in Black Culture, The New York Public Library, Astor, Lenox and Tilden Foundations. **Page 141**: Library of Congress. **Page 142**: Library of Congress. **Page 143**: Billy Rose Theatre Division, The New York Public Library for the Performing Arts. **Page 144**: Billy Rose Theatre Division, The New York Public Library for the Performing Arts. **Page 145**: The Granger Collection, NYC. **Page 147**: The Granger Collection, NYC. **Page 148**: Library of Congress. **Page 150**: Library of Congress. **Page 151**: Library of Congress; The Granger Collection, NYC. **Page 153**: Smithsonian American Art Museum, Washington, DC / Art Resource, NY. **Page 154**: The Granger Collection, NYC. **Page 156**: George W. Bush Presidential Library. **Page 157**: Photographs and Prints Division, Schomburg Center for Research in Black Culture, The New York Public Library, Astor, Lenox and Tilden Foundations. **Page 159**: National Archives/Double Delta Industries, Inc. **Page 160**: The Granger Collection, NYC. **Page 162–163**: Eric Etheridge. **Page 164–165**: Library of Congress. **Page 166**: Library of Congress; The Granger Collection, NYC. **Page 167**: Library of Congress. **Page 168**: Library of Congress. **Page 169**: The Granger Collection, NYC. **Page 171**: Library of Congress. **Page 172**: Library of Congress. **Page 174**: Library of Congress. **Page 175**: Associated Press. **Page 176**: The Granger Collection, NYC. **Page 177**: Library of Congress. **Page 179**: Associated Press. **Page 181**: The Granger Collection, NYC. **Page 183**: The Granger Collection, NYC/used with permission. **Page 184**: The Granger Collection, NYC/used with permission; The Granger Collection, NYC. **Page 185**: The Granger Collection, NYC/used with permission. **Page 187**: Library of Congress/used with permission; the King Center, Atlanta. **Page 188**: Library of Congress; The Granger Collection, NYC. **Page 189**: Library of Congress. **Page 190**: Fin Costello / Redferns / Getty Images. **Page 191**: The Granger Collection, NYC. **Page 192**: Brandon Kopp/MLK Foundation. **Page 194–195**: New York Daily New Archives / Getty Images. **Page 197**: public domain; New York Daily New Archives / Getty Images. **Page 199**: Bloomberg / Getty Images. **Page 201**: NASA. **Page 202**: Library of Congress. **Page 203**: Michael Ochs Archives / Getty Images. **Page 205**: Chris McGrath / Getty Images Sport / Getty Images. **Page 207**: New York Daily New Archives / Getty Images. **Page 208**: New York Daily New Archives / Getty Images. **Page 209**: New York Daily New Archives / Getty Images. **Page 210**: Larry W. Smith/epa/Corbis. **Page 212–213**: Alex Wong / Getty Images News / Getty Images. **Page 220**: Wilbur Jones

INDEX

Note: page numbers in *italics* indicate illustrations and captions.